THE 7 G

From

Death

to

JESSE LEFLER

ISBN 978-1-63874-050-6 (paperback)
ISBN 979-8-88616-581-4 (hardcover)
ISBN 978-1-63874-051-3 (digital)

Christian Faith Publishing
832 Park Avenue
Meadville, PA 16335
www.christianfaithpublishing.com

All characters appearing in this work are fictitious. Any resemblance to real people, living or dead, is purely coincidental.

Printed in the United States of America

Dedicated to the people who lost their way with Christ.

PREFACE

When God called me to do this story, I seriously didn't know what I was doing. Still don't. I have been through horrible pain in my life, some by stupid choice and others by chance. They hurt all the same in the end. I realized that I have some amazing people in my life with the most incredible experiences of life. I used the tools I had all around me. I am grateful I was able to meet them because it all came from a place of severe pain. In order to grow, I had to survive the rain. Just as there are seasons in the natural world, there are seasons in the spiritual. I hope that my pain can give you hope, a promise. I wrote this for God who wants to give it to you.

Try to imagine a life without the existence of time. It's beyond any human mind because, naturally, we want a beginning and an end. If there is no start, how could there be any finish? How does one accept the concept of "there always was?" That is the first thing to keep in mind when trying to grasp the concept of an ultimate creator. Everyone seems to want to put God in a box, and the truth is, it can't be done. He simply doesn't belong there and can't be contained there. He has emotions, knows all, and sees all. What if you could stay there, drifting into numerous possibilities?

To anyone who has suffered pain, loss, heartache, addiction, abuse, bad choices, dysfunctional family or you just never felt you fit in, I dedicate this story to you. Some of us have a hard time looking past our own loss and pain. We aren't getting married, we don't have the right body, the right job, or the right environment. Even those who seem to have it all together really don't. They are just better at hiding their dysfunction than those who live openly about their hurts and hang-ups. I have suffered just about every type of pain there is. Does that make me special? Not at all. I once had a psychologist tell me that I had gone through more in ten years than he had seen in any of his patients over a thirty-year career. I didn't know whether to be proud or to break down and cry.

Through all of those hurts and hang-ups, I chose to handle each situation differently. I knew what would really help me, but because I was so ashamed of the destruction in my wake, I couldn't face God. Sometimes I would work out to the extreme, running five miles every day, and sometimes I would try to find healing in men and broken relationships. There was always a short time of peace, but in the end, none of those were fulfilling.

I could never run enough, work out enough, fall in love the right way or be numb enough through an addiction. I knew I would find true peace in God. Interestingly enough, with all my pain, rejection, loss, and insecurity, God used all those things to help me with this story. When I finally decided to start praying, seeking, and asking for change in my life, requesting something so big I couldn't ignore it, along came an idea for a book. Since I asked for a big change, he came through in ways that didn't seem to think make sense. But in the end, when I chose to finally free fall and trust him, I saw that he actually does know and loves us.

The core characters you will read about in this book are actual people I know. Only 20 percent of what is written is deviated from their true testimony. The story is about the life they lead, with or without God, and the miracles the Holy Spirit did in their lives to reveal himself to them. He wants all of us to rely on him, no matter how ugly the destruction we have left behind us. With this story, he wanted to give you a reason to question, could there actually be a supernatural world that is unseen but very much alive? Yes! When you decide to allow him in, prepare for a journey you never thought you were capable of. He has given me every ounce of this story to write. He provided the people to write about.

I am positive that you will find yourself relating to several characters because of the choices they made. I pray this opens your heart to something you never thought was possible and breaks down all your walls. I pray that whatever Watcher is currently in your life or within your family line will be bound from distracting you. He wants to grow in a personal relationship with you and he wanted to say how much he loves you like a parent with their child. I pray this in his name, for the victory is God's. *He* is there. Seek him. He is the great I AM.

The story begins in heaven when the world was just created, and Lucifer is angry because of the attention God bestows to the humans. The humans didn't have the gold and flair, so he couldn't understand what was so special about them. He isn't about to bow down when he feels he was made to be worshiped too since he is known as Morning Star—the most beautiful.

Only in the very first chapter, a core character is speaking directly to you as the reader. She is setting up the breakdown in spiritual warfare. The following chapters become a bird's-eye view of the characters with their thoughts and feelings.

I hope you enjoy the journey! Remember to keep an open mind.

In the Beginning...
of the End

Hi, my name is Leilani Utua, and I want to introduce myself to you. I am a Guardian angel. Not the stereotypical angel that everyone seems to imagine. I don't sit on a cloud, playing a harp, jumping and singing like a fool. I am a warrior and a fighter for the light under God's reign, which means I am trained to kill. I have my weapon of choice because in spiritual warfare, bullets don't apply. You may be asking yourself, what would require a Guardian angel to fight and to kill against?

My mission is to explain what is going on in front of your very eyes that you have not been trained to see. The world is dominated by darkness and a spiritual battle. The days of Noah have returned, and the light, which I fight for under the Trinity Treaty, has forced us to just sit back and watch as you are tearing each other down. The world has become broken, and so many people reject the need for boundaries and morals. They keep showing intolerance and have become filled with hatred. I am here and need to warn you all about a war that is coming and the circumstances that will lead to this impending war. You must understand we wrestle not against flesh and blood but against principalities, against powers, against the rulers of the darkness of this world, and against spiritual wickedness in high places.

If you know anything about Christianity, you know that God banished Lucifer from his side in the heavenly kingdom down to earth. Lucifer didn't want to bow down to the new creation called mankind. What most people don't know is why. God endowed his love to Lucifer for the music he could create from within his body. His vocal cords produced a sound like a symphony and it embodied the true love of God. For example, just like an artist and his favorite piece of art that he perfected, Lucifer was God's highly favorite piece. All the musical instruments you see today originated from what God designed in Lucifer. He could actually create music that was visibly seen dancing in the air by his fellow angels he was surrounded with. The sound of the drums came from within his heartbeat, and the deeper he felt the music, the faster the drum would beat. He pulled the ligaments from his own body and created violins that could bring tears to any eye.

However, because Lucifer was given an incredible talent unlike any other angel was blessed with, he began to grow arrogant. He felt that he should be a God and worshiped as such. He kept growing dark and began to want to wage war and demand his own kingdom. He began to talk with his fellow angels, and due to his charisma, his incredible talent, and his beauty, he was able to gather a following. All angels have free will to choose, and most humans don't realize that. Unfortunately, passion and charisma can be used for great or horrible things.

To give you an example from human history, if you were to compare two leaders such as Dr. Martin Luther King Jr. and Adolf Hitler, you will see two men influenced by the light and the dark. Before you think I am saying Hitler was a great leader, what I am comparing is their ability to lead. Why were so many people moved by them? It was the passion behind their beliefs. People were not forced to follow Hitler in the beginning, but they eventually chose to because he convinced them that they were a superior race.

Anyone can easily be swept up in the river that was once a trickle because of mob mentality. Martin Luther King wanted all people to be treated as equals. They should treat one another based on character and never by color. He wanted peace and wanted to see all men to be treated as one. Martin Luther King Jr.'s voice spoke with grace and passion. He didn't preach chaos and destruction. People were beginning to see the error of their ways, and thankfully, with the invention of the television, Dr. Martin Luther King's message was able to transmit out to people he would never meet. Lucifer is an enemy with nothing but everything wicked from the depths of your worst nightmare. Ironically, it's why I was sent to you today.

Many of the angels didn't understand how Lucifer's heart became arrogant in the presence of God. Lucifer believed that he held a higher position than the rest because of his ability to create incredible and hypnotizing music. He wanted God's adoration centered on himself. He failed to realize his gift came from God as a blessing and not a debt. Lucifer changed rapidly once his heart began to grow dark.

As Lucifer's heart began to change with each passing day it, became clearly visible in his expressions, his body language, and most importantly, in the music. God had been anticipating the transformation but kept hoping Lucifer's heart wouldn't turn black. The situation all came down to Lucifer's choice. It always comes down to choice. God decided that he would approach him in the Grand Worship Hall when the time was right. Lucifer was losing his incredible gift, and the music began to play off key. Little by little, the notes would miss a beat or sound flat. The symphony that was once able to resonate within every soul was now losing its blessing.

The other angels who had not been a part of Lucifer's following instantly knew that there was something darker going on than just a few bad notes. They could see within his aura he began to fade, right along with the other angels he was influencing. His followers tried to stick together instead of conversing, laughing, and being a part of the fellowship with the others they had once considered friends. The angels who didn't choose to listen to Lucifer knew he was growing evil, and they began to ask themselves why he would allow the darkness to enter their hearts.

God addressed the angels by telling them to "Be still." The pain began to radiate in his heart as he replied, "They have the freewill to choose, and their choice will become their downfall."

Finally, when Lucifer and the other angel's auras had completely faded to a dark mist, God wasted no time in confronting them in the

Worship Hall. He was furious over the fact that his place of purity and cleansing was being desecrated by pride, jealousy, malice, and even hatred. It hurt God so deeply that the most precious and beautiful of his creations had become so wicked. Their hearts no longer had love, peace, patience, kindness, and especially goodness.

God entered into the massive Worship Hall methodically, looking all around, when suddenly, he laid his eyes upon Lucifer. His heart panged inside him. There was nothing left from the light in Lucifer's aura but a small neon blue flame. Lucifer's back faced toward God, and he was hunched over as if he was reading something with his head down. God stopped in his tracks and then asked, "Lucifer, why has the music changed?" Lucifer refused to turn and face toward him. God waited for a moment before he asked again with more authority, and the anger in his voice was unmistakable. "Why has the worship music changed?"

The sound of angered words coming from God vibrated off the walls and echoed throughout the hall. Lucifer slowly stood up, and after letting out a huge sigh, slowly, he turned his face to God. They both stared at each other, and neither spoke. Lucifer's aura was now completely black, and mistlike trails were floating and building around his body. There was only but a small dim light left within him. His voice hissed like a snake, a dead cold stare as he replied, "There is nothing wrong with the music." Lucifer paused and stared into the eyes of his creator. He didn't remove his gaze as he continued to answer, "Maybe there is something wrong with what you hear. Maybe you just don't appreciate the gift you gave me anymore?"

Tenderly, God responded, "Why do you feel this way? What caused such hatred within you toward me? What has brought about the violence that is within your heart?" God paused for a brief moment as he tried to hold back a tear. "I have loved you and made you a beautiful creation among all the others, yet when you look at me, I see nothing now but darkness there. You are completely in Eden, a beautiful garden. I have adorned you with every precious stone; garnet, ruby, topaz, emeralds, onyx, jasper, sapphire, turquoise, and beryl. You were anointed as a Guardian, but wickedness has now consumed you. Your heart has become proud on account of your beauty and talent. You are desecrating this sanctuary and bringing dishonor to my name," God replied.

It was as if on cue; all the other angels that Lucifer was able to deceive entered into the hall. This gave Lucifer a sense of power and authority, making him feel that he was superior to God. God looked around the Worship Hall, and his heart broke. He knew that one-third of the beings he created and loved so deeply were now lost to Lucifer's darkness. The dark mist then became a thick dense fog as it followed the other angels when they entered. Their expressions had become darkened, and their eyes no longer had any of the light within them. They all had made their choice to follow and listen to pure evil.

"You have made me to be the representation of worship, so I demand now to be worshiped!" Lucifer stated with arrogance. As wickedness grew in his appearance, he looked around at all the others that came into the Worship Hall. He continued, "They stand behind me and will worship me as their god, for they no longer choose you." He moved slowly closer to his creator.

Suddenly, there was the sound of a heartbeat in the room, beating faster and faster, struggling to keep pumping. Within a few moments, the beating slowed down and all but stopped. "You have mistaken my gift bestowed upon you as deserving of power, but as the heart stops beating, so will my tolerance for you and your arrogance and pride." God looked deep within Lucifer's eyes. He would not remove his gaze upon him as the words were spoken. Then suddenly, the heartbeat stopped. Lucifer started to lunge at God, and within that very instant, God's light came through his hand, and he struck Lucifer like a heavyweight boxer knocking down his opponent. All the other angels fell down with the blow as well.

"I made you what you are and make no mistake I will destroy what you have become!" his voice boomed with anger and pain. He then paused and continued to speak more calmly. "You are now cast from my sight, my throne, and this Worship Hall. I will make you crawl on your stomach the rest of your life, and you will be lower than mankind. You will be dirt among their feet, eating dust for your remaining days. Hear my words that you will never be allowed your

place at my side again." With the words spoken and his heart now fully broken, the tear he tried holding back finally dropped from his eye. When it fell and hit the ground, he cast them from his sight.

The next thing heard throughout the universe was an incredibly loud explosion. The sky completely lit up. When Lucifer and all his followers were thrown down, they hit the surface of the Earth and created an enormous crater hundreds of miles wide. Thousands of the now fallen caused the earth to tremble when they smashed to the ground. Within moments, they began to burn as if they had been doused in acid. Layers upon layers of their skin and some muscle melted off that left them completely blackened. The smell of sulfur permeated the air, and as they tried to stand up, the pain from the fire brought them back down to their knees. It was the first time they had ever experienced anything so painful and detrimental.

Their groans arose back to heaven, and then the voice of God came thundering through the skies. He was so sad and torn, his words spoken with a broken heart. "What had made you so great will now be your weakness. When worship is played, glorifying my name, you will not have any authority or ability. It will make you crawl like the snake you are and recoil from pain. As for the rest of you, you will no longer have the beautiful forms or bodies I gave you. You will be creatures designed from the darkness within your own hearts. You are banished to wander this world to be nothing. When the time has come, I will reduce you to ashes on the ground, and you will be no more. You have made this choice on your own, and now there is no coming back!"

The echo of his voice rumbled through the skies. There was dead silence, and suddenly, a tremendous strike of lightning shot across the sky. The crackling was so powerful that it was deafening as the tearing in the spiritual world was now fully split. God's heart broke that day. He mourned the loss of his creations which were once so incredibly beautiful.

When God created man, he made man in his image, yet he decided not to grant man with the same abilities and supernatural gifts that he had once given to the fallen. Unfortunately, some of the fallen had their own talents and abilities that they decided they would teach mankind when the time was right. With God's heart still aching from the loss of those he loved so much, he decided to bless man with every skill they needed to survive. Even though it hurt him, he would never force a creation to love him, so they were provided with the ability to choose freely. All the food he needed he would grant so the human body would be sustained and the nutrients that could keep them healthy. He gave man the ability to name all the animals within the beautiful Garden of Eden. He only had one rule to Adam and Eve: "Do not eat from the Tree of Knowledge."

Lucifer saw the creation of the humans and had nothing but distaste for them. As man began to grow and develop throughout history, Lucifer vowed he would take all his anger out on the humans. His hatred toward the Israelites was especially vile since above all others, they were God's chosen people. He despised and detested man with every fiber in his being. He made a vow that he would do everything vile to destroy mankind. So it was in that first moment he decided to take the form of the serpent and tempted Eve to eat from the tree of knowledge. God had called him a snake, so a snake he would become. Lucifer lied to her because he knew she was naive and childlike, a new creation, and he could manipulate her to disobey God. He set out for her because deep down, he knew how much it would hurt to destroy more of God's creations. They had no power, no special abilities, no glowing aura, and they were certainly nothing special to look at.

The fallen, behind their leader, began to be incredibly successful in his mission to draw the humans from worshiping God. As the time of man has carried on, throughout the centuries, mankind's heart has grown further from the God of creation. Mankind now lives for himself because his deeds can be wicked and selfish. It's easier to hide in darkness than to expose sensitive truth in the light. No one wants to be weak. I will agree that it isn't easy, though, to stay hidden when hearts have become numb to their own wicked actions.

The darkness is meant to make mankind believe that this life is all there is. He thinks it's best to live life for himself in the here and now because it contradicts what God tries to teach everyone. He gave us commandments to prevent us from the pain that comes along with poor decisions. It's not done as a punishment or to bring about guilt. It's comparable to when a parent takes away something from a child because they could get hurt or the consequences could be devastating. God doesn't want man to get hurt through decisions and actions.

It seems almost too simple to have two sides of nature—the light and darkness—yet they are both very complicated. Both sides have hierarchies just as in any military structure. Each piece in the structure is just as important as the next, and no one is considered more important than anyone else. There are natural leaders, and in the light, there is still human emotion but without sin. Everything is peaceful, funny, silly, and overall wondrous. Within darkness, there is pain, chaos, and loss. Nothing ever gets better, and everything only gets worse.

Starting within the light, the first level of defense is known as the Fruits of the Spirit. The Fruits of the Spirit's skill set is mostly comfort providing prayer, hope, and strength. When people walk through trials and tribulations, they can feel hurt, abandoned, confused, and oftentimes empty. The Fruits of the Spirit will get an assignment toward a person who is walking a path in life that takes strength and courage. They are the purest of the structure because they were the little children when they were alive. They also get assignments for people on earth to provide little treasures each day to help alleviate the pain. These little signs each day help during the tribulation or trial to get to the next day. They provide answers to prayers when someone has been seeking for direction their soul desperately needs. The little cherubs will attach themselves gently and will help out the person who just lost their job and desperately needs encouragement.

The Fruits of the Spirit have a counterpart within the darkness that has set out to do the exact opposite. Since God cast them to earth, they have formed their own structure. They were still so angry at being banished from God's side they have set out to destroy anything good. The longer they have remained on the earth, the uglier and stronger they have become. They are known as the Reeds of Death, and they hate man and have set out to influence man to be rude, selfish, and, of course, want man at war even within himself.

They snare, entrap, and entangle because their goal is to start a domino effect of destruction.

A major event such as divorce or death can start to break down any soul. Once the Reeds have hooked onto their victim, it allows and makes way for the next level within the hierarchy of darkness. Instead of rational thought, they are incredibly patient. Known as the Tortones, they linger and wait to see how the Reeds have afflicted the person, and their job is to place everything in your path to make you angry and frustrated. They can enter a life with any major or minor sin that began to develop in the hurricane of emotions. The Tortones take every opportunity destroy thoughts and to torture. They are genuinely out to make sure their victim fails and start to become miserable.

The counterparts within the light are known as the Momenti. These are the angels of the moment, providing the help that is needed. A person could be stranded in the middle of the night at a gas station, and let's say a person didn't have a purse, wallet, or phone. Suddenly, a man approaches out of nowhere and provides the money needed to get home. He asks for nothing in return and is never seen again. That angel takes full human form, and honestly, they can sometimes look ugly and off-putting. They will enter as one person or leave as another.

The Momenti are the reminder of the good things and the promises that God gives. Enduring a season of pain can affect even the best of people, and the Momenti can come in as a friend for that season. They provide support, friendship, and wisdom to help heal the heart, and God will do that occasionally to measure where your heart is. That's why it's so important to check your heart from time to time. Don't be so quick to judge surroundings and see everything for face value; it just may be a Momenti riding the waves of your true character.

The next and most physical level in the structure is where I come in and why I train to fight. Guardians are warriors, and we are sent to protect those alive, struggling day to day. Within both structures, the light and the dark, we can only influence. We are not allowed to interfere with a person's life because God gave man the

9

free will to choose. I know it's common for people to believe that their mom or relative who passed away watches over them, but that is not the case. If a mother was to be a Guardian of her own children and sees her child making mistakes that she knows will cause them pain, she will want to step in and intervene. Within the light, we just can't. If the light was to interfere, then that allows Lucifer the power and ability to then have almost full control of people at all times. Mankind has only seen a small fraction of his capabilities. So we have to remain vigilant to mind our side as much as possible. We are also not allowed to kill or wound any demons in the darkness, unless the person under their influence fully denounces and walks away from the dark.

Each Guardian is placed within a group of seven. There is always a leader, and the leader chooses their group based upon certain skills and abilities. I am one of those leaders and have carefully handpicked my group based on skill sets that I want for war. First, I have Big Ben who is the exquisite marksman. He is an excellent shot with his weapon and can hit his chosen target from almost any angle. I have JoAnne who is my problem-solver. Most Guardians, like people, look at a situation for what it is and focus specifically on what's in front of them; but she can always see through the problem and provide solutions. Before I get done trying to think of plan A, she has plan B, C, and D sorted out.

I have Nathan, aka Tank, because of his incredible brute strength. Even in the light, someone with supernatural strength is a sight to see. I have Reese who is my chameleon and can blend into any situation he is placed. He can hide in plain sight, which is a great advantage during war. I am about to obtain a new addition to my group named Kinsey. She will soon learn her ability and skill set as her training takes place. It is because of that ability and the lack of knowledge on how it works we are about to go to war. Now I know, including me, that only counts five, but we will be joined with the last members when the time is right.

Guardians are assigned to those who have similar personalities and have made the same type of choices and mistakes they're assigned person experiences. It is structured this way so we know and relate on a deeper level. Often, we have walked through the same pain, whether it was divorce, death, abuse, addiction, or rejection. Our compassion for our beloved people is above and beyond what could be thought of for a stranger. Believe me when I say we know our people so intimately. Our counterparts, however, are out to destroy in the worst way possible.

If you allow a Reed to enter into your mind and thoughts and don't denounce the thoughts, the door is opened for a Tortone to fester and grow in any sin or addiction. Unfortunately, once you have given in fully to the Tortone, prepare for a floodgate. Imagine a giant hole on the side of a home. The mind becomes the house with a hole. Now the fallen or Watchers have full control. These are the ones who are assigned by Lucifer to attack with no mercy. He created the Reeds and the Tortones so it would be easier to trip up mankind since he knew God's love for them.

Guardians have human emotion without sin, but we do know hate. We hate the pain the fallen cause. Our job is to kill and destroy them when they have entered into the person we guard. The catch is they have to choose to let them go and make them leave. So, in other words, your mind turns into actions and actions to habits. The key to notice is what habit falls under the light and what habit falls under the darkness. Just because it "feels good" doesn't mean it is good.

The Watchers can even be so strong. They stay in family lines. The sin of the father can pass to his children or even skip a generation down to grandchildren. They are everything that the darkness represents. Just as you are assigned Guardians from the light, the darkness has assigned Watchers. In many cases, two or three can be attached to one person. They don't play fair, and their job is to steal, kill, and destroy. They are shapeshifters, taking any form they please, except a permanent full human one.

Watchers can appear as a spirit or ghost to lure in those filled with curiosity about the supernatural. They will mimic voices and seem as though they are innocent children. This is done to deceive the people who are so vulnerable or have not been educated enough on how deceptive the dark can really be. God warns against seeking the supernatural, telling his people that it shouldn't be done. It is important, though, to be aware he doesn't say that it couldn't be done. This is one of his warnings because those searching will end up in a world they are unfit to battle without the power of the Holy Spirit.

The next level within the darkness are the lieutenants and Greater Demons. One is known as Belial. He is Lucifer's right-hand man. Belial was designed to feed upon the anger, rage, and war within mankind. With all the ugliness in the world, his dominance and strength are almost unmatched. Lucifer's left-hand design is known as Legion. He was formed to be the counterpart to the Holy Spirit. Since God's power can never be matched, Lucifer had to try and duplicate thousands of the fallen, combining them to be one. Legion is the eyes and ears of everything that is wicked throughout the entire world. Lucifer uses him as a spy gathering intel on his enemy.

There is also the Prince of Persia who is the driving force behind the tension in the Middle East. Since God recognizes the Israelites as his chosen people, Lucifer needed a demon to be cunning with wit and tenacious in strength. The Prince of Persia is wicked in his ways, devious with mankind and oppressive in his approach. He is the definition of a true terrorist and his power grows from the terror within the souls of his victims, and daily, he grows stronger.

The last of Lucifer's design is a Greater Demon that mankind has struggled with throughout history. Her name is Morajes. She was born from the perversion in the world. Her parents were the spirits of Sodom and Gomorrah. If God had not destroyed and demolished the cities, she would have had many sisters. Morajes is the reason sexuality is flaunted in mankind's face constantly. The more open sexuality is accepted, the stronger she gets.

In today's time, she is incredibly powerful. When adult entertainment became mainstream within the media, her power grew to a level that we Guardians had never seen before. The Watchers were attached to more and more families because of men's addiction, and women started to really believe this is what they needed to be in a man's eyes in order to be beautiful. The brokenness from believing sex gives anyone worth is enough alone to destroy the soul. Her goal is to lose all innocence. When she was instructed by her father, Lucifer, to go after children, she definitely became destined to destroy so many lives and families.

The good news is that the light is able to counter and defeat Lucifer's deadly officers. We also have the lieutenants and generals known as Archangels. Michael, Gabriel, and Itherial are the lead and command of God's army. They are considered brothers, and they have stood against the enemy of time and have never lost against the enemies in the darkness. You will get to know them as the lives of my group of Guardians comes to light.

Now I want you to sit back and watch the events that are about to unfold and lead to what will be known as the beginning of the end.

THE NEWEST ADDITION

The weather was absolutely perfect driving south on the 5 Freeway heading into San Diego. With the sun shining and a cool breeze dancing in the air, the weather provided the ideal setting to a great day. "Today is a true reason to celebrate," Kinsey said to herself. She had just been offered a job with a new career, and a new career meant a new life. An hour commute never really bothered her because she enjoyed the time to herself. The morning commute was bumper to bumper, and every fellow driver was still trying to wake up with either the local stop at the closest coffee shop, books on audio, or talk radio about the upcoming political debate. Kinsey didn't care for politics or even music on the radio. She loved driving with her windows down and music blasting from her iPod so she could sing at the top of her lungs and dance in the driver seat. She received the occasional honk from an entertained driver in another car which fueled the desire to entertain. Kinsey kept singing as though she was putting on a performance for the world to see; well, in traffic anyway. Music generally set her mood for the day, and today's music was especially upbeat.

Kinsey had been raised in a home with a God-fearing mother who made sure the family went to church every Sunday. Her mother spent many hours dedicated to work and to the church, especially in the youth groups. Her father was a moral man, but he struggled with organized religion due to his experiences in Vietnam. Kinsey never missed a Sunday at church or a Sunday night Bible study. There was no other option made by her mother, and Kinsey didn't mind since she had grown close with the other kids who were raised the same way. She never pushed her beliefs on anyone, but if she was asked, she gladly wanted to introduce people to the God she felt she knew. She had experienced numerous supernatural events that couldn't be explained scientifically, and those events only furthered her belief and her faith. The thought that if there was no God or something better than this life, then there wasn't anything to strive for, was too depressing of a thought for all the ugliness in the world.

Kinsey had long brown hair with red tones underneath, and though it was naturally curly, she usually straightened it out. In fact, she preferred to go against the grain. She had the hourglass curves that she was proud to show off because she didn't care to fit what Hollyweird called beautiful. Kinsey had blue eyes that could stare deep into anyone as she studied those who spoke. She was shorter than the average woman, but what she lacked in height she over-powered in personality. Stubborn, opinionated, quick-witted, and extremely sarcastic were the most dominant features of her person-ality. She found humor in most things people would get so offended over.

She was once told by a friend that she could make the pope come out of his shell. Those were the compliments she loved to hear. It took her years not to focus on the physical attributes because beauty can change instantly. What she held onto so dear were the observations her friends would tell her with regard to her character. They loved how her personality could draw people in.

Unfortunately, though, she had her insecurities too. On occa-sion, she would pretend and play the confident role yet internally would struggle because her mind could be her biggest enemy. It took her years to get to that point of knowing and loving who she was. She had to go through many changes in her faith and walk with God to come to realize it was who God said she was, not what the world says. It doesn't matter if it is good or bad.

Things had been rough, extremely rough for the past ten years, and her life was never really an easy ride. She struggled her whole life with bipolar depression, and because of the condition, she struggled with emotional highs and lows. She had lost everything she owned over a four-year timeline from a divorce and bad decision after bad decision. The pain from the divorce and the loss of everything she worked for made her angry with God, and she couldn't understand why. Her heartbreak caused her to blame God instead of just being patient and trusting it would get better.

Regardless of her circumstance, she did her best and continued moving forward. Finally, after spending a night in her car with her son, she knew she had reached rock bottom. Finally, she broke down and cried out to the God she had been running from to give her a way out. She was finally tired of running. Slowly, the blessings started to reveal themselves, and she was able to climb out of what felt like the pit of despair to better her situation.

A big source of pain was while everyone else around her had their mortgages and family growing in full force, she struggled with keeping gas in her car. The snowball effect started when she married a man who claimed he never loved her. The pain from the truth left her life to unravel, and her world that she thought she understood dissipated. He took her to her favorite restaurant for their anniversary and began their usual conversations about work, friends, and the drama that unfolds. Kinsey knew deep down he didn't love her, so she decided to just confront him right then and there. She figured it would give her some closure and possibly, for once, get an honest answer since she would catch him in lie after lie.

What felt like a tsunami of emotions that overcame her started when her husband confessed an affair with a woman he worked with. Though inside Kinsey died as the words were spoken, she stayed stone cold on the outside. She didn't want him to see one tear fall from her face. Love was all she ever really wanted. She didn't care about how much money a man made or that he was even the best-looking, just so long as he made her laugh and he loved and accepted her.

"Listen, I know you care about me, but you don't love me, do you?" Kinsey asked.

Her husband was completely thrown off guard by the question, but finally, he gave her what she needed: the truth. "I don't know if I ever loved you," he stated as he lowered his head.

Her blood instantly felt cold. She began to tremble slightly but tried to gain her composure. All she could think about was how badly she wanted to seriously stab him in the face and make sure he would always remember why he had a scar. She debated on what would hurt the most.

Kinsey thought for a moment and figured it would have to be something random, but the mark would need to be incredibly distinct, enough so that people would constantly ask about where he got it. *He isn't going to walk away that easy*, she thought to herself.

Her thoughts became more abrasive, and she did not care how crazy her thinking seemed as he sat and confessed his affair. *Maybe a fork, but I would have to have enough force that it would be deep and permanent. Hmmm, maybe the ones that are used while trying to pick up a pork roast out of a slow cooker. Those are incredibly thick and could do some massive damage.* Half of his words didn't even register with her because all she could focus on was the knife on her plate and the possible consequences of stabbing him in the eye and running away.

She had to file bankruptcy as a result of his foolish spending from large purchases like golf clubs when he didn't golf and a mountain bike that he would never ride. Back before data plans came with cell phones, he had also run up a bill so high when she went to pay, they said the bill was nearly six thousand dollars. "This has to be a mistake," she said as she called her provider. No, of course not. Just her luck: it was real. The graphic images that she found were not supposed to be found on a moral "man of God's" phone.

He ran up a bill looking at all kinds of sites no married man should go behind his wife and see. She broke everything he owned in the garage that night. It was not just because the bill was high; however, it was the reason that the bill was so high. The betrayal she felt destroyed her internally. She didn't understand why he wouldn't be intimate with her, but he wanted pictures and videos. Maybe he felt like he was cheating on his girlfriend with his wife, and that was the most rational thought she came up with. It was a pure slap in the face. So those golf clubs he cared so much about? All bent and broken. The Legos he wanted to build? All smashed by the golf clubs. The mountain bike that he was certainly never going to ride? Wheels off, frame broken, and pieces thrown everywhere. Vodka had definitely been her best friend that night, helping her to think she was acting completely rational.

He ended up a year later on marrying the woman he had been sleeping with, and all she could think to herself was, *Good luck.* Still, it left her slightly bitter on certain occasions when she would see couples who were married around the same time she was. They were still going strong and thriving. She was happy for her friends and always wanted the best for them. Still, she slightly felt herself die inside because she was dumb enough to marry a man who didn't love her. The embarrassment of her poor choices felt at times as if it was leaking from her pores.

Then, of course, came several relationships after him that ended in total disasters. She was angry and still hurt, never giving herself the time she really needed to heal, a common emotion many people feel when they have a hole so wide in themselves that they don't care what or who it is; it just needs to be filled. She had a tendency to gravitate toward the men that would make her feel good in the here and now, never really thinking they were suitable for long-term.

First, there was Steven. He swept her off her feet and made her believe that he would stick by her come hell or high water. She had never lived with a man before, other than her husband. With her history, she couldn't decide since she never wanted to get married again, she would give it a try and move in with him. One day, he just left and never came back home. She couldn't find him, and he never returned her calls. She was destroyed inside, and it felt like a full train wreck had crashed inside her. Not only did he leave her with no answer, but she had to ask herself, what was so wrong with her that she repelled the men she loved?

She ended up finding out six months later through social media he had married someone else. She felt another piece in her die inside. The abandonment was worse than what her ex-husband had done. At least her ex-husband had the nerve to face her. She knew she could be deadly with her tongue and wicked with her words when she got angry.

The truth of it, though, was she was incredibly broken inside. All that anger from those two relationships only made things worse. The next one was physically and emotionally abusive. He seemed so passionate and intense, but the truth was he was angry and insecure. He wouldn't work, so he stayed home, playing video games all day, messaging just about any girl he could. Slowly and unknowingly, he began to separate her from her friends and family.

One day, she realized the only messages or calls she ever had on her phone were from him. Kinsey had to check in and give a detailed account of her every move. Finally, one day, she had enough. She felt all her anger rise and fought back. This was not the smartest move and definitely not the man to confront. He instantly got into her face, screaming and throwing everything around the house. Kinsey didn't care anymore because she would not let him win this time. She was able to get several good swings in, though, before he finally got a firm grip on her neck. He grabbed her by the throat so hard that she could feel herself getting dizzy and almost passed out. He smashed her head into a picture hanging on the wall and then dropped her to the ground.

The choking had left her barely breathing. As she lay there, gasping for air, she coughed, but true to her personality, she looked up at him and flipped him the bird. She didn't care if it pushed him to go further because she finally had enough. Thankfully, she had been planning her escape route. That was finally enough for her. No more dating and no more moving in with anyone.

It wasn't about just the men she dated. She constantly hurt the people she cared about. Though she knew better, she couldn't always control her actions, but still, it was no excuse to go down the darker path. Kinsey just wanted to be like everyone else. She truly wasn't book smart because of the way her mind worked; she couldn't retain the information she would have to do for school, and as a young kid, no one got her ready in the morning or checked her homework at night. She was mostly left to fend for herself.

It became harder as she got older with a crazy mind working against itself to fight and be like everyone else. She was raised in a good Christian home, though, and did have parents who loved and supported her. Kinsey also struggled with self-image, and for years, it was all coming down to the pain. She didn't know how to love herself.

Kinsey knew the Bible and knew who God was on a deeper emotional level, but during those painfully lonely years, she was angry and running from him. Her whole world crumbled when her husband had told her he never loved her. A veil had been lifted from her eyes, though. She thought that when you were a Christian, you worked it out since God was pro-marriage. She truly believed God would have his hand in things and he would repair it. She didn't understand why he didn't step in.

After healing took place, Kinsey realized she was never supposed to marry him from the beginning. She actually questioned many times why she didn't even try to fight for her husband. She realized she had too much pride and was not about to beg for a man who didn't want her.

Kinsey had failed to remember from the days of her youth that there was a spiritual world she couldn't always see. Every time she made a bad choice, it started as an influence of evil. It took her years to fully understand what "holds every thought captive" meant in the Bible. Every single time she made a decision toward a relationship she knew she shouldn't get in, a domino effect would cause her life to start falling completely apart. She would barely put herself back together, then fall apart at the seams with every new heartache. She had finally had enough and began to grow stronger in her faith and walk with God again. She didn't want to run anymore because running was so exhausting. All it ever really did was leave what felt like a wide-open hole inside her body. It felt so void and empty.

"God, I choose you. I choose to forgive, I choose to let go, I choose to trust you, and I choose that you can make all of my past good," she prayed on the night she was forced to sleep in her car.

God had given her a gift the world would easily dismiss. Biblically, it was known as a prophetic gift. The Holy Spirit would speak to her in a still soft voice. It could easily be about a particular person or a situation without knowing the circumstances. She would cautiously approach and gently try to deliver whatever message she was supposed to convey. She found it easier to talk to a complete stranger versus a friend because she never had to worry about seeing the stranger again.

Kinsey knew with her checkered past that she wouldn't have the credibility. There were several instances when the Holy Spirit would impress on her heart a situation that a friend was experiencing, and she knew God was giving her the message so she could give a message of hope. It was just incredibly difficult because no one wants to look crazy. That was the downside to the gift when a person rejected the message.

Hearing that sweet voice and delivering a message to someone in need was so beautiful. There was no greater feeling than giving someone peace or a ray of sunshine through a hurricane filled with pain. She was all too familiar with that need. Unfortunately, the fallen don't appreciate anyone seeking out the God that banished them. When Kinsey was weak in her faith, an ugly and sinister Watcher would try to torture her every thought. What Kinsey didn't know was as those thoughts would come in, she allowed it to affect her mood and demeanor.

The Reeds of Death had been paving the way for the Watchers to come and stay. The Watcher would whisper and repeat her mistakes over and over again, like a broken record. The more she listened to the negative words, the more power they had. The negativity became apparent when she was in any unhealthy relationship with a man who had Watchers of his own.

Watchers have the ability to seek out the weak, any person with faith, or devour those with no faith at all. Finally, though...finally, things were going to change. She didn't have to depend on any man anymore. She was beginning to feel complete, giving her life back to a gracious God that granted mercy, love, and forgiveness. Kinsey, overwhelmed with emotion, was so incredibly excited for what lay ahead.

"All of it is over! I am getting my life back and ready to take over the world and conquer it once again." She smiled and laughed to herself, rocking out to her music as she yelled the words to absolutely nobody.

"Your family can finally stop worrying. You can give your two beautiful kids a reason to be proud of their mom, and you are real."

Kinsey slowly opened her eyes to a blinding bright light. She was standing alone in a room. Just standing. It appeared to be a hospital room. She felt weightless and slightly confused. The slow beeping of a heart monitor instantly caught her attention. She looked down at herself, and she was still in normal clothes with no hospital gown on her. Kinsey noticed that the bed in front of her had someone laying in it. She crept up to the bed and noticed a woman lay before her and was completely bandaged up. She didn't recognize the woman at all. She was badly burned and missing an arm. The woman's leg had been broken, placed in a cast, and there were cuts and bandages all over her face and head.

"Who is that? Wait, what am I doing here?" she asked herself out loud while she looked around the room. Her mind was completely blank. Why was she here? What was she doing before she was in here? A familiar feeling crept over, a feeling of how she had just walked into a room and completely forgot why she was there. Slowly turning, she stopped when she found herself facing a tall Polynesian woman. The woman fully caught her off guard. She had never seen her before, but Kinsey felt as though she should know her for some reason.

Her face was soft and incredibly kind, not to mention undeniably beautiful. The woman was standing over six feet tall with long curly hair. She was wearing a giant shark tooth around her neck, much larger than a great white. The woman had markings on her tanned skin and a design of a turtle on her right hand. Based on her looks, Kinsey guessed her to be a Pacific Islander. The woman was holding an odd-looking staff that was completely smooth except on the end. The staff was round, and shark teeth poked out from all directions. The woman dressed in what appeared to be military-type gear. The odd part to Kinsey was the woman wore turquoise. The color against her tanned skin caused her to stand out much more than she already was with the bright lights in the hospital room.

"I…umm… I'm sorry…do you work here?" Kinsey asked.

"No," the woman answered softly.

"Okay, do you know who this is? Because for some reason, I completely blanked out." Kinsey couldn't help but focus on the weird-looking weapon the Polynesian woman kept holding. She found it odd that hospital security would even allow someone in with a staff filled with shark teeth.

Maybe this is security? she thought to herself.

"Look closer, Kinsey," the woman said softly.

Kinsey felt herself freeze for a moment. "Who is she?" Kinsey asked herself. She had a photographic memory and never, not once, had she ever forgotten a face. She called it her rolodex of faces. As soon as she saw a face that looked familiar, it was like her mind flipped through the index. She would match up the face in her memory. It was a gift she was proud to have and wished she could have made some kind of career of. So why couldn't she remember her?

Kinsey turned back toward the woman and approached the bed slowly. She happened to notice the white board near the bed read "K. Rivers."

Hmm, this person has the same initials I do. Wait! Suddenly, she felt her blood go cold. "*No!* No, no, no, no, no, no…this is not real!" she said as she turned back toward the woman behind her. "This is not happening. I am in a bad dream and I am going to wake up any minute." She paused, waiting for an answer. "Or, wait, is this some kind of sick joke?" she asked as she looked at the motionless body in front of her.

"It's not a dream…or a joke, Kinsey. What you see is real." The voice was so soft and cool that every time she spoke, Kinsey instantly felt more relaxed. It made no sense, though. She couldn't get over the weird-looking weapon in the woman's hands. This had to be a joke. Who would come into a hospital with a pole full of shark teeth?

After a minute of silence, Kinsey finally replied, "What? Who are you? And what do you mean this is real?"

The woman approached Kinsey with the staff in her hand, and suddenly, a nurse walked in. Just as Kinsey was about to get the nurse's attention, she froze in place. She couldn't believe what her own eyes just saw. The nurse passed straight through the strange woman and rubbed her arms as if she was freezing.

Kinsey felt her throat drop down to her stomach. The Polynesian woman then approached Kinsey with gentle caution, and as she got closer, she placed her hand on Kinsey's shoulder. This made her instantly become comfortable and, surprisingly, very relaxed. With her touch, it was as if they were old friends about to embrace after years of a lost friendship.

"My name is Leilani, Kinsey, and throughout your life, I have been one of your Guardians."

For whatever reason, she couldn't explain why, but Kinsey actually believed her. She always questioned everyone about everything because there was little to trust in anyone due to her past. Now, for whatever reason, she easily believed that this was not only *a* Guardian but *her* Guardian. Maybe this was a really good morphine trip? That could fully explain her hallucinations. Not exactly what she had anticipated, but this was almost too much to register in her brain.

"So what are you trying to say? That this means I am dying?" she asked half-jokingly. She was hoping that this was still a part of some odd yet disgusting prank. The nurse was pulling up the blankets around the body in the bed into an upward position. Kinsey couldn't remove her eyes from all the wires and tubes connected to what was supposed to be her body. As she turned to face Leilani and to ask the millions of questions that were running through her head, the door opened again. It was her mom and dad. It wasn't until this very incredible yet unbelievable moment that Kinsey realized how aged and fragile her parents looked.

They walked up to the bed, and both of them tried to gently call her name. Everything she was looking at and watching still didn't register to her because Kinsey was not ready to die. Not after everything she lived through and the few suicide attempts.

"Kinsey? Kinsey, can you hear me?" her mother asked while placing her hand on top of her daughter's shoulder. The nurse placed two chairs by the bed and stated that the doctor would be in to see them in just a few moments. Her mom sat down and started to weep tears that looked like a floodgate had opened.

Kinsey's father grabbed her hand and called to her name with a more serious and demanding tone. "Kinsey! Kinsey, wake up!" He didn't say anything after and stood there, looking at Kinsey for several moments before he sat down. Finally, when he couldn't stand anymore, he sank into his chair. He began to fight back the tears as he gazed upon his daughter's broken body.

Kinsey couldn't help but to walk up to her parents and try to touch them. "I don't understand," Kinsey said with tears beginning to fill her eyes. She was horrified and couldn't hide the expression on her face. She looked back to Leilani for some kind of answer as anger began to build in her entire body. "What is this? What the hell is this? Tell me! Please. Is this some kind of sick joke?"

Just as Leilani was about to answer, the door opened yet again and interrupted the much-needed explanation to Kinsey. It was her two children, her reason to exist and her reason to keep fighting, especially when she didn't think she could. Her legs buckled from under her, and she went down to her knees. Leilani helped her to stand back up.

"We need to go, Kinsey," she said as she tried gently to pull her arm.

Kinsey shook off Leilani's hand and slowly walked up behind her two children. Kinsey had just spoken to her daughter that morning when she called to congratulate her. She was supposed to be meeting her this very evening to celebrate.

Her daughter, Grace, walked in the room, holding the hand of her much younger brother, Zerek. She instantly had tears in her eyes the moment she approached the bed where her mother's lifeless body lay. Grace stared at the heart monitor for a moment before she grabbed Kinsey's hand. She leaned downward. "Mom, can you hear me? Mom? Mom, come on, it's Grace. Open your eyes. Please, Mom, open your eyes! Zerek is here too. Mom, please?"

The pleading from her daughter caused Kinsey's parents to cry without restraint. Zerek, many years younger than his sister, didn't fully understand why his mommy couldn't wake up. Her family was concerned since he was nonverbal and was born with autism. Would he ever understand?

With a smile spreading on his face, he kept trying to get into the bed while grabbing onto her blanket. The little boy kept thinking his mommy was only sleeping or playing pretend.

Grace picked up her little brother and held him. He grabbed his sister's face, looked at her, and gently said, "Mommy wake up?"

Tears started to drop uncontrollably from her daughter's eyes. "Would you please take Z out for a minute so that I can have a minute with my mom alone?"

"Sure, baby," her grandparents said as they grabbed their grandson's hand and walked out.

Leilani stepped aside as they began to walk out, and Zerek paused to look up as though he was looking straight at Leilani. He smiled while looking up at the stranger and waved. His grandmother looked at him, slightly puzzled, and Kinsey shifted her focus back to her daughter.

Grace pulled the chair up closer to the bed and sat for several minutes. She held her mother's hand and lowered her head to pray silently. Grace then looked up with tear-filled eyes and grabbed several tissues on the table next to the bed. Kinsey braced herself for what Grace was about to say while sitting in the chair next to her. She had her daughter at a young age, so while everyone else she knew was going off to college and partying, Kinsey was a mom to a baby. There is a special bond between a young mother and daughter. Her daughter wiped her nose and after taking a few deep breaths, she began to speak.

"Mom." Her words were barely audible, but she tried to continue. "Mom, I need you to wake up. We have been through so much, and I need you here with me, and Z needs you here. I know there were times you thought I would be better off without you, but honestly, knowing there is a chance of losing you right now is killing me inside." Grace was struggling to say the words as she continued to pour out her heart. "I know you have always felt insecure as a parent compared to my dad. He may have given me stability through all of your craziness, but you still taught me to be strong. Even though you didn't always make good decisions, I know when it came to me, you really tried to do what was right. I realize now why you had me live with my dad. You knew it was better for me. I thank you for wanting to give me a better life, even though it killed you inside. Mom, you made mistakes, but you are still *my* mom."

Grace paused to wipe her nose and then began to speak with more determination, "I need you to fight this one last time for me and for Z. Even if it's just to fight with me, you need to fight. You have overcome a divorce, rejection, abuse, addiction, dealing with depression, and worst of all, having to struggle with thoughts of suicide. None of that matters now because I still believe in you, and I will always believe in you. We have been through so much together, and we have finally come out of all of it. Mom, please! You are supposed to be there for me when I decide to get married! You are supposed to help me pick out my dress when that day comes. I don't understand this, Mom, and I feel like I am dying inside."

Grace stopped talking for a minute and just stared at her mother. She felt like she couldn't breathe and wanted to believe all of this was a bad dream. When she gained strength, finally she continued, this time with more of an attitude and determination. "Mom, this is hard for me to look at you in this bed with all these damn tubes. Mommy... Mommy, please open your eyes and look at me. *Open them!*" she screamed out, hoping her mother would hear her. "Show me that you know I am here and show me that you understand me. Just grab my hand back. Please, Mom... I need you. Remember... Remember when you explained to me that the human heart is like a puzzle and each person in your life is a piece to complete it? Well, if you take away that piece, I don't know how I will make it. The piece you have in my heart is going to leave this massive hole and I can't make it through that without you. I can't replace your piece, Mom. It's only designed for you! Only you know how to walk me through all of this. P-P-P-Please, Mom. Please! Where is my brother going to go? What is going to happen to Z? Mom, I cannot accept this. It is especially after everything we have been through. You have to fight one more time." With those final words spoken, she rested her head at her mother's side and began to sob uncontrollably.

After watching her daughter and listening to everything she had to say, Kinsey had tears begin to fall like a Texas rainstorm. She wanted to hug her daughter and tell her that she was right there and that she wasn't going to ever leave her. Deep down, though, Kinsey knew it wasn't true.

Leilani stood at Kinsey's side, listening as her daughter spoke. She then crouched down to face toward her and said one more time, "Kinsey, we need to go. This only gets more painful the longer we sit and watch."

Ignoring her words, Kinsey turned to see that her parents had just walked back in with the doctor. She turned away again from Leilani and walked around the other side of the bed next to her body. The doctor approached her family, and they all braced themselves.

"See, now we will hear the good news and everything will be fine. He will tell them that I am just knocked out and I will be good to go after I heal." Kinsey looked directly to Leilani with hopeful eyes, begging internally for that to be the truth.

"Kinsey, your soul has already left your physical body. The only reason your body has a heartbeat is because your spirit is standing here. Let your family say goodbye and come with me," Leilani said with more authority.

The doctor looked at the family and spoke with a soft voice, all while knowing the news wasn't the best. The words spoken began to sound like a jumbled mess in Kinsey's ears. She felt dizzy and began to cry as the words *semitruck, brain-dead,* and *coma* were spoken. She couldn't believe what she was hearing, and most of all, what she was seeing. Her body was on a bed in front of her, her children seeing her physical form ready to pass, and her parents so broken and defeated by the reality of the moment.

"Pull it!" her father spoke with authority. "Living connected to a tube is no way to live."

Her mother looked at her father as he got up out of the chair and looked down at Kinsey's body. Her mother froze, barely breathing as she looked to her grandchildren.

Kinsey turned to face Leilani and snapped, "What the hell is this? Why is this happening? I have waited for years for my life to finally come together, and now this? Please, please, let me back in!" Tears kept dropping uncontrollably from her eyes.

Leilani stood solid in position, yet her eyes were still soft as she replied, "Kinsey, it's time to go. This only gets harder the longer you stay. I can take you away from the pain right now so you don't have to watch."

Almost as soon as the words left Leilani's mouth, Kinsey jumped on top of the bed and began to shake her lifeless body. "*Wake up, Kinsey!*" she screamed with such passion and filled with such conviction. Kinsey convinced herself if she was just able to wake herself up, this would all end. "Wake…up…right…now! I did not fight my way through so many years of pain and mistakes to die now! My kids need me. Please, *Kinsey*…please wake up!" She continued to shake her body's shoulders as hard as she could. The family and the doctor started to panic as it looked as though Kinsey's body was having some form of seizure. "*No, you can't do this! I'm not ready!*" she screamed, looking upward as if she was yelling this directly to God.

Grace picked up Zerek with tears blinding her vision and ran out the door. Her parents stood for a moment, and it was then Kinsey took a drastic move and slapped her own body in the face. Again and again, she kept hitting, hoping she would wake up.

Leilani had finally seen enough, grabbed Kinsey's arm, and everything faded to black.

WONDERS
NEVER CEASE

As Kinsey opened her eyes, her mind was completely blank. Leilani was at her side, holding her hand, and trying to help her to stand up. She was no longer holding the odd-looking staff anymore but had a weird-looking ball and string connected to her pants. Kinsey wasn't sure if she had fallen, but she couldn't help struggling to get up as she was taking in the new mysterious scenery. "How did I get here?" she asked herself. She remembered Leilani, but why couldn't she remember what just happened? She knew she was upset, but she couldn't figure out why.

When she realized she was standing on the outside of a wall, she was slightly surprised. Was she actually standing outside the gates of heaven? The sky was filled with stars shining like pure cut diamonds, yet it wasn't dark. The majestic view resembled an ocean of color untouched by man. In front of her stood two giant pillars. On the outer sides of the pillars was a solid gold wall glittering with more diamonds. On the inner sides of the pillars, the rods were made of platinum. Each individual rod was adorned in all the precious stones. The view through the gate suddenly caught her attention.

Directly in the middle of the gate, though, was a man who appeared to be blind. He was sitting at a cherry oak desk with a matching chair and a small lamp in the upper left corner. His eyes were white, showing no color, which slightly took Kinsey off guard. He was dressed in a white suite with a golden tie, gold shoes, and cufflinks that were shaped as music notes. He had a large book in his hands, and as he sat down at the desk in front of him, he smiled the instant he knew they approached him at the desk.

"Leilani, is that you, girl?" the man asked as he began to open the book and start flipping through the pages.

"You know it is, Ray!" Leilani replied, chuckling as Kinsey joined Leilani's side, still trying to look through the gate.

Ray looked toward Kinsey and instantly laughed, "Oh, I see we have a fighter today! This one is especially feisty, ain't she?" Ray asked with a smile.

"You have no idea, Ray! She has been having a headache sometimes, but she has a big heart," Leilani replied.

As Leilani and Ray spoke back and forth to each other, Kinsey kept trying to get a better look through the gate.

She could hear people but she couldn't see them. It took her a moment to realize that the man had just addressed her. Leilani and Ray were looking directly at Kinsey and waited for a response.

"I'm sorry"—Kinsey paused, focusing her attention—"I didn't hear you. What did you just say?" Kinsey asked. She focused on Ray and noticed something lying near him on the ground. She peered around the desk and discovered that a gargantuan lion was on his side, licking its paws as if it were a house cat.

Leilani and Ray's eyes followed Kinsey as she crept up to the giant beast. Kinsey didn't feel afraid, which caught her off guard. She slowly approached the lion as if it was a gentle kitten. Just as she was about to pet the top of his head, the lion looked her right in the eyes. Kinsey stepped back as her heart began to pound in her throat. She realized that this was no kitten or house pet. The lion stood up, stretched its back with a huge arch, his claws retracted, and Kinsey thought his paw was bigger than her head.

Ray and Leilani continued to watch, entertained by the visitor's curiosity. The lion focused his gaze into Kinsey's, and for a few moments, they both stared at one another. He was studying her. Then he slowly approached and began to nuzzle her legs and lick her hand.

"I see you met Mittens!" Ray started laughing, thinking his own pun was funny.

Kinsey then petted the gentle giant as he kept circling her legs. He was as smooth as velvet with his mane perfectly trimmed. Kinsey felt the heavy vibration under her hand and couldn't believe the beast was actually purring.

"You actually named him... Mittens?" Kinsey asked, dumb-founded by the thought. The giant cat rolled over on his back, paws upward to signal her to rub his belly.

Ray and Leilani laughed to each other as Ray flipped through a few more pages in the book he was holding, then suddenly stopped. Noticing his demeanor change, Kinsey stepped away from the giant cat and stood in front of Ray. As she looked down at the book, she saw there was no writing on the inside of the pages. Upon closer inspection, she saw it was written in brail.

"Are you Kinsey Rivers? Born on February 21, 1981, in California? Daughter to Janelle and Reggie? Mother to Grace and Zerek?" Ray asked in a serious businesslike manner.

"Yes," Kinsey stated as she felt herself slightly tense up. It reminded her of the feeling like she was doing a job interview, which she always hated.

"Do you think your name is in this book, Kinsey?" Ray asked with an authoritative voice.

Kinsey thought for just a moment and then finally answered, "Yes, I believe it is."

"Why do you *believe* that it is?" he asked with a touch of sass.

It took her a minute before she answered. Flash images shot in and out of her mind of the horrible mistakes she had made. She felt so unworthy and began to think she didn't deserve it. Before she responded, she remembered all the verses she ever read in the Bible. Those words became her only hope to get out of bed each day. The horrible mistakes and choices really made her question why she deserved to walk through the gate. Then a thought shot through her mind. She read during her darkest days and remembered, even though she did those things, she was still forgiven. A sense of peace came over her, and then she answered, "I believed with all my heart that God was real, and as a child, I asked Jesus into my heart. I even rededicated my life as an adult. I had years and years of horrible decisions, hurting people, running from God, and I was so broken. I own my mistakes. I just wish I had a chance to make what I did right while I was still alive. I had to remember it was who God said I was, not what people said. His word promises the only way to the Father is through the Son. Though I did many things wrong, I was forgiven. I take that back. I *know* my name is in that book," Kinsey stated proud of her answer.

"That's what I wanted to hear, baby. Ha, ha, ha! That's the right answer!" Ray replied with a smile on his face.

Kinsey couldn't help but notice his hands moving across the page and decided to ask, "What are you reading?"

"I'm reading about your life, sweetheart, your good and your bad, your ugly, your pretty, your pain, and your laughter. I know as much about you as Leilani does now. You had a strong Guardian for a reason."

"Ray, may I ask you a personal question?" Kinsey approached with slow caution.

"Of course you can, baby girl," Ray answered while petting his big cat.

"If I am at the gates of heaven, I remember from reading we are supposed to have a new body, right? So why are you blind?" she asked.

"I choose to stay blind, baby girl. When I was alive, I saw things no man should ever lay eyes upon, things that would make my mother ashamed. I was anything but a moral man. I was living the fast life and lost my sight in my older years after decades of drinking, women, and drugs. I was a musician and singer and relied on sight to play instruments and gaze upon beautiful women. It wasn't until after I lost my sight that I began to grow as a man. I came to learn a need to see men and women through God's eyes. My other senses gave me abilities I never knew were possible. My sense of hearing more than tripled in intensity. I could hear a pin drop. I could tell exactly who was approaching in my direction by their walk. I could even tell a high arch in their foot or a completely flat foot.

"I could sense when someone was uncomfortable or excited by the movement of their body. Best of all, my common sense and my sense of honor helped me to become the man God had destined me to be. I was able to play any instrument with no problems at all after I lost my sight. So I stay blind until the last person enters through the Golden Gate, the same gate the Messiah will walk out of when the time of mankind ends. Don't let Mittens fool you, though, he's my personal protector and stands guard at the gate with me."

Kinsey absolutely loved his answer. The fact that he still had the ability to choose what he wanted was not lost on her. He had free will in the face of God, and his decision was to stay the man God destined him to be. "Thank you, Ray, you seem like an awesome man in my eyes—no pun intended!"

Ray smiled back at Kinsey as he stood up. He shook Leilani's hand, then shook Kinsey's hand. "Go in, baby girl, and go see your friends and family. They have all been waiting for you."

Kinsey's heart fluttered at the very thought of seeing what few family members she did have that had passed away. In one year alone, she had three members of her family pass. She did have a friend pass away, and it was the hardest thing for her to grasp. To get to see them again almost scared her because what would she say? And what would they say? Had they been watching her this whole time? That would be incredibly embarrassing if that was the case.

Leilani matched Kinsey's pace as they slowly walked through the gate. The gate slowly closed while Mittens began to lick Ray in the face.

The sight was incredible. Kinsey had to stop for just a moment so she could take everything in. Her and Leilani first began to pass through a field covered in every flower that had grown under the sun, even hybrids she had never seen painted in every color. Sunflowers in green and purple, tiger lilies in black and silver, orchids in blue and orange, and, of course, her absolute favorite—cherry blossom trees everywhere.

Cherry blossoms were significant to Kinsey because they represented new beginnings. In her past, new beginnings were constant since it took years for her to actually understand what the right choices were. A gentle breeze came through the air, and the perfume of all the flowers resonated her senses. The smell reminded Kinsey of spring and how fresh nature would smell after a rainstorm. All the petals that gathered the drops of water sparkled like an open jewelry box reflecting light directly off the gems. The ocean view of colors resembled the waves of the sea as the breeze brushed over all the delicate petals. Kinsey wanted to stop and smell the roses, literally. She wanted to pick them, but she felt that maybe she shouldn't. They each looked so incredibly perfect in shape, size, and color, and she didn't want to disturb the delicate beauty.

As they continued to walk along the path, Kinsey couldn't help but ask, "Leilani, do Guardians usually escort someone into the gate?"

"Of course we do. It can be an overwhelming feeling to know where you are and who you have left behind. So our job as Guardians is to guide you when you first enter into the kingdom. It's almost an overload of information a person has to take in, and Guardians are with you to make the transition as easy as possible."

"Why does Ray sit at the gate? Especially with a lion?" Kinsey inquired and giggled to herself, realizing saying it out loud made it humorous.

"Well, that's where it gets a little tricky. Every Guardian is required to bring the ones they guarded to the gate, and those who are not in the book are sent away to a place of darkness and waiting until Christ returns. Those with the ugliest of hearts who were selfish and full of pride, the lion instantly reacts, signaling Ray that something is off. Some even argue with him, but no one wants to argue with a lion. The lion is for Ray's own protection."

Kinsey took her words in for a moment and imagined how awesome it would be to have her very own pet lion that wouldn't try to eat her.

As Leilani and Kinsey kept walking, they came upon a waterfall unlike any a person had ever seen or imagined in their wildest dreams. Vegetation was growing around the vast pond, collecting the mystical water. Several hundred flamingos stood in the water toward the shallow end while toucans, parrots, and macaws were up in the trees, surrounding the entire field. Small finches flew past her as she stopped to look at the water. It was three waterfalls gathering into one capacious pool. The first waterfall to the left was sliding down huge boulders, and each boulder was perfectly circular and smooth.

The water sliding down was a sparkling seafoam green and had immense fish swimming through. The waterfall to the right was a perfect rainbow of color—luscious red, soft pink, lavish orange, dashing yellow, gorgeous green, electric blue, and royal purple all flowing together in the fall. The middle waterfall was crystal clear and through the spray, numerous indefinable sea creatures were visible, their fins large as sails on a ship. The water, though, was actually going up instead of down.

Suddenly, what resembled a great white shark swam upward, and there was a man riding its back. He waved through the fall at Leilani, and she waved back. Kinsey couldn't help but just sit and watch and asked, "Who was that?"

"That's one of my brothers, Cronk. He loves food and water! The only time he doesn't have food in his hand is when he is in the water. He doesn't say much either, but when he does, he is hilarious," she stated with a smile.

Leilani stayed at Kinsey's side while she continued to just take in the beauty and magic of the three falls. "Do you know what those three falls represent?"

Kinsey shook her head no as she kept staring into the hypnotizing water.

"Well, each one represents a piece of the trinity. Jesus is known as the 'cornerstone' or foundation of faith, so the boulders in the first waterfall represent him. The rainbow waterfall stands for how God's Word will never be void, and he has never broken a promise. He gave us a rainbow after he flooded the world and promised to never do it again. The third represents the Holy Spirit."

"Why does it go upward, though?" Kinsey inquired.

"The Holy Spirit defies reason and science. He is everywhere at all times. He raises up the people as they lift their faith and prayers up to God. Faith makes a fool of what makes sense. Those who really let go and just believe get to see the miracles he will do for those who believe in him."

Kinsey thought on this for a moment, and as she took in the scenery with wiser eyes and full appreciation of the beauty lying before her. She was excited to see what was about to come up next. As they decided to continue walking, the path came to a curve, and Kinsey could hear on the other side people were talking. She could hear numerous voices all speaking together and laughing. Her heart began to beat rapidly since her whole life she had always wondered what heaven would actually be like. As they rounded the corner, Leilani stepped slightly back so Kinsey could take it all in.

It was indescribable. She came face-to-face with a modern-day outdoor marketplace. Food stands all aligned up, one right after another, bartering fruit, vegetables, and even sweets. The aroma of peppermint, strawberries, and chocolate tingled her senses. Along the other side, booths were lined up with merchants trading freshly picked flowers that she assumed came from the field she and Leilani just walked through. Women were trading jewelry made with all the precious stones and gems from pearls to platinum. Several booths had women exchanging fabrics made of silk, leather, polyester, cotton, satin, velour, and even fleece.

Laughter echoed throughout the area while music was played in the background. Kinsey couldn't make out the language of the music, but she definitely loved the beat. It made her want to dance and celebrate. The people within the marketplace were dressed in all different periods of time. Some women looked as if they came from Greece with the white and purple robes and the adorned hair in jewels. Women were even dressed in turn-of-the-century clothing with Victorian dresses high up to the neck. Others dressed like they came straight from the concert at Woodstock—bell-bottom jeans, tie-dye t-shirt, sandals and all.

A beautiful person of color passed by Kinsey and Leilani in a cocktail dress from the 1950s. She held her head high and a purse in the corner of her arm with white gloves while holding the hand of a little boy following behind her. A cheerful Hispanic woman who was bartering fabric exchanged a beautiful necklace with the woman and little boy. "Thank you," the little boy said as he took the fabric, and they walked away. Kinsey loved absolutely everything she saw.

The humor was not over her head as she realized it was all women doing the shopping. What she noticed more than anything is they were all laughing and getting along. Some even started singing together in a different language. It didn't matter race, color, personal style, or even time period from which they came. This is how mankind was supposed to live—a world without sin, without drama, without pain, and without exclusion.

As Kinsey and Leilani passed through the marketplace, she couldn't help but stop and look at the chocolate-covered strawberries. Her mouth began to water. The strawberries were monstrous in size and the sweet smell of the chocolate combined with citrus engulfed her nose.

"Would you like one?" the woman in the booth asked. The woman looked as though she was from India and wrapped herself in pure silk adorned in gold with jewelry coming across her forehead. She was absolutely beautiful. Kinsey's first reaction was excitement and true joy knowing that she would be able to eat her favorite delicacy. The next reaction was to grab one of the delicious treats, but she realized she didn't have anything with her to barter or trade. As if knowing her thoughts when Kinsey hesitated, the woman smiled and handed the giant chocolate-covered strawberry over to her. "Please, go ahead, and when you begin to barter, you can come to me first."

Kinsey smiled and thanked the woman and promised to come back as soon as she could. She grabbed the delicious fruit and took a bite. The juice was so overwhelming in her mouth. The sweet taste from the chocolate and the strawberry was the perfect combination. Neither overpowered the other, and with each bite, it kept getting better. Leilani grabbed one for herself. "I'll be back before sundown with some pineapple." The woman smiled again, and the two of them began to continue the walk through the market.

As Leilani was biting into her strawberry, she began to explain how the marketplace actually worked. "My brothers and I grew up in Hawaii, but our parents were Samoan. So we usually barter in pineapple, surfboards, carvings, and we raise sea turtles. So when you need clothing, food, or just the occasional precious personal gift for someone, you barter and trade. No money exists. The currency is the item. Jewels, of course, are held in a higher regard, so I would give her two pineapples and a surfboard for a piece of beautiful jewelry. The trade balances out because it takes time to grow the fruit or make an item out of hand, so it all evens out when you come to barter. Everyone works, everyone contributes, and everyone has a job that they do."

"Surfboards and sea turtles? So there is a beach? I have always felt so incredibly at peace, lying on a beach, and reading a good book," Kinsey stated as she closed her eyes, trying to envision herself lying on a peaceful beach and getting herself lost in whatever world the book created.

"Of course, Noah is one of the best surf instructors, and he will definitely teach you to hang ten!" Leilani replied with a smile.

"Noah's Ark? Noah, you mean, right?" Kinsey couldn't believe it. Thinking about the man himself sailing through water, it sounded like one of the coolest things she could have never imagined. She secretly fantasized in her mind Noah speaking the native California style, "Dude," and the thought made her giggle.

"Exactly. Sounds silly, but he could really catch some waves like no one has ever seen."

Kinsey laughed again at the thought of a man with a long beard and robes trying to climb on a surfboard.

They continued walking, and suddenly, all Kinsey could hear was the sound of children playing. As they turned the corner out of the marketplace, Kinsey found herself, stopping to stand in awe and wonder of an area dedicated completely to children. Thousands upon thousands of children were running around, and Kinsey couldn't believe the magnificent playground, so many happy little cherubs running around, castle towers high into the sky with an infinite number of slides coming from all directions. She gazed at a wading pool that periodically created waves for the older kids to swim in. Jungle gyms as far as she could see with swings, merry-go-rounds, and monkey bars. She smiled at the thought of being a child in such a magnificent place. She thought about how a child would never know pain, never know what it felt like to cry, and never having a broken heart.

Kinsey focused on several girls in tutus and tap shoes, displaying a performance for their friends. Kinsey was so enamored by the joy of the children she didn't notice two small children at her side. She looked down at the little girl and boy and smiled. The boy reached for her hand, and the little girl looked up at her.

"Hi," Kinsey said. She knelt down, and as she did, the little boy wrapped his arms around her. Kinsey hugged him back, thinking the child just wanted a cuddle. Nothing could have prepared her for what happened next.

"Hello, Mommy," the little boy said.

Kinsey instantly let go to look him in the eye. She didn't understand why he thought she was his mother. Leilani gently touched Kinsey's shoulder, and suddenly, old memories that had been buried deep down flooded her thoughts. In Kinsey's younger years with the many experiences of a broken heart, she found herself with two terminated pregnancies. These two children...were hers. The reality sunk her heart like an anchor. What could she say? What apology would ever do justice? And how could "I'm sorry" ever atone to these two beautiful babies?

Tears began to fall from her eyes, and she felt a pain stabbing deep in her heart.

The little boy lifted up her head as he spoke softly, "Mommy, why are you crying?"

Kinsey couldn't find the words. The little girl finally approached her, hugged her, and held her face in her tiny hands. Kinsey stared into the girl's big beautiful green eyes as she said, "Mommy, don't be sad. Great-Grandma has been with us, and she has been taking care of us." The child then wrapped her delicate arms around her mother's neck as tight as she could. Kinsey felt so much warmth in her heart.

Those awful memories were shoved down so deep because Kinsey never wanted them to come back up. All she could do was just hold the two beautiful children. She looked up at Leilani who smiled back at her and mouthed the words, "It's all okay. You have been forgiven."

Kinsey smiled and leaned back. Wiping the tears from her eyes, she asked the little girl and boy, "What are your names?"

"My name is Saige, and his name is Jaxon," the little girl stated with pride.

Kinsey instantly smiled. Those were the names she had thought of shortly after the terminated pregnancies. Saige sounded whimsical and light, while Jaxon sounded determined and strong. "Do you want to come with me to go see Great-Grandma?"

They both smiled while shaking their head yes. Saige grabbed Kinsey's right hand while Jaxon held onto her left hand. The four of them continued forward to the next destination.

Kinsey looked over and saw another woman being approached by three children. The mother was crying hysterically and laughing. Leilani noticed Kinsey watching and began to explain the situation. "That woman lost her children in a brutal and horrible way. A man kidnapped them and took their lives."

How terrifying that must have been. The poor woman had all of her children taken from her. She never got to teach them to drive, go to a school, dance, or even become an adult. "She looks so happy and she can't stop holding and kissing them. It's beautiful," Kinsey stated with a smile.

Kinsey looked at Leilani and wanted to ask why she didn't warn her. Such an intense moment was about to take place. Then she realized she wouldn't be able to fully appreciate the beauty of the connection and reunion. These were her babies, the babies that she was pregnant with and the babies that God had blessed her with. She was too selfish, scared, and unwilling to trust that God would help her each step of the way. Here they were, her little cherubs.

Another tear dropped from her eye because these children were so excited to see her. They weren't angry with her for the decisions that she had made, and in her heart, that gave her peace.

"Come on, Mommy, you're walking too slow!" Jaxon said as he began to pull on Kinsey's hand.

She smiled and asked, "Do you wanna race me?"

The two children screamed and ran ahead of her. *How could this be?* Kinsey thought to herself. She felt it was almost too easy, and that was definitely something Kinsey was not used to. She decided to just enjoy the moment and let go of all the heartache she had from the past and not ruin something so precious. The kids ran through a courtyard, shadowed with a plethora of trees, golden benches, and numerous families walking through, laughing, and talking together.

Just ahead as Kinsey was running behind Saige and Jaxon, she was mystified by a colosseum that resembled a place where gladiators fought. She felt like she had stepped back in time. She found herself staring at a marble structure where gladiators had once fought. An admirable archway was heavily crowded with people entering through. It was a grand structure handcrafted all in marble, embellished with designs of horses. The area had a depiction of four horses outlined in gold with riders upon them.

The first horse, white, decorated with white diamonds, pearls, and quartz crystals. Upon his back, a man wearing a crown on his head, designed in gold, while holding a bow with arrows. The second horse was red, adorned with garnets, rubies, red jasper, and red sapphires. The rider on his back was wielding a sword with a dove falling to the ground. The third horse, black, was decorated with black diamonds, onyx, and obsidian. The rider upon his back was holding a scale that was off balance, a bag of wheat on the lighter side of the scale and gold bars weighing down the other. The last horse was made with nothing but gray stones. On the back of the gray horse was a skeleton in a black cloak. They were magnificent, majestic, and downright ominous. Kinsey suddenly realized they represented the four horsemen of the apocalypse.

Hundreds of thousands of people were heading toward the entryway. Kinsey, surprised, realized she had not noticed anyone else around them when she ran after the children. It shouldn't be a surprise, though, considering how many people die each day, let alone their family members to greet them. Men and women of all ages and nationalities kept passing through the archway. The children, Kinsey and Leilani, all had smiles on their faces as they entered the massive colosseum. The entry hall grew dark for a moment, but it didn't stop the excited chatter between friends and relatives.

Suddenly, the archway opened in front to enter into the colosseum. Kinsey became overwhelmed by the crowd, the music, and the excitement—tears of joy were falling uncontrollably. The sound of all the people echoed throughout the arena.

Reactions from numerous reunions were astonishing. Leilani placed her arm around Kinsey and asked, "Are you ready to see your family?"

Kinsey answered with an emphatic, "*Yes!*" as Leilani led them in the direction of her family. Kinsey couldn't help but to keep looking at as many homecomings as physically possible. The sound radiated throughout the colosseum of loved ones being reunited. The first people she saw melted her heart and weakened her knees. An older woman, possibly in her late seventies, kept working her way toward a man who appeared to be her husband. The woman, so aged and frail, started struggling to get to her husband. The woman kept limping, but as soon as the couple touched hands and embraced, Kinsey envied the true love they had for each other. Then the most astonishing thing then happened. As the man and woman were in each other's embrace, they began to morph and change. When they let go and looked into each other's eyes, they looked young and vibrant again. The man was incredibly handsome, and his wife was stunningly pretty.

"You're as beautiful as the day I met you, Helen!" the man said as he kissed her sweetly on her lips.

"I missed you so much, Jack," the woman said back, looking dreamily into his eyes. She looked like she could have been a classy pin-up model from the 1940s. He grabbed her hand, and the woman, along with what appeared to be her Guardian, walked off to see the rest of her family. It was a pure and beautiful moment, and Kinsey was so grateful to witness genuine love that remains long after death.

"Gigi!" Jaxon and Saige yelled as they ran through the crowd to hug their great-grandmother and grandfather. Kinsey knew Jaxon called this woman his great-grandma, but she wasn't prepared visually by her appearance. Kinsey's grandmother, Joyce, passed away when Kinsey was twenty-four. It was the only grandmother she had a relationship with. Kinsey's father never cared to have his family involved with the insanity his sisters brought upon themselves. He rarely ever spoke of them. Kinsey assumed there was a falling out at some point, and they just never reconciled.

Kinsey felt so grateful that her grandma set the example of what a Christian mother was supposed to model for her kids. Joyce was the reason Kinsey's mother spent so many years involved in the church. Joyce laid the foundation in her belief by training her children in the way they should go. So when they grew older, they would not depart from it. Joyce stayed single and prayed. If God would allow it, another man after God's own heart would come along and love her.

Kinsey remembered instantly that one day in her seventies, a neighbor named James Mason came to her house and asked if she wanted to go on a walk. They started walking every day. Every day, for weeks, he would walk next to her. One spring morning, James surprised Joyce and asked her out on a date. Kinsey joked around and told her grandmother she was grounded and not allowed to date, all while Joyce laughed like a young schoolgirl. Since Kinsey never had a grandfather in her life, she grew a special bond with James. After a year of dating, James asked Kinsey's father for permission to marry his mother-in-law. She stood there behind James, shaking her head while her eyes sparkled. She lived the last ten years of her life like she was a young woman again.

Now here she was with her grandmother. She had the warmest and cheekiest smile. Her body was vibrant, young, and beautiful. Next to her was a man Kinsey assumed to be her biological grandfather. "Hello, baby," she said, hugging Kinsey.

Kinsey started to cry tears of absolute joy. "I missed you so much, Grandma," Kinsey replied.

She didn't want to let go for several moments and as so many others were around, reconnecting with their relatives and friends.

Her grandmother stepped back. "Kinsey, this is your Grandpa Richard." Kinsey couldn't help but notice he was a handsome man. He reminded her of a movie star from the fifties with his slicked back hair and gray suit. Joyce matched his look by wearing a green cocktail dress with a seam that ended at her knees. She was actually surprised by how nice her legs looked.

"Hello, Kinsey, it's wonderful to finally meet you," Richard said as he embraced Kinsey. Then out of the corner of her eye, she saw James. She stepped away from her Grandfather Richard and took a couple steps back to see James. James was also a good-looking man, now in his younger years, and standing next to him was his first wife. Kinsey hugged him and was introduced to his first wife, Victoria.

"Hey, troublemaker!" Kinsey heard a familiar voice from behind her.

She turned and saw her Aunt Judy. She was wearing the similar clothing Leilani was, except instead of the light teal, Judy wore the color red. Judy passed away the same year her grandmother and James did. She was dying of cancer, and on December 25, Kinsey's cousins, Sondra and Josh, woke up to find their mother went to sleep and didn't wake up. They hurt, of course, by the loss of their mother, but several days before she passed, she stated all she wanted for Christmas was to be with Jesus. In Kinsey's mind, that was the most incredible gift anyone could get. To ask God to escape the pain of cancer and be brought home to meet her maker. That was the year she literally lost half her family.

Kinsey ran up to Judy and couldn't help but to keep hugging her tightly. Kinsey kept saying how much she missed her and how many times she wished she had been around. She just wanted someone to understand her. Her aunt spent many years angry with God because the true love of her life, her husband, had an affair and divorced her. Kinsey was all too familiar with those emotions. No one else in Kinsey's life had been through a divorce, so no one could understand the feelings and emotions that a person is forced to experience during such a loss. Her sister's marriages never fell apart, so as supportive as they tried to be, no one in her family could relate, except Judy.

Her aunt was an interesting person altogether. She was the hardest working woman anyone had ever known, other than her own mother. They were true workaholics, and Judy was a skilled handyman. The problem, though, while Judy stayed angry and blamed God for her divorce, was she ran down a path of absolute despair and destruction. She became addicted to drugs and alcohol to cover and mask the pain and brokenness she felt from the rejection.

Judy had as many failed relationships as Kinsey, knowing every single one of those men were absolutely not good for her. Sometimes, the empty hole filled with everything horrible was better than not filled at all. In Judy's worst years, she became a drug runner for a well-known biker gang in Southern California. It wasn't until Judy was shot and almost killed by this gang that she finally had enough and surrendered herself back to God.

Some people, when they come to the end of their rope, get lucky enough to have a complete transformation. Judy was one of those people. She was able to instantly quit drinking and had no withdrawal from the drugs. From that day forward, she never looked back upon her past but kept her eyes pressed forward, looking to the God that gave her his grace.

"I checked in from time to time, but Guardians can't stay with family members. I made sure Leilani gave you a good swift kick to the butt when you needed it. I was around more than you realize, kiddo," Judy stated as she pulled away from Kinsey.

Leilani smiled and replied, "Believe me, Kinsey, that was more often than not!" They laughed together and bantered back and forth for a few more moments while Saige and Jaxon kept running around the adults, playing as children do.

"Kinsey?" came a voice from behind the three of them.

Kinsey turned around and saw the only friend she ever knew to pass away. "Christina, I didn't know you would be here to see me too!" She embraced her friend, and as she pulled away, Christina was also wearing the combat gear. Kinsey found the combat clothes an interesting choice, except instead of being in turquoise like Leilani or Judy in red, Christina was in purple. Kinsey became curious why they were each wearing clothes that appeared to be for battle, yet they all came in different colors. She didn't know military gear had other options.

Kinsey began to look around, and then she looked at the people who were around to greet her. Her grandparents introduced her to family members she never knew she had. She watched several men and women with over twenty family members and friends, greeting those who recently passed as they came in. Kinsey was grateful for the little family that she had, including the one friend there for her. "So are you a Guardian too, Christina?"

"Yes, actually, I am. You know me. I never turned down a good fight," she said with a contagious smile. Christina was another person Kinsey wished she could be when she lived on earth, incredibly talented, and she was as beautiful as she was deadly because of her practice and skills in martial arts. She trained for years and intimidated Kinsey by not only her looks but also by her skill. Christina had a heart of pure joy, and her smile was so magnetic.

"Leilani and I have trained together several times, and she is a great sparring partner!" Christina said with a smile.

"What do you train and spar for?" Kinsey inquired.

Judy, Christina, and Leilani all glanced toward each other, neither wanting to answer at the moment. Just then, Joyce walked up with the children. "Come on, Mommy, there is someone else you get to meet," Saige said, pulling on Kinsey's hand.

"Are you going to come with me?" Kinsey asked. She kept feeling slightly nervous, looking at her family.

"Of course we are. Now you get to experience the best part!" Judy said as they began walking over to a long rectangular table in the center of the colosseum. Kinsey had not noticed the table originally when she had passed through the crowd. As they approached, the noise throughout the colosseum became a soft murmur. Suddenly, the only people Kinsey could now see were her family members. Everyone else disappeared. She wondered where everyone went but found herself more intrigued by what was directly in front of her.

The table was immaculate and made of pure gold. It appeared to be an elongated desk. Beautiful carvings adorned across the front, embedded with precious gemstones, similar to the stones in front of the colosseum. Instead of the horses, the carvings depicted a man upon a chariot of fire. Directly in the middle on the front of the table was a carving of a symbol that Kinsey did not recognize. The table in front of her had fifteen seats total with men sitting in every single seat, except the center seat was empty. The empty chair appeared to be a throne designed in gold with purple velvet. Kinsey was disappointed that there was no one in the seat. To the left and to the right of the empty throne were two men, monstrous in size. The two men had to be at least three feet higher than the rest of the men.

The man on the right was tanned, clear blue eyes with sandy brown hair, while the man on the left was also tanned, green eyes, and slicked back black hair. Both men had straps across their chest with the top of what appeared to be a weapon peeking above their right shoulders. For some reason, Kinsey was intimidated by them. The man to the right stood up and set out for Kinsey to shake his hand. She approached the table slowly and shook his hand.

He held on for a second longer and looked deep into her eyes. Leilani, Christina, her Aunt Judy, and the rest of the family stood directly behind her. It was dead silent, and Kinsey wasn't sure if she should say anything. Even Saige and Jaxon had stopped trying to play and had grown silent in their observation.

"Kinsey Rivers, my name is Michael, and I am honored to meet you," he said, standing up. The man on the left stood up and out-stretched his arm to shake her hand as well. "My name is Gabriel, and we want to welcome you officially home." Kinsey's family cheered, and the men sitting at the table clapped along with them. She breathed out a sigh of relief, and a few tears dropped from her eyes out of excitement. This moment resembled no more sorrow and no more pain.

When Gabriel and Michael stood up, they stood twelve feet tall and well-proportioned from head to toe. They were each wearing white relaxed pants, no shirt, and gold sandals. Both men were made of pure muscle. They had markings on their arms so unique in their patterns. She was looking more intently and taking in their appearance. Upon closer inspection of the straps across their chest, Kinsey noticed there was writing. It was in an unfamiliar language but was fabulously artistic.

The difference between the two weapons they were wearing was Michael's was white gold with topaz, sapphire, and aquamarine while Gabriel's weapon in gold was adorned in emerald, peridot, and jade. Michael noticed Kinsey was focused on his weapon, so he withdrew the largest sword she had ever seen from his back and placed it in front of her.

Michael then explained, "All angels have weapons, but only three of us have swords made in this way."

Kinsey began to wonder where the third person was. Then it hit her. Who was this person? As she gently approached, she ran her fingers across the sword and admired its beauty.

He then slid the sword back into the holster and continued speaking, "Kinsey every person, when they meet us, are given a specific job and responsibility. These jobs given are based upon your life on earth and how you honored God and his kingdom. These men have observed every word spoken from the heart, every sin hidden in the dark, and any act of kindness that wasn't always convenient. These men are the twelve apostles who sat with Jesus, and each one of them knows your strengths and your weaknesses. They know every single moment you were knocked down as well as every moment when you got back up to fight. The information they provided to Gabriel and I help determine what skills you have that would be best suited for God's kingdom," Michael said.

The shock of the statement first made Kinsey freeze because she was actually looking at the twelve men she read about. Not only that, but now, every moment of her life had been accounted for. She looked at each one of them individually trying to figure out who was who. These are the men who followed Jesus, the men he broke bread with, and best of all, the men who witnessed his miracles. Here she was, only a few feet from them.

Kinsey's mind began running about ninety miles an hour, thinking of all the situations she chose right and definitely remembered all the times she was less than stellar as a Christian. She always let her mood swings determine who would be a victim in her monstrous anger. Kinsey tried to convince herself that she was also kind, giving, and genuine. On many occasions, she stood up for the underdog, and Kinsey was never afraid to speak up and tell when she would see something is off or not right. No matter how many mistakes or how many times she messed up, she still tried to be the best person she could be. What mattered most is what she did when she stepped out in her faith, how many people she led to believe in God, and most importantly, when she was to deliver a message God had asked her to deliver.

"Kinsey, I am sure you are aware you made poor choices that led you down many lonely paths." Michael continued to speak, "If only you had listened to the wisdom sent down from your grandmother when you were supposed to, your peace would have flown like a river or like the waves of the sea. God knew, though, what decisions you would make long before you made them. You dealt with rejection over and over and over again, and we know you were too embarrassed to speak up. You decided to completely surrender when God was giving you one last chance. You took the years of pain and made it into strength instead of becoming a victim. We have agreed that you will be"—he paused for a moment, she assumed for dramatic affect—"a Guardian!"

Screaming came from behind Kinsey. The shock of the screams made her jump. Her Aunt Judy, Christina, and Leilani instantly grabbed Kinsey and hugged her. Judy high-fived Kinsey. "I knew it, kiddo, I knew it!" Saige and Jaxon ran up from behind her and hugged her legs. The rest of her family cheered her on, and Kinsey assumed, based on the cheers, this was a good thing.

Each of the twelve men were smiling and clapping along with the family. Then Michael handed her a small trinket. It was oddly shaped with a hole in the middle. As Kinsey grabbed the unique item, she had so many questions, starting with what was the little item and what it was for. She wanted to sit and ask who each one of the men were. Before she had a chance to approach the men, Leilani grabbed her hand and said, "Come on, Kinsey, we have a lot of work to do."

Kinsey turned around and suddenly the table with the apostles and the two archangels were gone. Her grandmother hugged her and told her, "We love you and we will see you later. Don't worry about the little ones. We will take care of them, and they have their own work that they do. Leilani will explain everything, and we will see you tonight at dinner."

Kinsey wanted to ask where she would meet them or how would she find them, but just as she was about to open her mouth, they were instantly gone. Christina hugged her again and whispered in her ear, "Just wait, Kinsey, you haven't seen anything yet." Her friend kissed her on the cheek and disappeared.

Judy looked at Kinsey and with hopeful eyes told her, "There is a reason you have been chosen as a Guardian. All that pain on earth wasn't for nothing. Remember that I love you, and I will see you at dinner later." Judy was gone just as quickly after she hugged Kinsey.

Leilani wrapped her arm around Kinsey and said, "There is so much to teach you, and you will love being a Guardian."

As they walked out of the colosseum, it seemed so much larger than before now that it was empty. She wondered how many people actually died the same day she did. How were Michael, Gabriel, and the twelve apostles able to see each and every single person day in and day out? Then she remembered God was outside time. He created time, and she needed to take God, Jesus, and the Holy Spirit out of a box and remove all boundaries. Now absolutely everything was possible. She smiled with the thought and followed Leilani out of the colosseum.

ITHERIAL

"Izzy," God said to Itherial as he greeted his messenger with a smile.

Itherial had been awaiting the Father while standing outside the Trinity Falls. Izzy walked up upon the king, kneeled before him, then stood back up. As he arose, a small dove flew off of his shoulder and gently glided into the garden outside the falls.

"I got your message. You wanted to see me?" he asked. Itherial dressed in the same clothing as his brothers, Michael and Gabriel. The loose flowing pants stood out against his darker skin. His sword upon his back was slightly different since it was made of Tungsten and outlined in platinum. The beautiful sword was decorated with black and white diamonds that shone brightly against the sunlight. Itherial stood twelve feet tall, just like his brothers, except his skin wasn't white, the muscle in him chiseled to perfection. The only difference with him is that he had once lived on earth.

While he was alive, he was average height, standing around five-foot-ten. He had a small muscular build, light-colored eyes that had a tint of gray in them. Itherial was good-looking and had a smile that radiated whenever he laughed. His face was kind and his laughter was contagious. Due to his intense heart as a servant and his love for the Lord God kept his hand upon him, and he was a well-respected man in life.

When Itherial entered heaven, his welcome was different than all others because God wanted to see him first. Itherial was special. His purity of heart was rewarded because he never allowed the color of his skin to define who he was as a man. In Itherial's eyes, it was who God said he was, not any white man who hated him nor any black man who stood beside him. It was only God. Even during his time of racial tension, he was a man after his Savior's own heart.

At the time of his death, it was a beautiful Mississippi morning in the spring of 1941. That morning, Itherial opened his eyes and instantly smiled. He loved the morning more than any other part of the day. He loved the way the sun would slowly creep up into the horizon and shine upon the colorful countryside. Every aspect of his surroundings became clearly noticeable when the sun lifted up into the tranquil blue sky. The glimmer from the Mississippi river sparkled as the water ran down stream. The dewdrops delicately sat upon the pink, red, yellow, and white roses his wife so tenderly took care of in the garden. Some people love sunset when it's comfortable, cool, and the day is over. Not Itherial. In his eyes, every sunrise meant a new beginning. Even if the night brought tears, joy was sure to come with the morning. He was known for being a man that everyone considered warm and cheerful. Itherial never missed a moment for a good joke or practical prank. People couldn't help, though, but to laugh and smile with him.

He loved to put on music first thing in the morning and listen to the best swing and blues jazz on the radio. Itherial would turn the volume up so loud that it would carry through the whole house. With his upbeat and carefree demeanor, he would dance and sing as loud as he could and, of course, it would wake up his wife and three beautiful children.

Itherial worked as a delivery man, and his days started early. He wasn't just an average delivery man, though. He worked for the newspaper, the grocery store, and even delivered coal in the winter. He started early in the morning and was busy until late in the evening, and he did it all without complaint. Every boss he had was white but treated him with respect. It was the contagious smile and aura he gave off that they just liked and trusted him. His bosses were more concerned about making money than only serving white neighborhoods, so they were smart to hire Itherial.

He would represent the three companies he worked for and did so in a professional way. Itherial was a form of physical advertisement. He had the ability of a true salesman and brought the men he worked for more money due to his welcoming smile and undeniable charm. He was grateful that he was able to see his friends and service those he loved. He wore a generic uniform but always kept a touch of class with his favorite black fedora. He delivered the coal at the end of the day since he was rarely left clean after his final home drop-offs.

Usually on his last stop of the day, he would visit his best friend's house. He and Walter had known each other since they were children. Walter gave him the nickname Izzy years ago when they were younger, and they never really knew why, but they knew the name just fit.

"Come in and relax for a minute. You work too hard," Walter said as he opened the door for his friend to come in.

Unfortunately, Itherial was incredibly tired. "Not tonight, old friend. I have been doing more deliveries than usual, and I just want to go home to the Mrs."

Walter looked at his friend, and he could see how tired Itherial really was. He noticed on that particular day his eyes didn't seem to have the same sparkle that usually shined through when he spoke.

"All right, man, take care, and don't work yourself to death. Be blessed," Walter stated as he closed the door when Itherial walked away.

Even though Itherial was hardworking, he always took time to pray. He prayed consistently over his children and wife, of course, but he prayed for the times to change. He saw so much hatred with the discrimination, yet he made a choice to never let it get to him. He was tested constantly when he would hear men say racial insults, but Itherial had to let it slide off his back. It took him years to get to that point. In his younger years, he was constantly allowing the anger to get the better of him. Itherial's father raised him by example and actually taught him to not allow what any man said to define him. Only God's view mattered.

Itherial served in his church every week, and if he could, he volunteered in any way to help. The church congregation, including the pastor, loved when he led the service because Itherial had an unprecedented gift to speak. He was requested to lead the service on multiple occasions because of the passion in his words. His selfless acts among his fellow church members never went unnoticed. If anyone was in need, Itherial was glad to help in any way, but he always made sure he spent quality time with his family.

He had three children at the time who were fourteen, ten, and six. The youngest one, a total surprise, but Itherial never allowed himself to worry. His wife, Ruth, always needed Itherial to help put her anxiety at ease. He knew God would provide a way to take care of the family. Jacob, his only son, was the eldest. He could occasionally get a little unruly as a typical teenage boy, but he would still show respect to his father.

When Itherial asked him a question, Jacob always answered with a, "No, sir" or "Yes, sir." He was the protector of his two younger sisters, and Itherial always made sure Jacob understood his position as an older brother. He was strong for his age and taller than most boys he went to school with. He was attractive like his father and had an angelic voice when he sang.

Itherial's oldest daughter, JoAnne, was such a joy to him, and she took after his love for music and his playful sense of humor. She had his eyes and smile, and he would often call her Annie Jo. She would gather all of her dolls as her audience and put on music performances for them. JoAnne even made it a point to have white and Black dolls in her audience because it was important everyone sat together. Her brush was her microphone, and the world was her stage. Her imagination and curiosity made her unique and wise in the way she saw the world. Itherial believed in his heart and soul that JoAnne was going to be a warrior. She had a boldness that he admired, and it was apparent she would live an incredible life.

His youngest daughter, Sarah, was unlike her sister or brother. She was shy, cautious, and didn't trust people. Itherial never understood her canniness toward strangers and those she knew. She was the observer and didn't talk to complete strangers like her sister so freely did. If the family was out and about, headed to school or at church, Sarah attached herself to her mother's hip. Itherial hoped that one day, she would come out of her shell and be just like her older sister. The young girl didn't have the same bond with her father as her siblings, and Itherial hoped that one day she would break away from her fear and step out into the world with confidence.

The morning of his death, Itherial woke up a little earlier than usual and had an unfamiliar feeling that he just couldn't shake off. He didn't play music like he normally did and instead wanted to settle himself in silence. He was restless and felt outside his comfort zone. He got down on his knees and started to pray because the feeling just wouldn't go away. He figured this wouldn't wake anyone and allow them to enjoy extra sleep. As he made the decision to do so, he felt a small tap on his shoulder. Slightly startled, he turned to face JoAnne.

"I had a bad dream, Daddy," JoAnne stated as she looked at him with pleading eyes.

He could see in her stiff body language that the dream must have had an effect on her since she was holding onto her favorite doll as tight as she possibly could. He gently grabbed her hand, kissed her on the head, and said, "Everything is better now, Annie Jo. Daddy will always protect you."

She was considered a daddy's girl and instantly smiled since he knew she considered him her hero. Itherial stood up, held his little girl's hand, and proceeded to the kitchen to eat breakfast together.

The sun shining brighter than usual helped Itherial feel better, especially after praying. Unfortunately, though, he still couldn't shake the thoughts that something was off. JoAnne babbled away about the latest play she just finished writing. She was so excited to show her daddy that she wrote him a song. "Daddy, I worked all Sunday on my song for you. Tonight is the big opening. Make sure you wear your hat and bring Momma. Let's say it's a date."

Itherial smiled at his little girl, and the feeling subsided momentarily as he got ready to go to work.

The Mississippi river ran alongside the group of homes where Itherial lived, and the only way to get into town was to cross a massive bridge. Large trees were located at both ends of the bridge, causing visibility to be limited to cars coming from opposite directions. The bridge was the connection to all the local stores, schools, and, of course, the three places Itherial worked. He drove a 1941 Plymouth Woody Wagon that he was blessed to have through his hard work.

Unfortunately, though, as he walked outside this particular morning, he noticed he had a flat tire.

Odd! he thought to himself as he inspected the tire. There was no indication last night that anything was wrong. "Well, I guess maybe this is why I woke up so early," he said to himself. He proceeded to check the back of the car and realized he didn't have the spare because he had allowed Walter to borrow it recently. "Oh, well, I'll take the bike today," he said to no one, looking around.

Itherial hated driving on the bridge due to the young drivers who had a tendency to be reckless. He always tried to cross as quickly and safely as possible. On this particular morning, there was a young girl making her way alongside the bridge, heading toward his direction. Itherial thought it was strange that a child was up so early and out, alone and all by herself. She couldn't be any older than JoAnne, and he instantly got a sick feeling in his stomach. As Itherial was riding toward her, he noticed a car full of teenagers speeding into the bridge. His gut feeling told him that they were about to hit her due to the limited visibility.

The driver slammed on the horn, scaring the little girl frozen. Itherial grabbed her just in time so she didn't get hit. The teenagers sped off, hollering and laughing, leaving the little girl scared and crying. Itherial held her while he ran outside the other end of the bridge for a moment until his heartbeat slowed down. As he was about to put her down, she held onto him tighter, screaming, wrapping her arms around his neck.

"It's okay, baby girl. It's all okay now. Izzy here. You're safe now." He kneeled down on one knee and placed her feet on the ground. She was still crying, but the sobs had slowed down. He recognized this little girl and had seen her playing at the grocery store he made deliveries for. He decided he would just take her with him and drop her off.

Coming from the opposite direction, Itherial didn't see three white men in a red pickup truck. They didn't happen to see the drama that had just unfolded, but what they did see was a black man holding a little white girl, crying. Itherial instantly knew that the outward appearance of the situation did not weigh in his favor. His intentions and actions were honorable, but an explanation would do no justice to help the situation. He stood frozen, heart pounding in his ears as the truck stopped, and all three men began to climb out.

"What in the hell do you think you're doing?" said the first man who stepped out of the truck. His Southern drawl was thick, and his words were slightly slurred with the huge piece of dip in his mouth. He had a shaved head with a scar that ran across the top and a long beard that was unkempt. He was wearing a white tank top that had yellow stains under the arms and appeared as though it had never been washed. His jeans were rolled up over his black shoes with a hole in the toe. He spat out the dip in his mouth after he spoke and a small remnant of the dip remained in his beard.

"I don't want any trouble," Itherial spoke, trembling as he stepped back from the little girl. The girl was too young to really understand what was about to happen. His heart broke as he looked down at her and spoke, softly saying, "Run home, little girl...as fast as you can."

The innocent girl hesitated, still scared. He knew these men were going to hurt him, and as a father, he didn't want a child, so innocent, to watch something so evil. She looked into his kind eyes, and it was as if then she fully understood him and she did as he requested.

"Looks like we're gonna have to teach you a lesson, tar baby," the second guy spoke with the same thick Southern accent as he got out of the truck with the third man following. The second man had a red baseball cap on along with overalls and no t-shirt, holding a beer. The last man from the truck was the driver wearing what appeared to be a work shirt for a local gas station or mechanic shop. As he stepped out, Itherial noticed he was incredibly tall, standing at about six-foot-three, and he made Itherial's heart pound uncontrollably as he approached.

"No lesson to teach here. That little girl almost got hit by a car, and I was just trying to keep her from getting hurt," Itherial tried to explain. He slowly kept backing up, knowing it wasn't going to do him any good. He contemplated running back into the bridge and making it to a place he could hide, but where could he go? Any place he tried to run to could end up getting someone else hurt. He debated on jumping into the water, except he couldn't swim. He could sense that death was closing in, and he didn't have time to debate which scenario would possibly be worse.

"Well, I didn't see that. Did you, Fox?" the first man said, spitting his dip again as he spoke looking at his friend in the overalls.

"Nope, all I saw was this man trying to take a little girl. What about you, Ben?"

Ben said nothing as he just stood and stared at Itherial, making sure that his presence and height was intimidating.

"Are you really that dumb to grab a little white girl? I didn't see no car, and you gotta be dumber than dirt to think we would buy a story like that," Fox said as he walked up to Itherial with a wrench he was holding. He kept hitting the palm of his hand with the tool and slowly looked at the other two men.

Itherial kept trying to slowly back away, but Fox knocked him out quickly with the wrench before he was able to run.

When Itherial opened his eyes, he was on the ground. His head throbbed, and his whole body ached. He could see the cover of the bridge above him and could hear the water running below. He was sure he had a couple of his ribs broken because it ached when he tried to take in a deep breath. He was covered in dirt and had the copper taste of blood in his mouth. His hands were tied together, the same with his ankles. When he tried to move, he noticed his neck was restricted. There was a rope around his neck. The three men were hollering at each other and laughing as they opened their beers and prepared to push him off the bridge and into the river.

"You're either gonna drown or choke to death today!" Ben stated as he smacked Itherial in the face.

Blood started dripping down Itherial's nose and ears, and his face was incredibly swollen. Then Ben lifted him up and placed him on the bridge's edge.

Itherial was barely able to stand, but he gathered all the energy he could and began to pray. "Lord, I know with all my heart that you are real. I ask that in this moment if I am to die that you forgive me for any wrong I have done. I ask you to forgive these men for their ignorance. I am not ready to go, but God, if it's my time, I wanna go quick and not feel any pain. Let my children grow up to see a different world than what I know." Tears were streaming down his face as he prayed, for he knew that as soon as the pickup truck started to drive, he was going to be in severe pain. The engine started, Itherial braced himself, and Ben with his monstrous foot kicked Itherial off the bridge.

As Itherial opened his eyes, he felt no pain. In fact, he felt amazing. He felt strong, and his face wasn't bleeding anymore. He looked around and was amazed by everything within his view. He saw people from all time periods, and they smiled at him as he gazed upon them. He was standing in a monstrous colosseum, and he didn't pass through the gate as all others did nor did he see the table with Michael, Gabriel, and the twelve apostles. Suddenly, his knees were weak, and he dropped down as he saw the Almighty God sitting on his throne. As he looked around, it was like he was in slow motion.

Before the throne were two Seraphim standing proudly to the left and the right of the King. The wings on the Seraphim were indefinable, like nothing Itherial would have ever imagined. Each of them had six wings. With two wings, they covered their faces, another two covered their feet, and the last two were spread completely out. Itherial gazed in awe as each set of wings were enormous, stretching out twenty feet long. They were white as snow and outlined in fire. Suddenly, Itherial could hear the most beautiful music he never encountered before coming from behind the Seraphim.

"Itherial," God called to him as he trembled and admired the view. Itherial felt excited and scared at the same time. His heart raced the instant his name was called. He stayed on one knee, and tears dropped from his eyes uncontrollably to the ground as God spoke to him.

"My dear Izzy, I have taken so much delight in you. Your worship to me was always the sweetest sound because your heart was always pure. I know in your life you wanted to do what was right in my eyes, and you did. You are one of the few people throughout the history of mankind that rarely gave into sin, and because of that, Lucifer had a target on your back. Your kindness, hard work, attitude, and love for me has reached many people, and as a result, you have brought all them into my kingdom. You will be reunited with your family and friends one day."

Itherial instantly thought of his wife, children, and friends. All of their faces flashed into his mind, and God began to speak again, knowing his thoughts. "Izzy, you planted seeds with deep roots. Your children may stray, but remember, you gave them the foundation, and they make their own choices. I wanted to see you first because I have a special job for you."

With the words buzzing in his head, he smiled because God chose *him* for a special job. Of all the people in the world, what made him wonder what made him so different?

"I want you as my personal messenger. You will deliver my messages and provide hope to those in desperate need. These people are significant because of who they will affect in their lives. I gave you the ability to speak and make people laugh. You were a delivery man without complaint, so as your reward, I want you personally to deliver my words I need my people to know. Sometimes it will be an image, maybe a dream, but I will ask first, will you do this for me?"

Itherial froze. Was he joking? Did he really just ask that? He asked himself to take everything in. Itherial stood up and wanted to ask details, specifics, like who and when. He was so excited but decided to just trust that all in time, he would grow to understand more. "Yes, Father, I will do as you ask. I want to serve you any way I can." Soft tears fell from his eyes because he rejoiced that he would never have to suffer again from pain.

Since every person is given a job or responsibility based upon their gifts and talents, God used Itherial's gift to help other people in the kingdom. Itherial had the ability to reach hearts, and those hearts would listen. When he sang worship in the Worship Hall, some people were brought to their knees from the Holy Spirit working in them. Itherial could gather a whole crowd just by the start of a story. God loved that his smile was so contagious and could light up any room. He was so energetic and animated it was a true talent that would never be wasted.

Only two of Itherial's children came to join him, and unfortunately, his wife and his youngest daughter did not. Ruth never had faith of her own. Her belief and faith had always been dependent on Itherial. She came from a broken and abusive home, so she felt like he was her knight in shining armor. Slowly after his death, she stopped taking the children to church and began to fill her life with alcohol and despicable men. Sarah was too young to understand everything when her father died. She was never taught God's love through her mother, so she grew up thinking she needed a man's love to provide and care for her.

Ruth kept men around her children constantly. When one man was tired of her and the children, they would find themselves in a new home with a new disgusting man. Jacob and JoAnne were able keep their faith and their belief. It was too depressing for them to think this life is all there is. The God their father taught them about just had to be real. They didn't always make the best choices, taking a few wrong turns with the pain of life. They knew deep in their hearts what their dad taught and showed them what was real. Jacob never stopped singing. He would sing to his sisters the songs their father used to belt out early in the morning.

He felt closer to his dad when he sang. He wrote songs to pierce the heart so others could feel what he experienced. JoAnne had several years of trying to fill the void of a missing daddy, but her brother was always able to bring her back to her roots. Sarah suffered in silence. She didn't say much at all, and no one ever really knew what was going on inside of her.

When they entered into heaven, the two were so excited to be reunited with their father. Itherial cried tears of joy to see his babies again and hold them. Jacob became involved with the Worship Hall and began working on building the houses for those who needed new homes built. JoAnne became a Guardian chosen by Leilani and tends to some of the fruit trees for everyone to eat.

The present morning, Itherial felt something was different when God requested to see him. As a result of so many encounters, Itherial now had bright blue eyes and white hair. The light that radiated from the Trinity Falls reflected in Itherial's eyes. There was a fragrance, an aroma that was so pure it made his senses tingle and grow warm. Itherial never got over the feeling that warmed his heart every time he met personally with God. The gentle breeze that came from the Father's words were comforting and sweet. How anyone could not believe such a God existed was beyond his understanding. Itherial saw God in everything he did and everything he experienced while he was alive.

"Izzy, my faithful servant, I always enjoy our time together. However, today, a serious message must be delivered to your brothers, Michael and Gabriel. As we have discussed previously, the time has come, and the final days of man are upon them. Lucifer has been allowing his Watchers to interfere into man's heart because he knows his days are numbered. I have observed his actions go this far, but today begins the mark of Revelation. The child was born, and the Watchers are trying to close in and find him. Lucifer doesn't know who it is yet, and we need to keep him distracted. This child's family is the key that opens the door for the Trinity Treaty to break. This is what you have all prepared for. I trust you, dear Izzy, to support your fellow brethren and not to be afraid."

It wasn't beyond Itherial to question the Father when he asked him to deliver a message. Itherial never doubted what God instructed or said. There were moments, though, when he had no clue what the message would mean. Many times, he would be given just one word or a vision with no explanation. Regardless of the minimal information, one of the reasons he loved delivering those types of messages was because the person would know instantly what the message would mean.

One of his favorite memories was when he was sent to a single mother struggling to pay bills. She had been praying about whether to leave her current position because of a better paying offer or stay where she knew her position was safe. She prayed consistently for an answer. It was Itherial's job to whisper in her ear, "Don't go for the money." The mother instantly knew to stay at her current company, and in time, she came to learn that the other company failed to thrive and, shortly after, closed. Itherial didn't know what was being offered to her, but when he watched her reaction to the answer, he felt a pure sense of joy. The type of joy that gives goosebumps because their emotions are so powerful. His favorite part of delivering a message was it could be anyone, and he never knew ahead of time who was in need.

The very first message turned out to be the most important of all. When God sent him, Itherial was overcome with excitement. He kept asking himself, who could it be? And what would he say? When he arrived at the location, he froze. He was puzzled by his surroundings and kept thinking it was a mistake. God didn't make mistakes, so why was he here?

He was standing in front of the White House. Itherial slowly crept in through the doors, thinking at any moment someone was going to stop him. Yet no one did. He wasn't really sure where he was going, so he began walking around. He took his time, observing every person that passed him or passed through him, still expecting to be seen or noticed. Slowly and carefully, he looked at statues, paintings, and kept peeking his head into the different rooms.

Suddenly, Itherial knew where he was going and made his way into a bedroom. The bedroom was immaculately decorated with cherry oak furnishings, paintings of the most beautiful tapestries that Itherial had only dreamed to see in his lifetime. The bed was built for a king, and Itherial instantly thought of his family. He joked to himself that his wife, Ruth, and his children could all easily fit together on the bed in beautiful slumber.

Suddenly, a man entered the room, and Itherial's first thought was to panic. As the man passed through him, Itherial laughed. It was going to take a few trips back to earth to remember that he could not be seen. He did not recognize the stranger who walked in. A young woman knocked on the door, and as the man told the woman to enter, Itherial watched intently and was caught off guard when she called him "Mr. President."

This made Itherial confused for a moment because Franklin Roosevelt was president when he died. Who was this man? Itherial had to remind himself time in God's presence was not the same as time for people.

He then noticed a desk matching the rest of the furnishings in the room and crept over to see if he could see a date. A notebook lay opened with scribblings of small notes with important dates. Itherial's eyes widened when he read the date—October 1, 1947. Itherial had been dead for six years, and it felt like no time had passed at all.

The man acknowledged as the president was named Harry Truman. Itherial studied him as he finished his conversation with the young woman and then indicated that he didn't want any interruptions for the next three days. Truman took a breath and proceeded to his desk. He sat for a moment, closed his eyes, and didn't move for a couple minutes. He looked tired and decided to just let himself slump in the chair. Truman's body language was screaming to Itherial that the president of the United States was exhausted. Truman sat for just a moment and then began to pray out loud.

"Lord, I am tired. I do my best for this country and do my best striving to be the man of God that you called me to be. I know it is only by your grace that I even made it this far. I am just a Baptist from Missouri, yet you saw me fit of all the men around me to run this great nation. I know it is no coincidence that I am the thirty-third president. No one else may see it, but I do, and I see that as a sign that you are always with me. I have tried to serve the people, your people, as best as I can. I am feeling deep within my soul that I need to ask you about your people. What do you want me to do? You know the dangerous situation in the Middle East, and your chosen people will be destroyed if I make the wrong choice. Over these next three days, please guide me, confirm for me, and speak softly so that I may make the correct decision."

He finished his prayer and looked outside the window in front of him. The sun shining through the glass gleamed upon a document that the president had brought in with him. He began to read, and with Itherial's curiosity getting the best of him, he read over the president's shoulder. The Israelites requested to become their own state and allow them back and return to their promised land because of their help to win in war. This was no small decision to make. Tensions in the Middle East were no different today versus thousands of years ago.

Truman requested three days before he would announce his decision. When he was done reading the document, he set it aside to the top corner of the desk and pulled out from one of the drawers his Bible. The fragile book reminded Itherial of his own Bible. The pages were crinkled from the occasional water drops and the sides, frayed and worn. Small notes were written on the sides and important verses highlighted and dated. Suddenly, Itherial knew what the message was and knew to stay by the president's side for the next three days.

During those next few days, Itherial stayed particularly close to the president's side. When the Holy Spirit warned Itherial someone was coming to talk Truman out of his decision, it was Itherial's job to create a distraction so Truman wouldn't give in. Itherial worked off of memory and kept directing the president to the books in the Bible that predicted God's chosen people would come together again. Scattered from all corners of the globe, his people would all reunite in one day. The majority of his time was spent in Isaiah, Daniel, and Ezekiel. At the end of each day, as the sun went down, he got down on his knees and prayed.

Truman felt the time was now for God's chosen people to claim their land back. Many of the men within his cabinet stated if he did such an act, they would resign. He would be marching the United States straight into another world war. The opposition that he was facing was tearing him up inside. He wanted to do the right thing, knowing the right didn't always translate to easy.

On the third day, Itherial directed Truman to the story of King Cyrus in Babylon. He gave the Israelites their homeland for the building of the second temple. Truman read through the book of Ezra, and suddenly, Itherial whispered his final words to the president. He had to do what the Holy Spirit was leading him to do. Since Truman had prayed and fasted all three days, God honored his request and finally gave him the answer. Itherial whispered, "Be as King Cyrus, and God will bless this nation you lead."

After the final words came through, it was time for Itherial to leave. He took one last look at the president, and he couldn't hold back the smile spreading on his face. Itherial was overcome with joy and began to praise, giving all the glory back to his Almighty God. President Truman now had his answer, and he began to address the State of Israel to the United Nations.

Over the upcoming decades, the Israelites faced many battles with the surrounding nations. Lucifer was so incredibly angry that Truman had fulfilled the prophecy toward God's chosen people. So Lucifer made sure that the minute Israel became their own state, he declared war against God. He would attack those God loved most. Lucifer was choosing a losing battle. Even though the countries that attacked were prepared for war, Israel still had victory over its enemies. When Israel gained independence on May 14, 1948, they were attacked by a handful of countries at once, starting with Egypt, Syria, Lebanon, Jordan, and Iraq; and even though Israel was ill-equipped for battle, they still won. God always keeps his promise, and he has protected the Israelites day in and day out as war has been waged against them. One of the following wars that was declared against the Israelites from the same six surrounding nations in 1967 was won by the Israelites in six days. The world was stunned that the singular country was able to not only hold their ground, but they won against nations in literally six days.

Itherial also had to experience dark moments in life as well with people who were so broken. The message wasn't always historic but still life-changing for the person he was sent to. The one that weighed the heaviest on his heart was when he was sent for what he called a special delivery. God would tell him to just go, and he would know what to do when he arrived at the destination. The sight was dreadful. There were two shapeshifting Watchers in the home, and they had been tormenting a young woman. As he arrived, the Watchers instantly retreated. Itherial had authority, and they knew he could easily destroy them.

The creatures were persistent and set on holding their place in the home. Itherial withdrew his sword, and it started to burn with a black flame. The two shifters shrank in size and form into small animals with sharp claws. As they tried to swipe at him, he moved his weapon faster than lightning and cut the paws off the creatures. They screamed and howled in pain and left behind a dark murky sludgelike puddle of blood as they raced to leave. Itherial swiped his weapon across the puddles, and they dissipated. He began to pray throughout the home, touching every doorway and window with frankincense and blessed oil so that those two Watchers could never come back.

Suddenly, the woman came around the corner. She looked to be in her late twenties and had a small Watcher on her shoulder with its tail wrapped around her neck. With a face of a baboon, claws of a tiger, and teeth like a shark, it could easily be someone's worst nightmare. It squealed and screamed so loud when it saw Itherial that the woman stopped to turn her head as if she heard the noise. Her hair was disheveled, and she was carrying a knife in her hand. Her expression on her face was stoic and her movement robotic. There was little Itherial could do since he couldn't interfere. She was choosing to listen to the Watcher, and Itherial had to wait until the message from God came before he could react.

The room he followed her into was in shambles. The TV was on the floor with movies scattered all about. Several picture frames were smashed and had been knocked off the wall. By the sight of the melee, Itherial knew that a fight had taken place and someone took a good pounding. He took another look at the young woman, and he could see the red marks on her neck as if she had recently been choked. Itherial was overwhelmed with empathy, and the only time he experienced a person's pain was when he was sent to a person so empty inside. Itherial was no longer able to experience human emotions such as pain, anger, or sadness, but he understood that helping the living means he experiences them with every human he helps. He wanted to hold her and tell her it would all be okay. He wanted her to know there is always hope. She started crying deep sobs, and her makeup ran down her face.

The Watcher then wrapped its tail around her arm and whispered something inaudible to Itherial inside the woman's ear. She reached into the cupboard and grabbed a bottle of Jack Daniels and started to walk back up the stairs toward her bedroom and into her bathroom.

Itherial followed behind her as the creature upon her shoulder then placed its tail in her head. She turned the water on to take a bath, and Itherial couldn't understand why the message had not yet arrived. She pulled out a bottle of opiates and swallowed several pills with the whiskey. Her face clenched as she swallowed the first gulp. She repeated the action over and over again with rhythmic motion as the Watcher kept spinning its tail faster and faster in her head. She could feel herself sway slightly in front of the mirror in the bathroom as she observed her face and neck. She slowly traced around the handprint on her throat.

Suddenly, she screamed out in pain, and Itherial felt as though he was just punched in the heart. He ached, and his thoughts were rapid. He stopped to pray for a moment and asked the Holy Spirit to be back in control of his own emotions, for he had never experienced something so deep and empty.

She noticed a marker that had been left by her little girl since she was always coloring by the tub when her mother took a bath. She slowly climbed on top of the bathroom counter after she reached for the black marker and began to write lyrics from a song she knew on the mirror. As she wrote, she kept singing the morbid tune over and over again.

The Watcher kept whispering in her ear while on her shoulder, and the nasty creature kept his eyes dead center on Itherial. Itherial couldn't believe such lyrics existed, and his heart sank as she wrote:

I just want to say goodbye and disappear with
no one knowing.
I don't want to live this lie and smile to a world
unknowing
I don't want you to try, it's not enough to keep
me going
I will be fine... I will be fine for the very last
time.

Itherial froze as the letters appeared on the mirror. He instantly prayed, asking God what the words were because he didn't want to watch this! It was hands down the most painful moment he had ever seen. She didn't even take off her clothes as she submerged herself into the tub now filled with steamy hot water. She stared into the knife, gazing into a hazy reflection, and continued to mumble the words to the heartbreaking song. The cold dead stare of the Watcher became a warning sign to Itherial as the woman made the first slice into her arm.

Tears began to run down his face. He didn't understand. How could someone experience so much pain and want to die? He continued to silently pray and began to sweat as he watched her cut into the same wrist over and over again. The cuts kept going deeper, and he could see the blood rush and the veins pulsing. She screamed out again and again as she cut herself repeatedly. The Watcher looked Itherial dead in the eyes as she kept cutting and laughed as much as he possibly could.

"Just let me die, pleased, God!" she begged with pure desperation in her soul.

Itherial, completely horrified, began to feel his body go heavy. What was he supposed to do? He couldn't interfere and because she was listening to the Watcher, he was limited on the ability to influence.

The bathtub became fully brown, and the woman dropped the knife by her side. Her clothes were fully soaked from her own blood, and her eyes started to close. She could feel her heartbeat in her chest slow down. Then in a low voice, she prayed, "Jesus, please forgive me. I can't go through this anymore. Yahweh… Adonai… Elohim… please take the pain away." Then she slid into the water.

Itherial finally had what he needed to take action. Within a blink of an eye, he grabbed his sword and burnt the creature from the black flame off the woman's shoulder. When the Watcher jumped down, it continually howled in pain. The Watcher shaped into another form that resembled a squid and stretched his leg to grab onto the woman again, but before the suctions from the legs got to her, Itherial stabbed the Watcher straight through the head. It squirmed for only a single moment, then turned into the black sludge and disappeared.

Itherial knelt next to the bathtub, grabbed onto the bleeding wrist, and as he did so, he said the words, "Yahweh Rapha. Heal the mind, heart, and body." The cuts on her wrist then slowly began to close. It was at that exact moment the message finally came through. He whispered softly into her ear, "You're not going anywhere. God still needs you here. You have a purpose."

The woman began to sob deeply again as she put her arm into the water. She then howled out from the horrific pain of the open wound exposed to the hot water. Suddenly, the young woman stopped crying and lifted up her arm. The gashes had completely healed, and there was nothing left on her arm but a few small red lines, barely visible.

Itherial, overloaded with emotion, cried alongside her in the tub. He thought of his own daughters along with his wife, Ruth, and couldn't begin to imagine the pain this woman felt. He could see in her eyes she had fallen into an abyss of pain. He prayed over her quietly and slowly. He saw her expression start to change. He placed his hand into her stomach, and she began to profusely vomit all the whiskey and pills she had consumed. He stayed by her side for a few more moments and felt just as exhausted as she did. He made sure she was okay and had thrown up the rest of what she had consumed.

It was time for Itherial to leave, but he took one last look at the blood-soaked woman, and her face became permanently sketched in his mind. When Itherial returned home, he knew he would never forget her face nor would he forget that moment. He didn't understand how someone would just want to give up.

Today, however, was different. He would be seeing his brothers, two of his fellow archangels that he always delighted in seeing. They could banter back and forth about his white hair against his darker skin or joke with him how he sounded like a dying seagull when he sang his worship. It was all in good fun as close brothers and friends should be with each other. There was no pain, no offense, no malice, jealousy, no hidden motive when someone spoke, and that is the beauty with the pure of heart.

Itherial loved his brothers because every time they got together, there was always an abundance of laughter. This time felt different, though, because he knew the message had to be on the serious side. He knew the end times were upon them, and no one in the kingdom knew exactly how everything would start. They knew it would be a spiritual battle before the physical battle, and everyone on earth would feel the impact.

"Brother!" Michael called out as he saw Itherial enter the colosseum. "Look. Gabriel, the old man decided to pay us a visit!"

Gabriel looked up and waved Itherial over to him. Itherial slowly jogged over, and Michael couldn't help but to take a jab. "Look at the old man trying to run. Don't hurt yourself, Izzy! A man your age needs to take it easy."

Itherial brushed off the banter and replied, "You only wish you looked half as good as me. No contest, hands down, I am the prettiest between the three of us."

The three of them laughed, hugged, and asked what called for such an occasion that Izzy would meet them in the colosseum.

"Well, he asked me to deliver a message to you two specifically today. He was actually more serious than usual," Itherial stated.

Michael and Gabriel looked back at Itherial with concern. "What do you mean? What did he want us to know?"

"Well, from the sound of it, the time is officially here. The boy has been born, and Lucifer has been trying to close in on the family. I don't know what tactics he will use, but I do know he will stop at nothing to find him. The last time I spoke to Jesus, he was on his way up to the mountain above the falls for some alone time. When we were in the Worship Hall, he wasn't singing either. He had his eyes closed, silently rocking back and forth. I had a feeling something was up. I just didn't realize it would be now," Itherial said with all seriousness.

"Okay, but what does that mean to us specifically?" Gabriel asked.

"We have to throw Lucifer off the family's scent until the time is right," Itherial stated as plain as he could.

"I guess we can have a meeting with all the Guardian leaders and the Momenti so they can be aware that the child is starting to grow up. It's important we need to resume business as usual. Tell all of them not to give anything away by speaking out in the open down on earth. The Watchers are always listening," Michael stated, looking back to Gabriel.

"He didn't give me the specifics to the story. He knows Lucifer is wanting to get his hands on the family so bad he can taste it. Just make sure that the Guardians check in more often. It will happen spiritually within our world before it hits those on earth. So I guess we have to ask the fighters to report any weird activity. Any group that has less than seven, we need the leaders to share with the rest of us anything they see that could indicate the family he is born from," Itherial said.

"Why doesn't God want us to know who it is? Shouldn't we know so we can protect and guard them more efficiently?" Gabriel inquired to Itherial.

"This is where it gets tricky. There are some Watchers who can hide even from Guardians. There are only several thousand Guardians who can actually have the ability to see them, and all it takes is one slip of the tongue, thinking they are safe. If they want to discuss it, it needs to be here and never down there," Itherial stated with all seriousness.

"Good point, old man, the eldest is usually the smartest," Michael poked, trying to lighten the conversation, all the while knowing how serious this moment really is.

"Please don't forget the prettiest," Itherial stated with a smile. "Well, I will see you guys later! Places to go, people to see, and messages to deliver."

Michael and Gabriel waved goodbye to their brother, and for several minutes, they didn't say a word. They were alone in the colosseum, and the silence was deafening. Michael looked at Gabriel for a moment, and both angels suddenly realized after all these years, it was finally here. Through several millennia, centuries, and decades, they have been preparing for this moment, and now, it had finally come. Both knew there would be people who would suffer for their beliefs and the sacrifices they would make for the God they loved. These two were the originals who watched Lucifer fall. They knew now, though, that with the time of man coming to an end, they would need to be prepared for whatever Lucifer would throw their way.

They were close with him before the fall and once called him brother. They both knew at some point they would have to fight Lucifer again, and though they hated who he had become, they once loved who he was. Would they be able to do what they needed to? They turned toward the grand opening of the colosseum, and neither of them spoke a word as they headed toward the Guardian's training school to speak with each of the leaders.

IN THE SHADOWS, DARKNESS LURKS

The morning sun just began to shine upon the desert horizon over a remote village in the Middle East. Ten men stood directly behind ten men that had been pushed and forced down to their knees. The men were blindfolded with black sacks on their heads with their hands tied behind their back. One by one, the ten men on their knees had been ripped from their homes throughout the night. They were accused of being traitors to the current corrupt leader. The victims had been tied and blindfolded, and they each were accompanied by their Guardians who were trying to provide peace in this moment. The Guardians held their position alongside the terrified victims and kept still as the perpetrators kept screaming and shouting at their captives. As the men sat on their knees, frozen with fear, they kept silently praying to provide themselves with strength and comfort.

The aggressors were accompanied by monstrous Watchers crouched upon their backs, feeding off the violence within the men's hearts. The nastiest demons, made from the depths of worst nightmares, each had grown to the size of gorillas. They were biting into the men's bodies, feeding, clawing, and whispering into every single one of the evildoers' ears. Each bite from the darkness consumed their hearts and diminished any desire to restrain the pain they were about to accomplish against their victims. The attacker's actions were not only influenced by the Watchers but driven by a Greater Demon known as the Prince of Persia.

Fear overcame the many innocent people as they observed and witnessed good men and women tortured for nothing more than standing up for their beliefs. They had jaw-clenching anxiety of who or what could be next. The women and children of the men stood by, helpless at the sight of their loved ones about to be executed. The victims elected for execution and refused to conform to laws enforced by a corrupt government. Anyone that did not submit themselves to the will of the devious leaders was executed and some tortured to be made an example of.

Lucifer was making his rounds as he usually did, checking into looking into the hearts and souls of the families filled with terror. He fed off their lack of hope in the desolate places throughout the world. Legion, Lucifer's left-hand man, maintained his position permanently at Lucifer's side. Lucifer needed to design a demon that was capable of spying in as many places in the world as possible. Legion's appearance didn't have a touchable physique. He was instead a transparent smokey gray mist that resonated a human form.

The trails of the mist spread further and further away to seek out devastation and despair. Faces were visible, and the thicker the mist became, the more faces could be seen. Lucifer, incapable of omnipresence, designed Legion to be his eyes and ears throughout the world. Their strength kept growing stronger, rising steadily each day as the world continuously rejected away from God.

"Something you may want to see, Lucifer," Legion hissed as the countless number of souls returned back into one form. His voice echoed like a howling wind of a thousand whispers into an ear. He had the ability to quickly scan through the locations throughout the people of the world, tormented by the dark prince, and report back to Lucifer everything he saw.

"Oh? What has my bloodhound found?" Lucifer questioned in a cold smooth voice. His unforgiving stare pierced deep and empty as a half-smile spread across his face. The expression made him look even darker than usual. He was petting two enormous dogs that he referred to as his hounds of hell. The giant beasts were on a leash made of fire that only Lucifer could hold and the only one with the key to unleash their destruction. The hounds' frames, comparable to the size of bears, each had two horns adorned upon their heads. One of the dogs looked up and growled at Lucifer's words. Lucifer bent down at the beast beside his leg, and with a cold breathy voice, spoke, "Don't worry, Abaddon, I would never replace you and Mott. You are my very own death and destruction." He scratched behind their ears.

As he looked back up to Legion, his facial features changed. Lucifer dressed himself in a black pinstripe suit with a single blue rose in his left jacket pocket. A black fog consistently hissed out of his collar, sleeves, and down by his ankles. The fog danced about his body, and wisps of the dark smoke followed him wherever he went. He kept his shoes shined to perfection. His thick black slicked back hair didn't change his appearance, and his eyes had a cold dead stare with an abyss of emptiness.

"The Prince of Persia has continued creating chaos in the East. He's been inducing terror amongst all the innocent. He would like you to see the latest conquest," Legion said.

Lucifer looked appeased by the request, and with the snap of his fingers, he, Legion, and his hellhounds appeared at the location of the ten men with the swords and their victims. The Guardians beside the men stiffened by the sight of Lucifer. He knew they couldn't do anything to him, and he also knew that he could antagonize them with literally a snap of a finger. The Watchers connected to the men with the swords and swelled up in size with the presence of their master. Their claws and fangs sunk deeper into the men standing, causing readiness for the slaughter.

The Prince of Persia welcomed Lucifer by bowing down on one knee and kissing his hand. A true prince to his core, the prince adorned himself with vibrant gold that danced among the blue and purple in his wardrobe. The only piece to his body exposed were his eyes. The reflective green eyes stood out among the rest of him. They were deep, and his heart was truly hardened for the thousands of years he stayed among the sand in the desert. The Prince of Persia fought relentlessly to destroy people and was excellent in his endeavors.

"I thought you might want to witness the slaughter of the innocent, along with the weakness of the Guardians." The Prince of Persia stated as he stood back up, glancing backward. The Prince met Lucifer's gaze and then turned toward the massacre ready to take place. The Prince of Persia remained in control and became the driving force behind the chaos in the Middle East.

"Oh, a beheading! How generously fun," Lucifer stated loud enough for all the Guardians to hear. He pointed his finger toward the men, and a deep black mist sprayed from his deformed scarred finger. The mist changed into wormlike tendrils that fell to the ground and began to squirm. The black tendrils wiggled past and around the Guardians, and as much as they wanted to stop the slimy sludge, they could not. The black worms crawled up the legs of the men standing and stopped right at their chests and bit into their hearts. If there was any doubt or hesitation in their souls to behead the men in front of them, it would now disappear. Lucifer snapped his fingers once more, and their swords swung down, and all of the heads came off the men blindfolded on their knees. The Watchers each screamed and howled as if a great victory was just achieved.

Lucifer sat for a moment and glared at each one of the Guardians. They showed absolutely no fear toward him, and the look in their eyes was as if they were challenging him. This was something new. He had never seen any angel be bold enough to sit and glare at him. Lucifer, Legion, the Prince of Persia, along with the hounds of hell, starred as the souls of the bodies arose and left with each of the Guardians. The families of the victims were each screaming and crying as they tried to tend to the bodies of their loved ones. The massacre empowered the Prince of Persia as he fed off the blood of the slain.

"Those rodents," Lucifer hissed through clenched teeth, and as his anger rose, his skin started to turn ashy and black. Calming himself, he turned toward Legion and stated, "Well, let's go home, boys, we have more important matters to discuss." As soon as he snapped his finger, they were yet again gone.

He had the best of all the darkness within one location. The world had grown so thick with desperation to become a star, people willingly ready to pay the price, even if it meant bending and breaking their core values. The world was now a "me, me, me, what can be done for me" society. All the drugs, vanity, and self-righteousness were so commonplace that he had no need to even visit and feed off their sin. He had a buffet all lined up and became easily provided by his Reeds of Death. As the world began to become so focused on themselves with social media, it was apparent people had grown incredibly insecure. There was no privacy anymore. Lucifer had little work to do. The Watchers easily latched on so deep into those who rose up in fame.

His home was a mansion and a residence that no one could get in or out of. Lucifer made himself out to be a mysterious neighbor no human ever saw. Majority of those in Hollywood were only concerned with their own affairs, so Lucifer was able to come and go as he pleased. Over many decades, the darkness in the world was reaching levels so high that his Watchers had very little work to do within the county and even state as people were doing wicked deeds all on their own. Their lies, tax evasion, cheating, drug abuse, and gang-related crimes alone in the Los Angeles area were enough to destroy a small country.

Each one of the "sins" all started with a simple thought to do the wrong thing. As it began with the fall of Adam and Eve, every situation came down to a choice. If Lucifer had anything to do with a choice, he would make sure in his hierarchy no one would ever miss an opportunity to influence the wrong one.

When he returned to the mansion, his daughter, Morajes, was waiting in a stunning sparkled red sequence dress. Her hair was long, luscious, and blonde. Her body was the lustful dream of any man born under the sun and the broken desire of every woman striving to obtain her physical structure. In front of humans, she was able to portray hazel eyes that could seduce either man or woman. Through spiritual eyes, they were pure black, and nothing was in her but darkness created by her father. Her frame, tall and slender, had the curves in all the right places.

As Lucifer and the others came in, she was sitting on a black velvet chair with cherry oak legs. Her legs were crossed, and she held a wine glass of dark liquid. It was the only thing she was actually able to consume. The liquid was the blood of the innocent taken before life began, and the liquid gave her power. She stood up and greeted her father as he came in.

When God destroyed her parents, Sodom and Gomorrah, she was only a small child and was left for dead upon the sand. Lucifer found her and decided he would focus and raise her into a woman of pure destruction. He stood upon the sand, and she looked up at him with a single black tear rolling down from her deep empty eyes. Lucifer wiped her tears, grabbed her hand, and decided to raise her as his own. He raised her to believe that God had no compassion because if he did, then her parents would still be alive. He showed her in his twisted fatherly way he was good. This was not the usual father-daughter relationship, though. It was perverse, abusive, and broken. He wanted her to grow to have no feelings of sympathy, compassion, or kindness. He taught Morajes to hate anything that was of God—goodness, kindness, patience, peace, and most of all, love. He raised her to feed off of lust and perversion.

As she grew into a seductive demon, she was able to entice any person who had any kind of obsessed sexual desire in them. She was the rise and fall of every porn star, and not a single girl was able to escape her grasp once she took hold. Morajes was merciless, especially toward little girls because she never got to be one. She had nothing but distaste toward humans and pure hate toward God. She didn't ask to be raised the way she was, but Lucifer also raised her to target those that tried to follow after God and crush them in their weakest area. Her job was to knock them down as hard as she possibly could, and with Lucifer as a father, nothing less was to be expected.

She embraced her father and kissed him intimately. "Hello, Daddy," she stated right as she grew close. Legion glared as she embraced Lucifer, and she purposely looked him in the eyes. Belial, another Greater Demon, had just entered into the mansion and pushed his way past Legion and the Prince of Persia. He bared his sharpened teeth as though he was a wolf. Morajes noticed his presence and fixed her eyes upon him as she kissed Lucifer again.

Lucifer pulled away and led everyone into an underground conference room unable to be seen by any mortal or angelic eye. The walls were made of a blue fire, and it danced as smoothly as running water. Several statues were mounted in the corners that paid tribute to Lucifer. Upon the fire wall, a painting displayed people who were frozen in time and the horrible mistakes they had made, moments that left their mark throughout history from King David lusting after Bathsheba to Hitler attempting to eradicate the Jews. The painting continually changed like a billboard on the side of the freeway, advertising the greatest seductions of mankind's greed and sin.

Lucifer proudly displayed the painting. The greatest people throughout history had fallen from God's glory, and it was his success and pride that kept him going. It was never enough, though; lusting for more pain and desperation made him stronger. Lucifer would gaze upon his winning moments to give him more power and motivation in any destruction he set out to accomplish.

Belial was the first one to speak as they sat down in their seats. His anger vibrated through the base in his voice as he was still agitated by watching Morajes kiss Lucifer. Each chair was designed to fit the different Greater Demons, the conference table constructed with the bones of innocent children and victims of the most evil acts in mankind. As Lucifer sat in his oversized black velvet chair, Belial instantly demanded to know why they had been called together. His temper could be detrimental to his surroundings, and it was unwise to agitate such a beast.

"Why have you called us here?" he roared. The horns adorned the top of his head, unmatched by the gargantuan and unbreakable size. His eyebrows came to a point and his face, long as a horse. His upper half of his body mimicked the structure of a man, yet his skin was red. The lower part of his body was animalistic. Where feet would usually stand had been replaced with hooves. His legs were muscular with the strength of a rhino. He did not like to be called away from the anger he fed off of in the world. The anger in recent years kept elevating, and Belial was the driving force behind it all. The destruction caused by Belial within an innocent soul became a monstrosity, raging like a bull, tearing everyone down around them. The tips of his horns started to turn auburn as his anger became visible. Of all the demons within the darkness, Belial was physically the strongest and merciless.

"Belial, have you noticed a change with the Guardians lately?" Lucifer asked coldly toward the beast.

"What do you mean? What kind of changes? Why would I care to notice a change in the Guardians? They are no match for me," he commanded with his voice raising and the tips of his horns starting to turn red.

"Watch yourself, Belial," Morajes stated with her hollow eyes staring back at the beast. She placed her hand on top of his, and his horns turned back to black.

"Always takes a woman to tame a beast," Lucifer stated with a sinister smile growing across his face.

Legion gazed upon Morajes' hand and then spoke, "I have noticed lately that there is a change in the air, a shift in dynamics, and unfortunately, the 'believers' seem to see it too." More pastors are coming out and explaining the words spoken in Revelation, and though most people believe they are crazy, others are starting to listen. They are rising to a new level in their faith or they are completely denouncing the God they once trusted. The Watchers can't seem to understand the predictions, and lately, even I have had trouble. We have been following the Guardians everywhere, but they are consistently keeping to the rules. The one thing I have personally seen is they have become daring and bold toward the Watchers. The people they are assigned to are starting to stand their ground more than usual."

Lucifer cut off Legion from continuing to speak, and his annoyance was clear as he spoke. "I care only about what the Guardians are doing alongside their humans. Ugh, the people they help are nothing. They are fickle, easy to be swayed, and each one has their price. I will never understand his love for the vile creatures," Lucifer stated as his eyes began growing red.

"Father, don't worry. Not a single Guardian or an army of Guardians would be able to influence man against me. Christians are considered intolerable, and that now makes them the enemy to the world," Morajes spoke her words smoothly and soft as silk. Pushing her chest upward, she continued, "Every show on television is more daring and pushing impurity and sexuality to outdo one another. Sex sells. It's now the norm, and there is nothing God's people can do about it." She began stroking Lucifer's arm.

"You are right, my child. In this world, you are the treasure and prize all women wish they could grow to be. You are the perfection that all men lust for. I know you have been able to convince the masses how they live should be accepted and normal, but let us take it to the next level. We need to start exposing children and animals. Let's see how dark the human world really is. No child is left untouched by the sins of the father. No one is immune to any of the fallen," Lucifer said.

As Lucifer finished speaking, and the words still lingered in their thoughts, a Watcher entered in the room through the blue fire. Lucifer almost smiled as he saw the creature come crawling up to him. "Feassure, my favorite fallen lizard, have you anything to tell me?"

Feassure was a unique fallen Watcher—quick, stealthy, and had the ability to blend in the background. He had wings of a dragon with the skin of a snake. His eyes lacked emotion as he appeared to have a blank marble stare. Since Feassure was blind, this made his other senses more alert to everything around him. Since only a small percentage of Guardians had the same ability to hide in the spirit world, they were the only ones able to see him. With Feassure's ability to hide, he could easily attack the weak while he preyed upon their fear, and most of all, depression. Those suffering under his influence were unable to get themselves out of bed.

Feassure made sure they stayed in their self-loathing and darkness. He devoured their loneliness, draining their spirit internally when he pierced a hole in their souls. His victim's blood would feel cold and there was rarely any relief from the desperation they endured. His power was stronger against the youth in recent years for the generation so caught up in social media they allowed their measure of worth to be determined by how many likes they got on a picture. The days arrived swiftly when the Internet determined who they were in the eyes of the world.

The blank stare in the middle of his eyes were welcomed by Lucifer, and Feassure smiled with a grin of razor-sharp needles for teeth that were tipped with blood. He just had a fresh feeding of a celebrity who died of a drug overdose. Feassure spoke in a language that only the darkness could understand. His ability to communicate was taken from him when he caught on fire during his fall, and his tongue burned off as he was cast out with Lucifer. He never recovered from the reptile scars to his skin. Lucifer considered him as his own personal spy and was appeased when the spying dragon entered into his presence.

Feassure had been lurking and blending into his surroundings to try to spy and listen to conversations among the Guardians. In the past couple months, the Guardians had been discussing a change. Something big was coming. They were happier and less cautious around any of the fallen. He heard them discuss that a Guardian would shift the spiritual world, but most importantly, the boy Lucifer was looking and waiting for had been born. God hid the Messiah from Lucifer and all the Watchers, but this time, Lucifer would stop at anything to find the child. Each Guardian kept guessing and discussing among themselves which group would be assigned to him and his family.

Feassure decided to follow a particular group of Guardians as they entered into a church. The Guardians acted so excited and animated because for centuries, this was now the prophetic time they had all been trained and waited for.

It was Easter Sunday, and the seats were filled more than usual for the holiday. Feassure crawled his way into the church, and he had to replace a Watcher attached to a man with a severe pornography addiction. Feassure had no authority in any location of worship and would catch on fire if he entered by himself. The man that was allowing the Watcher to latch itself onto him had free rein to go anywhere the man went, so Feassure had to trade places with the Watcher and entered into the church on the man's shoulder.

"I keep wondering who it will be. I can't contain my excitement anymore!" said the first Guardian. "I am so tired of watching the pain and brokenness in this horrible world."

Feassure methodically and slowly slid down the man and crawled up the wall toward the front of the church toward the three Guardians. He needed to get closer in order to hear the three Guardians speaking to one another.

"I personally think it will be a Guardian of incredible strength. I mean, it makes complete sense. Since the boy is marked as a huge bull's-eye on a target, it would require impeccable strength. Don't you think?" said the second Guardian.

"Well, that's not entirely true. Sometimes even an ordinary person can be asked to do incredible things. Personally, I think it will be a Guardian who is a planner. They will have every step of the way planned, and I think they will know internally they were chosen for a family of this importance," said the third Guardian.

The worship team was playing so loud, Feassure was struggling to hear the conversation. Suddenly, he lost his grip on the side of the wall. He landed on a drum and had to instantly jump off and blend into the carpet of the church. The pastor had a colossus of a Guardian that was once a sumo wrestler while he was alive. Since pastors are meant to be a shepherd protecting their flock, they can sometimes be the most vulnerable to the Watchers attacks. God always assigns their personal Guardians to be monstrous in size, gifted, and, of course, incredibly strong.

Taiho, the sumo wrestler, stood above the demon with a spear in his hand. Feassure didn't count on the pastor's Guardian having the ability to see him. Taiho took his weapon from his side and stabbed downward, right near Feassure's head, and without missing a single beat, Taiho smiled and said, "Oops, I missed. Wanna see if I miss again, little lizard?"

Feassure was terrified, frozen in the place he lay. He noticed the three Guardians had caught sight of him, and their first instinct was to draw their weapons. Before they could get a chance to destroy the demon, he scurried off as fast as he possibly could. The Guardians chased him out of the church, but Feassure's ability to camouflage in the background made them quickly lose his tracks.

Feassure headed to Lucifer's home and crawled into the room slowly and fearfully, knowing Lucifer would be hysterical as soon as he told him what he found out. Feassure spoke slowly, dreading to tell Lucifer the events that had just taken place. The others around the table could only stare, trying to figure out what the lizard with wings was saying, and whatever it was didn't make Lucifer happy.

"*What?*" he screamed at the small creature as it cowered before him. The walls made of fire raged hotter and brighter as he continued to scream at the creature. "Did they say who? Did they say when? Can you tell me anything useful?" he demanded from Feassure and smacked him down to the ground.

Morajes tried to speak as though honey was dripping from her lips toward Lucifer. As she tried to calm him down, he instantly slapped her to the ground next to Feassure. Standing above Morajes, he screamed louder than before, and his rage continued, "Don't you dare talk to me like you are equal with me or even above me!"

A dark mark grew on the side of her face, but after so many years of his abuse, she had grown numb to his outbursts. She could sense that Belial was becoming angry above her, so she gently placed her hand on his leg while she tried to stand back up and keep him calm.

"Legion, we need to start following the Guardians. Doesn't matter where they go, just be on alert. We need to know every conversation and pay close attention to anyone who has an abnormal gift. I know their aura will be different and they will have some form of a special talent." Lucifer, at this point, was pacing around the table and beginning to sweat. His slicked-back hair had fallen down to his sides, and the sweat began to dampen through his suit. As he kept pacing around them, he continued, "Morajes, you need to release your full power. It's time to entice girls younger into adult entertainment. Children need to be exposed so they can become numb at a younger age. Belial, you need to cause as much chaos as possible. Prince, you need to make sure the radicals are extremely prepared. Legion, you will need to stay by my side as I want a report at all times."

The present situation reminded Lucifer when he tried to stop at nothing his attack against the Israelites when President Truman declared Israel their own state in 1948. Lucifer knew with this significant moment in history, his time had become limited. His every attempt to destroy God's chosen became vengeful. He was angry then, but his anger was different compared to his present situation. This moment came down to fear and rage. None of the Greater Demons had ever seen him this worked up. The dark mist that usually surrounded his body turned blood red, and the more he thought, the thicker the mist became. For the first time since he had been banished to the human world, Lucifer became terrified.

Morajes took a moment and allowed his emotional explosion to set in. He just gave away his fear. She finally knew his weakness. Throughout the several thousand years he raised her, she only saw his destruction, his anger, and his ability to cause so much despair. She never thought she would see the day when her father, the fallen angel who found her as a child, would expose himself to be vulnerable. Thoughts raced in her head, and she concluded it was time she would have to follow the Guardians. She knew everyone had a weakness, and the trick in this situation was to find what made a Guardian vulnerable.

Morajes began to lightly tap her fingers on the table. Lucifer realized she must have had an epiphany. The devious smirk on her face was all the confirmation he needed. She was the true whore of Babylon. The only task he trusted her with was to make the world's sexuality and perversion grow. He designed and constructed her to be the woman she was today, and he couldn't understand why he hated her for doing what he designed her to do.

Lucifer stopped in his tracks and instantly smiled. "I know exactly what we will do! Abaddon and Mott!" he yelled, getting both of the dogs' attention. They looked up to him with their ears straight up, and he continued, "I want you to sniff out the blood of a fresh Guardian. Follow the scent of anyone, even if they are surrounded by six other members." He paused for a moment, and as he turned around, his teeth became fangs, his eyes darkened, and then he screamed, "*Go!*"

The hounds of hell ran out through the fire, and Lucifer turned his attention back to the rest of the group. He calmed himself, smoothed his hair back, and then spoke in a cold stony voice,

"Time is on our side. It most definitely is." As Lucifer started to walk through the walls of fire, he began singing the song he loved from the 1960s. The others around the table sat in silence as his voice changed while he sang the tune, "Time is on my side. Yes, it is."

The Prince of Persia and Feassure quickly left after Lucifer and Morajes instantly looked at Legion, then over to Belial. "Did you see what I saw just now?"

Neither demon wanted to speak for fear that Lucifer would hear them.

"Well, I know what I saw, and I already know how we can take this world for ourselves." She stood up as she was talking and ran her nails across Belial's horns and head. She slowly and seductively walked over to Legion and began to stroke his hair. "Boys, it's time to really show this pathetic world our power and ability. He is just the director, but we are the keys, boys, we are the keys to making everything happen, and now we know his weakness."

Legion and Belial looked to each other, uncertain what Morajes was trying to accomplish. Both the demons knew she was a liar and incredibly selfish, so why would she want their help? As if it was an unspoken agreement between them, they would not respond to anything she stated or questioned.

"Just give me a little bit of time, boys, and I will give us everything we want." She walked out through the fire that burned red as she crossed the threshold and began to sing the same song her father sang. "Time…is on my side. Yes, it is."

SIFU XIANG LAU

Xiang Lau was in the middle of the martial arts school, practicing his tai chi as Itherial walked in. Quite some time had passed since the news came out about the boy Lucifer was after. Itherial came to provide the information to Lau himself because this was his best friend. He had come to learn when Lau had his eyes closed and was gently swaying to the light music, he needed to just be still until Lau was done. Lau would perform only to his thoughts and to unwind from the stress from training the Guardians. As a Sifu or master in martial arts, he taught the Guardians to defend themselves and fight against the Watchers.

Lau began to train at a young age and mastered fighting skills southern kung fu style. His movements were fluid, precise, and careful. Each step and form came as natural to him as breathing. He earned the title Sifu at a much younger age than most men in his village during the many years of practice and training. He enjoyed the challenges of hard work along with sparring against his friends and fellow villagers. He had a desire that burned within him to perfect his technique and become absolutely flawless. A man that he considered his uncle spent countless hours training him to become not only an incredible martial artist but a warrior.

Lau had been born in 1830 in China, located in the Sichuan province near the Yangtze River. The land provided an abundance of natural vegetation for their food. Fruit trees, berry bushes, rice paddies, and most of all, fish from the Yangtze River kept the province fed. The Sichuan province was so desirable that the villagers had to learn martial arts in order to protect their homes. They were simple people and lived a lifestyle that was peaceful. They didn't care for the outside world nor the treasures it was rumored to provide. As long as each family had a home, food, and worked their share for the village, life was great. They were each taught several different trades. In case one of the households fell sick or injured, another group or family would help pick up the slack.

Over the years, many warlords, including the British, tried to take over Lau's land because of its abundance in provisions. They fiercely protected themselves since they valued their independence and farmlands. They were fortunate enough to have an enormous mountain range protecting the north and west which made it impossible to try to gain any access from the treacherous terrain. The Yangtze River protected the south, so any attempts at a surprise attack would end the minute anyone from the village saw a ship. So the only point of entry was from the east, down a pathway much too small for horses or a large invasion. They used small and sharpened nails melted together to form spikes on all sides. They would scatter the nails very hidable from anyone coming in. They were melted and combined to stick out in all directions to be a more effective defense tool.

Only the villagers knew where to walk to avoid the pain and shock from the tiny but effective weapon. This action warned Lau's village ahead of time if anyone tried to enter. They knew it would be hard to maintain silence with several nails stuck in their feet.

In Lau's village, they trained women in kung fu for the projection of the children which were considered the future and most valuable. Lau had the honor of becoming included into an elite group, trained for special missions when rumors would grow regarding a possible invasion. The men, from time to time, would make their way to the nearest village and try to get an update on any possible new intruders. Village elders decided the future or fate of the men for protection missions.

The elders taught the men, women, and children their kung fu was not just about martial arts but about military skill. They would have to learn etiquette, sportsmanship, the art of the sword, and train with many other weapons. The men and women learned even the most common item could be used as a weapon. They were also taught infiltration, psychology, chemistry, acting skills, and how to travel through enemy territory by learning accents and dialects. If any of them ever got lost in the wild, they were taught to taste the ground of pathways. This was used to see how often a particular path was traveled by tasting the salt from sweat or any recent animals passing through.

The elite members specialized in pills against hunger which they combined from rice, buckwheat, tea leaves, and sometimes fish blood. Lifelong diets were strict among the most disciplined to have no onions, sweets, or garlic and instead vegetables, tofu, nuts, and other odorless foods. The wrong meal could easily be their last as body odor could cost these trained men their lives. Passing gas would be no honorable way to die before their time.

Lau had been raised to give honor to his ancestors and never had a need for religion. While he was growing up, Christian missionaries passed through his province, and he found them to be curious and odd. His whole province was intrigued by the newcomers. The missionaries were always kind, polite, and often provided the village with a fair trade from the outside world. He was as intelligent as he was talented, so he was able to pick up some English and started to learn about a man named Jesus Christ. The man was weird in Lau's eyes. He couldn't understand how the death of this one man saved the souls of those who believed in him? How would he fit into their heart? When he was able to understand more English, he was given a book called the Bible. With what English he had learned, he tried to read. The stories he read about were confusing.

When Moses kept going to Pharaoh, yet God hardened his heart, Lau thought that it was not only cruel but went against everything the missionaries made their God out to be. At least Buddhism made sense because it was a way of life. What he put out into the world he would receive back. He would pray that his ancestors would watch over him so he could bring honor to the family name. He was mindful of his thoughts and actions. He didn't want any bad karma to come back upon his family, so he worked hard to be not only a good man but one day an elder in his village.

Even though the missionaries came in peace, the warlords saw the traveling Christians as an open doorway to enter due to distraction. The village would have their defenses down, and all the oppressors needed was a golden opportunity. When they found the chance to infiltrate, a desperate battle was sorely lost. Lau's fellow men were taken over, and he himself felt the cold hand of death upon him. Something strange happened inside him, though. In a split decision, he prayed out to the God the missionaries taught him about. He wasn't sure what made him do it, but in his heart, he decided to try. He asked himself, "What would it really hurt if I were to die anyway?"

After he prayed, a dark-skinned angel presented himself before Lau. Itherial stood over him, smiling with his hand stretched out. The angel's dark skin was unknown to Lau, and he was distracted from the sword wound to his side. Massive blood loss and a slow heartbeat began to encase him. A strange feeling surrounded his whole body. He didn't know how or why, but his heart was overcome with peace as he kept his eyes on the angel before him. Lau reached for Itherial's hand, and his soul instantly left his body as they headed for heaven.

He became so overwhelmed when he entered through the gate with Itherial he cried. Just like Itherial, though, God wanted to see him first before anyone else. Lau wouldn't have any ancestors or family members who would be waiting for him. He fell to his knees in the presence of the Almighty God of the Israelites. Tears filled his eyes, and every muscle trembled. He could not move until he heard God say to him to stand up. God began to explain why he sought out for him through the missionaries and explained that it wasn't by chance Lau was able to learn English so quickly.

God thoroughly explained what he was looking for in what he wanted from him. Lau was one of the best warriors in the world and the top throughout mankind. God specifically chose men and women from all countries, different time frames, and different fighting styles to train the Guardians. Every Guardian wouldn't be assigned to one of those leaders, but God chose Lau for his skill set in kung fu.

Lau became taken aback by the request. He knew he was good, but he didn't think he was "training a kingdom" good. He felt proud but humbled himself. Realizing it was a serious commitment and he didn't take the request lightly, he sat for a moment and finally responded, "If I am going to help your kingdom to become true warriors like my fellow kinsmen, I get to speak my language." He had grown tired of the missionaries and British who tried to force him to learn English. The only time Lau chose to speak English was toward a new student and to the dark-skinned Angel who brought him to heaven and eventually became his best friend.

"My brother. How are you?" Lau asked, smiling when he noticed his friend. He quickly walked over to greet Itherial. Since Itherial was the only one he spoke in English to, he would try to speak slowly and clear because of the respect he had for his best friend. They hugged, pulled away, and started to walk toward the back of the training school where a small kitchen was located. Itherial followed Lau to the back room and sat on a pillow delicately set beside a table close to the ground.

Itherial loved the little kitchen because of its Chinese design and how well it reflected his best friend. The table had been talentedly crafted in pure jade with a design of a dragon upon the surface. Itherial loved looking at the dragon because the colors consistently changed, but the eyes adorned in rubies always stayed the same. Lau reached for his teapot and began to pour the tea, and as he sat down, Itherial began their conversation.

"I had to see Michael and Gabriel, and I have constantly been on the move since then. I'm sorry that I wasn't able to come and see you sooner. I decided to make sure I could visit today," Itherial stated with a smile.

"So, you come…to tell me…a message?" With each word spoken, he looked deeply in Itherial's eyes.

Itherial was always surprised for some odd reason how discerning his best friend really was. Lau learned to read the eyes of a friend or foe and know the soul deep within that person. That talent is what made him an incredible opponent in war. Somehow, he was able to always be two steps ahead of his enemy, and that gift was attributed from God.

"Well, my friend, yes. Yes, there is something you should be aware of," Itherial answered.

"I have heard Guardians talking lately…about changes in the wind." Lau looked down, sipping his tea. "I have not asked what others know because… I want to hear from my brother first." He looked back up into Itherial's eyes.

"The time is finally here, Lau. The boy has been born. I have been waiting for this moment since I first became a messenger, and I need to know, is it weird to admit that I am slightly afraid? I know how bad the world is going to become, and it scares me for those still lost down there. I hurt for the people who will suffer." He paused for a moment to study his friend, then continued, "You fought against enemies during your life. Weren't you ever afraid?"

Lau studied his friend's face. He could see the growing concern in his friend's eyes as he answered honestly, "I think it would be unwise to…underestimate *any* opponent as I *always* teach the Guardians." Lau lowered his cup after taking another sip. "The winds are shifting and the tide changing. There will be much suffering, but we know who holds the hearts of winners." Lau placed his cup back onto the table in front of them. "Come with me, brother."

Lau stood up and headed toward the back of the school and out into a garden. He intertwined his fingers behind his back as he started toward the door. Lau held the traditional hair braid, known as a queue, that his forefathers had, and Itherial noticed how long Lau's queue had grown. The braid currently grew to Lau's waist and gently rested upon the top of his hands.

As the two men stepped outside, hundreds of cherry blossom trees were swaying with the soft sweet breeze that filled the air. Small petals gently fell to the ground and all around the two men. Itherial followed close behind Lau as they began to walk on top of a koi pond. Numerous fish swam under their feet, trying to nibble at their toes. Two cranes were slowly walking through the garden alongside Lau, waiting to be fed. The lining of the garden was made of bamboo, and in the corner was a small panda bear rolling in the grass and starting to make her way toward them. The panda stopped at their feet, and Lau rubbed her head.

They continued through the garden until they came upon a bench, and as they sat down, Lau kept the playful panda at his feet but turned toward Itherial. He then presented a small golden sphere. It hovered above Lau's hand for a moment, and without saying a word, the two men placed their pointer and middle finger on it, and they were instantly taken to the final moment in Lau's life.

Bodies completely surrounded the two men. Lau slowly made his way past the men he grew up with, worked with, and trained with. Lau was even looking down at the enemy that lay before him and remained silent while he placed the sphere back into his pocket. He crossed his hands behind his back in his usual fashion and began to walk again. Itherial followed his friend and didn't remember there being so many bodies when he presented himself to Lau.

Flies had already begun to seek out the smell of the decaying bodies from the summer sun. He methodically walked through his fellow countrymen as if he had walked this same path thousands of times before. The truth was, he had. The sphere he carried with him was his moment of death. He could touch it at any time and be taken to that moment, and Lau consistently went to see those he loved and lost.

Itherial was watching Lau and was unable to gather his thoughts as he looked around at all the dead bodies. There were so many questions he wanted to ask his friend as they looked upon the morbid scenery, but he wasn't sure where to start.

Lau stopped in his tracks, and he stated slowly, "Brother...do you know where we are?"

"No," Itherial answered softly.

"We are in a...cemetery," Lau stated as he stood over several more bodies.

"Most wars always end with a mass grave, I suppose." Looking around at all the blood, Itherial felt himself become slightly queasy.

Lau, still motionless, began to explain why he kept returning to this moment in time. "Brother...this place is not a cemetery because of everyone who died fighting. It's an actual cemetery...where my ancestors...were laid to rest."

"Ironic, don't you think? To stand in a cemetery, and this is where your final moment of your life is?" Itherial asked as he walked up alongside Lau. "Gives a chill down the spine just thinking about it."

"Let me show you these final moments, brother…and tell me what you see." Lau took out the golden sphere from his pocket and spun it slightly to the left. Suddenly, all the men who lay dead before them were moving in reverse. Itherial and Lau stood completely still as Lau's last battle played before them. He touched the sphere again, and it stopped spinning. Itherial's eyes widened as he watched his best friend in a battle for his life. Itherial could see in his eyes that he fought with honor, heart, and so much passion. He couldn't believe how incredibly fast and talented Lau was.

God always chose average everyday people to accomplish incredible tasks. The job didn't always require the strongest, best-looking, or even the smartest. It was the power and authority that came from the Holy Spirit within the man. Itherial finally realized, watching his friend fight, just how talented Lau really was. He was taking on two men at a time and moved as if he was water, completely fluid with every strike or step. Itherial watched in pure awe of his best friend.

"How many times have you come back to this moment, Lau?" Itherial turned to face his friend, wanting to look him deep in his eyes.

Lau stayed silent for a moment and finally answered, "Too many times to count, brother."

"Why do you come back to this place of death and war?" Itherial didn't quite understand why *anyone* would want to witness their own death over and over again. The very thought brought back the copper taste instantly back to his mouth from the moment of his own beating and death.

"I come here every day…to watch my fellow men fight…and to watch the enemy. Every day, I am here. I study different men… and their movements. It is always best to know your opponent so you know what to train for and how to train. It is why I must be strict with the Guardians so that they do not lose focus. I also observe to see…if they share the same skill with the men I knew. I do this so I know each counterattack and customize what is the best strategy for each individual."

Lau never ceased to amaze Itherial. Underneath a simple man who loved kung fu and drinking tea was a cunning and decisive leader and warrior. Itherial believed him to be the deadliest weapon when the final war would come. He fought like a caged tiger that had been tormented, and the instant the beast would be let out, he would devour the enemy.

"Come closer. There is something…you must see." Lau placed his hand on his friend's back and directed him toward the final moment in his own personal fight.

They watched Lau as he took on the two men, striking and kicking in any way he could. Lau was quick and fluid. Then suddenly it was as if he was drunk. He couldn't focus and began stumbling. He was struggling to see, and just as quickly as it started, the fight ended. Lau fell with a sword wound just below his ribs. He lay holding his side, and the blood gushed through his fingers. He was stabbed again by the two men he had just been fighting. As he lay on the ground, Itherial's eyes widened as they watched him reach out his hand and then go limp.

"What happened to you? You were so quick, and then it was like you lost your footing, rocking back and forth," Itherial stated, still looking at Lau's limp body.

Suddenly, they were both distracted by a voice calling in the distance. Lau pulled out the golden sphere again, and as both men touched it, they were back in the garden with the panda gnawing on the bamboo as if it were a dog's chew toy.

"Sifu Lau, are you around?" the same voice asked again.

Both men headed back into the school, and they saw Leilani walk in with someone they had never met before. Itherial stopped in his tracks the minute he got a better look at her face. It was her…the one with the Watcher on her shoulder trying to kill her. He couldn't help but to try and look at the wrist he helped to heal.

"Sifu, I would like for you to meet Kinsey," Leilani stated with a bright smile.

Lau approached Kinsey and shook her hand. "Is she to be my new student?" he questioned in Cantonese.

Kinsey was surprised she understood what he said. She gazed upon all the weapons that had been aligned neatly along the wall and placed perfectly apart from one another. Some she recognized from all of the martial arts movies; some she did not. She always found kung fu to be incredibly fascinating because of the discipline it took to achieve the level of skill true warriors attained. She found herself walking along the wall and stopped dead in front of two Chinese broadswords. They were stunningly beautiful for a weapon, the handles handcrafted of jade with a design of a dragon carefully carved with immense detail. Diamonds had been placed on the top side of the handles with two garnets placed as the dragon's eyes in the center. The sword's blades mirrored Kinsey's reflection, and she could not remove her eyes from the beautiful weapons.

"Yes, she was just assigned today, and I wanted to walk her over to meet you. I have to head back out and get the rest of my group," Leilani stated, suddenly realizing that Kinsey was not at her side anymore.

Lau, Itherial, and Leilani noticed the trance Kinsey was locked in. Lau walked up beside her and asked in a soft voice, "You appear to be hypnotized by the beauty of the broadsword."

Kinsey could not remove her eyes from the masterpiece in front of her. She didn't answer him and kept studying the dragon. It began to move and dance. She reached out to touch the dragon, and when her finger was placed on the handle, the jade turned red and formed itself to the shape of her hand. She pulled both swords off the wall, and the weapons felt as though they were a part of her, an extension of her arm and hand.

"It appears…that her weapon…has already been chosen," Lau stated in English, breaking Kinsey out of her trance.

"Oh, I am so sorry, I probably should have asked first" Kinsey stated while placing the sword back on the wall.

"I don't think I have ever had a Guardian obtain their weapon this quickly," Lau spoke again in Cantonese. He began smiling back at Leilani and Itherial who were both amazed how drawn she was to the weapon. "I am Sifu Lau, and I will be training you how to fight and how to use those swords," he said in Cantonese.

"Nice to meet you, Sifu Lau," Kinsey stated with a warm smile. "I don't know how good I will be, but I am sure you will see what kind of train wreck you're working with. The swords are beautiful, and thank you for letting me use them."

"You will not just be using them. You now own them. They belong to you. Each student obtains a weapon that was made specifically for them, and don't worry, students start off with the basics. In time, you will learn your strengths and also learn areas for improvement." Lau spoke so quickly Kinsey was amazed she could keep up with words spoken in another language.

"You mean... Oh, wow!" She paused, completely surprised. "Thank you so much," Kinsey stated to Lau. She noticed that the other man with Lau had not moved or said a word since she walked in. She walked up to him and introduced herself. "Hi, I'm Kinsey, do you teach as well?"

As Lau turned from Kinsey back to Itherial, he noticed that Itherial still had not moved from his position when the two women entered the school.

It took Itherial a moment to respond, and then he finally answered, "Itherial. And, no, Sifu Lau is a good friend of mine. I came by to have a quick chat with him before I have to head out." He couldn't help his emotions in the moment. It was her. The girl in the bathtub. Flashes came into his mind—the marks of her neck, the words on the mirror, and the cuts upon her wrist. He couldn't help but notice the twinkle in Kinsey's eyes that was once dull and dark from his encounter with her. Itherial then realized he needed to go about his day, so as he left, he stated, "See you guys later. I have some deliveries to make." He looked at Kinsey one more time and walked out.

As Itherial walked out of the school, Lau couldn't take his eyes off of him. He started to wonder what had caused his friend to respond so strongly to someone he had never seen before. Then it dawned him that maybe this was a person Itherial was sent to help.

Either way, Lau knew that it was only a matter of time before he would talk to Itherial about his new student.

"Kinsey, all I ask is that you push through the training. It will be hard, but over time, you will learn the art of being a martial artist," Leilani told Kinsey.

"Great, so when do I start?" she asked as she looked back and forth between Leilani and Lau. She then looked down at the swords in her hands again and gently swayed the weapons around, and she noticed that it felt natural.

"We will start now. I have some comfortable clothes for you, so come in and stretch to warm your muscles. You will have regular workouts along with the others, but I will start you out on the basics today. Go ahead and set the swords back by the wall, and we will begin." He spoke so quickly it took Kinsey a minute to register his words.

"Well, I'm off. You will meet the rest of the group later, Kinsey, but for now...stretch!"

Lau looked back to Kinsey to show where he had more comfortable clothes that she could change into. She was still wearing the same clothes that she had died in, and that was definitely the most awkward thought. She quickly changed and couldn't believe the way they felt against her skin and smiled. She walked out of the back room and smiled back at Lau. She sat on the ground and began stretching her legs from holding her feet. Lau walked up behind her and pushed her down further.

Leilani waved to Kinsey, told her to have fun and they would meet back up later, and left the kung fu school.

GETTING

ACQUAINTED

Leilani raced up over the hill that led directly toward a majestic beach with smooth waves and crystal-clear water near her house. Dolphins displayed an aquatic performance as they leapt out of the water for entertainment. The sand was smooth and warm upon any bare foot, and the tropical scenery was mesmerizing. She headed to gather all the Guardians in her group to meet their newest member. She knew Sifu Lau would keep Kinsey busy, so she had plenty of time to round up the troops.

First on the list was Reese, and he lived in an adorable cottage along the shoreline next to her and her brothers. Their home was massive in comparison to Reese's since she and all her brothers occupied the home.

Every time a new Guardian joined her group, Leilani preferred to gather everyone as one big welcome home. She, of course, included her brothers to meet the newest addition and make them feel like one giant family. Her brothers added that tasteful seasoning to complete the perfect meal. They were big, loving, funny, family-oriented, and most of all, pure in heart.

"Reese? Yo, Reese!" Leilani yelled from outside the cottage. She didn't hear a response, so she yelled one more time before she opened the door. Her urgency to get the group rounded up outweighed her hesitation to just enter the house. She yelled out as she opened the door and called his name again. She could never get over his incredible artistic skills with interior design. He had a sense of flare when he was alive, and that wasn't about to change after his death. He had designed his home from the ground up. Reese built his home with his own hands, and Leilani's brothers helped with the foundation. He decorated with all sorts of beautiful fabrics with varieties of colors and textures.

"Come on, dude, we are going to be late. I know you think it's fashionable and all, but remember, we have a new member today." Leilani paced around his house as she waited for him to come down.

"Coming, darling!" Reese yelled from the top of the stairs. "I was just practicing my form and was in the zone. You know, when I'm in the zone, it's my time alone," he said as he started walking down his spiral staircase. He was dressed to kill in his light-blue Guardian combat gear and against his tanned skin and the outfit, it made his blue eyes stand out more than usual. His blonde hair was styled to perfection, and as he approached Leilani, he spoke again.

"Okay so I have been dying for you to tell me about our newest member."

He sat at the bottom of the stairs, tying his boots, and placed his Tai Chi sword at his side in the holder. "Male or female?"

"Female! I already told you that!" She stood in front of him for a moment, looking down at him fiddling with the last shoestring, and then opened the door. "Come on, buddy, let's roll because we still have to get the others."

"Yes, dear, yes, dear, I'm coming." He finished tying his boots and stood up. As a joke to Leilani, he turned to the side and asked, "Does this make my butt look big?"

Slightly annoyed, Leilani answered, "Yes, now let's go get Annie and Big Ben."

Reese looked himself over in the mirror and slightly flexed as he did so. He pointed to his image in the mirror and said, "Hey, good-lookin', go get 'em today." He winked at himself and just caught Leilani's eyes roll as she walked out the door.

"Okay! Wait up, wait up." Reese matched her speed and continued to ask questions about the newest member. "Okay, so give me the big D, the details, the scoop, the skinny—tell me all about her."

As he reached Leilani's side, they began walking up the flower-covered hill and back down toward a narrow pathway. As they continued, they kept tracking toward a path made of smooth round stones, trying to keep their balance.

"How old is she? Was she married? Did she have kids? Was I ever on an assignment that helped her?" Reese wasn't paying attention while he began to walk backward and kept looking directly at Leilani for his answers, and before Leilani could warn him, he fell backward into a pond.

Leilani started laughing so hard tears were rolling down her face. She almost fell over laughing. She couldn't believe he was so distracted he missed a complete area of water.

"Ha, ha, yes, very funny. Oh, gross, this is horrible. Could you compose yourself, please? This took forever to put together this morning," Reese said sarcastically. He began to get annoyed as he tried to stand up but began to sink down into the sludge. It took several attempts to get him out of the pond since his boots were stuck. Leilani knew how important his appearance was to him, and it made the moment even funnier. Not that he was vain about it, but he took pride in the good looks that God had blessed him with.

"Great! Just Great! Yeah, go ahead and keep laughing. Ha, ha, ha." Reese couldn't help but try to hide his smile, knowing deep down, it really was hilarious. He was not remotely paying attention as he walked alongside her. He was just filled with so much excitement because they had not received a new member to their group in years.

"You know we are going to have to go to the marketplace so I can get more clothes, right?" Leilani tried to hold some form of composure, but the more she tried, the harder she laughed. Finally, after she was done giggling, she got him out of the water. "Okay, let's go get you some dry clothes. But, wait, are you sure you don't want to go back home and grab another set of your gear?"

Reese sheepishly smiled at her and said, "No because it gives me an excuse to get a new set. I need a new one anyway. I have been proud of my current ones because of the stained blood of the

Watchers. I have been tearing it·up lately, and although it's cool to have those stains, most of them are ripped and falling apart."

They headed toward the marketplace, and Reese got excited when he could hear the thousands of bartering and trading women. Each one of them seemed to enjoy seeing him soaked as he walked past through all of them. Reese always headed toward his favorite merchant and friend, Debbie. He went to do the double kiss to her cheeks, and the moment she saw his clothes, she instantly said, "Nope, take those off, and put on the fresh set I just made for you this week. You've already worn out several sets I made for you. My Lord, did you fall in? Did you think swamp water is an actual color? I mean I am gifted, but I am not a magician. There is very little I can do with this now. Lord, you sure do know how to stretch the boundaries when it comes to fashion," Debbie said in one breath while picking up the articles of clothing.

He went behind a curtain so he could change in private, and as he did, he could hear Debbie and Leilani giggling. To make sure they knew he was annoyed, every time he took one piece of clothing off, he would toss it out toward Debbie. Every time she picked one piece, he threw two more articles out. "Debbie, will you be willing to patch up some of my gear so that I can continue to wear them with pride? I worked hard to earn those stains, and I love having them as a sign to the other Watchers that I mean business." She was the only one with unique fabrics in all the colors that he loved, and she was the only one who truly knew how to repair his gear with as much stitching as possible so he could continue to wear the stains of blood from the Watchers.

"How in the world did you seriously get these so soaked? Oh, sweet Lord, they are starting to stink. Wow, I wish I saw that, though. It would have been hilarious when it happened," Debbie said.

"Yeah, he decided to take a dive after all those hours of working on his hair." Leilani giggled through her breath.

Reese poked his head through the slit and looked at her with the evil eye. Then after a moment, he smiled and said, "It was pretty funny, actually. I'll admit it."

Debbie kept picking up the clothes and then told Reese, "I'll have the items cleaned for you, and you can pick them up later. In the meantime, I'll make several more sets of your combat gear since you are your biggest customer." The truth was she had the best fabrics and could make an outfit out of anything.

Reese, finally dry and dressed, stepped back out from behind the curtain and flexed one more time to Leilani as a joke. He kissed Debbie cheek to cheek, and she waved him off.

"Great! Darling, you look fabulous. Can we go?" Leilani asked, turning her back to him as she spoke.

"Yes, Lili," he stated with an evil grin, waiting for her to respond.

Leilani stopped dead in her tracks and slowly turned back to Reese. He knew she could not stand the nickname her brothers gave her when she was younger. It was the same as if they were calling her a sissy girl. Leilani considered herself a tomboy growing up and definitely had no desire to be compared to a sissy little girl.

"You're a dead man, Reese! When we go to practice later, better sharpen that little pocket knife you call a weapon 'cause it's gonna be go time, pal," she stated, pointing to his weapon at his side.

"Pocket knife, huh? We shall see which is more practical in combat. Your staff of shark teeth...or my handy sword," he stated back to her.

"All right, we can beat each other up later. We really need to go get Ben and Annie," Leilani stated with determination.

Leilani and Reese raced out of the marketplace and passed through the children's playground. They smiled as they passed by, listening to all of the kids running around and laughing together. Leilani spotted Jaxon and Saige and waved. They waved back for a quick moment and went directly back to playing with their friends.

"Whose kids are those? I have never seen you wave to them before," Reese questioned, looking intently at Leilani.

"They are our newest member's little ones, Saige and Jaxon. She still has two left on earth, and I have kept her constantly on the go. Once it hits her that she can't watch over her children, she will get distracted. It's crucial that we keep her focus on training until she finds her own niche. You know, like we all eventually do. I just want to keep her eyes on our assignments," Leilani replied.

"They look adorable. Wait a minute. Were these children that she—" Reese stopped as the realization hit him.

"Yes!" Leilani said quickly. They all knew everyone had a past. There were just some subjects that tended to be more sensitive than others. Leilani had no desire to dredge up dark moments of their newest member.

Realizing the sensitivity to the question, Reese, in his usual fashion, switched the subject back to what he really wanted to discuss. "So she must be pretty. I mean, those two kids were adorable," he said, facing Leilani, trying to read her face. Her expression always gave away her thoughts, and she definitely didn't have a poker face. She wasn't the type of Guardian to hide her reactions, and sometimes her presence in a room said everything without speaking a word.

"Well, we are all pretty, Reese, remember?" she stated quickly. She knew deep down he would keep asking about her looks while she was alive, and he wouldn't quit asking until he got an answer. "I think she is, and while she was alive as well," Leilani finally replied.

"Don't worry, you will always be my pretty Polynesian. No one could take your place other than Annie!" Reese nudged into Leilani's side.

She gave him the sideways glance and kept moving toward the courtyard outside the colosseum. "I am almost positive Big Ben and Annie are working on target practice. It always amazes me for a man who never misses his mark, he consistently keeps improving on his kill shot from all angles."

"Well, he is a perfectionist, and being one myself, I completely get it," Reese stated while placing his hand over his heart.

Leilani stopped in her tracks and looked Reese dead in the eye. "Did you just say you are a perfectionist?"

"Of course, doll, you know how I am about my cozy cottage and all my designing. Every color represents something special and unique, and I would not rest until my home was laid to perfection. Now, stop stalling, and let's go get Big Ben and Annie. We have a new member to get to know." He smiled at Leilani. He turned his head and quickly headed toward the archways into the colosseum, directly below the designs of the four horsemen.

Instead of the family reunions, God designed the colosseum so that if Guardians were escorting the most recent death, then all that would be there would be family reunions. But if Guardians were going to practice, then all that they would see would be the other Guardians practicing. There were Guardians of all talents and abilities practicing best kill shots with their weapons. Mostly men filled the arena due to the fact that God designed men to be strong for a reason. He wanted them as the protectors and providers. It wasn't anything against women, but the perfectionist females took up a good portion as well, trying to outdo their male counterparts.

The females that got assigned as Guardians were mostly due to the fact of the amount of pain they endured while they were alive. It takes a lot to go through PTSD, pain, depression, abuse, and abandonment, especially if they were mothers. Several thousands of Guardians were running up and down the colosseum steps while others were running through thousands of different obstacle courses. The courses were set to keep them on their toes and to expect the unexpected. Watchers were unpredictable, and the fact that they could morph and shapeshift didn't help. So the more training the better.

The Guardians were already physically fit and in excellent shape, but some habits die hard when fitness is a big part of a human's life. Big Ben and Annie were among those who practiced daily in the arena. They were a duo that was uneasy to separate. They spent every waking moment practicing, eating, and training when they weren't sent for any missions.

Reese and Leilani scanned the arena looking for the dynamic duo. With each Guardian assigned different colors to represent skill, strength, and personality, they were looking for a yellow and dark blue blur running around. Yellow represented intelligence, and dark blue was for nobility. Leilani's teal represented Zen and leadership. Reese's light-blue color was for comfort and kindness. Tank, along with the rest of Leilani's brothers, wore black to represent strength.

Big Ben's height could be intimidating, but his structure was slender and chiseled to perfection. He had an intense stare with his dark blue eyes. He was a no-nonsense type of personality when it came down to his assignments and was able to easily discern who a person was before they revealed their true character. He wasn't a man to make idle chat and cut straight to the point. As a perfectionist, and while he was alive, he had an uncanny way to know when people were lying or telling the truth. He was an observer while he was alive and he always based his trust on someone's actions and never on their word.

Even though he was intimidating, it didn't mean he didn't mean he didn't have friends. He handpicked those he truly liked, whether they were funny, hardworking, loyal and, most importantly, had no drama. He had been involved with a couple friends in his younger years that could have gotten him in serious trouble. It took just once, and he never spoke to them again.

Annie, or Annie Jo as her father, Itherial, called her, complemented Big Ben with her dark skin and smooth braided black hair. She had incredible curves with a toned body to match. Her eyes were kind and sincere, and she was the only woman in the universe who could match such a strong counterpart. Just by a simple touch to his arm, he felt the sense of comfort a person needed when heading to help his assignment against the Watchers.

"I think I spot them," said Leilani as she was squinting toward one of the courses on the other side of the colosseum. Reese looked over, agreed, and they began walking.

Big Ben and Annie each had their weapons out, slicing and smashing themselves through the animated course. The supernatural shapeshifting creatures popped out to simulate and move as the Watchers do. They would shift from one form to another, making it difficult to attack, but the goal was to help the Guardians prepare for the inevitable fight that would eventually take place against a Watcher.

Big Ben used two different weapons to fight against the creatures that popped up in the simulator. He had one for a long distance and another for a close encounter. The long-range weapon, a spear, had been sharpened to a perfect point. The weapon had the capability to pierce through any surface. After the weapons sliced through the flesh of a Watcher, it would bend into a triangle and boomerang back to him. He had to constantly keep his eyes astute to his surroundings because it was only to him that the spear responded. If another Guardian got in the way, it could cause serious damage. His close-range weapon was a circular ax that had the ability to literally cut a Watcher in half. Big Ben loved both of his weapons, and as he was finished running through the course, Leilani and Reese approached.

"We have a new member today, right?" Big Ben asked.

"Yes, we do, and we still need to find Tank," Reese said, scanning the colosseum, looking for a giant black blur.

"Tank's here with your brothers." Ben pointed over to another course that the strongest and massive Guardians practiced in.

Leilani's brothers were monstrous in size, and wherever they went, Tank went. Annie came out of the obstacle course, placing her weapon to her side. "Hi, Reese, Leilani. Are you ready to go see Lau? Is she still with him?" Annie had her hair pulled back when she trained to keep from getting into her face. The yellow against her black skin brightened her appearance and usually made her easy to spot.

"Yes, I dropped her off about an hour ago, so she should be working up a good sweat by now. I'm almost positive she is dreading that I ever took her in there," Leilani stated as she was walked over toward Tank and her brothers.

The others followed her, and as they approached, all of the Utua brothers howled, *"Ua li gumz!"* It'd become a family slang term as kids which meant, "What's up, bro?"

Leilani and the others smiled as her pack of brothers jumped down off the obstacle course. As usual, their massive size always left an impression and slight tremor through the ground. They banged their giant staffs with shark teeth against giant shields made of prehistoric turtle shells. The shells were massive and completely covered each one of the men that held them. All of the brothers had markings on their skin, except for around the face. Their arms and their legs were each uniquely designed, and every single one of the Utua clan had a marking of a sea turtle on their right hand. Tank stood out with his white skin and lack of hair. He bore the same markings on his skin, including the turtle design when he was added into the Utua family. His weapon was unique among the others, though, since he was given a massive double-ended battle ax. Tank could cut through anything with his weapon and leave some serious debris in his path. That is what earned him the name Tank.

Leilani had been assigned to Big Ben, Annie, Tank, and Reese, and wherever she went, her brothers went. The brothers didn't have their own individual groups because they all stuck together. That was their request when assigned as Guardians. They had been through hell as kids because their mother was a drug addict. She had child after child, and when she did, they all ended up with different relatives and they all just wanted to be together. Leilani was unique in this family. She was the only girl and she was the youngest. She had been gifted, incredibly levelheaded, could read people, and she bore the skills of a true leader.

When Reese first arrived and met the brothers, he was so overwhelmed with their enormous stature that he decided their names needed to fit their appearance. Reese had a knack for giving someone a nickname that suited the personality of the person. It was never to put someone down; it was more about the fact he felt closer to a person when he could give them another name, and his eyes made the person unique. Starting with the youngest of the brothers, which were twins, the names given were Thud and Thunk because for whatever reason, they always kept tripping and they always bonked a Watcher on the head to knock them out. The twins kept their hair in two long braids down the sides of their heads. Cronk always had food in his hand.

The name Grunt was given to the brother who never spoke, and his long curly hair slightly hid his face. Mongo only spoke Samoan, leaving his hair long and flowing down his body. The eldest, Poni, was the *Matai* or Chief of the clan and kept his hair in a tight bun above his head. Each one of them were incredibly handsome, and they all had hazel eyes. At one point, they all wondered if they had the same dad since they all looked so much alike. They didn't believe so, but since their mom never became a part of the kingdom, they wouldn't get the chance to ask her until the final battle was won.

"All right, we are all here, so let's head over to see Sifu and meet the new member. She may be overwhelmed when she sees you guys, so try your best to not scare her, my dear brothers," Leilani stated directly to each one of the beasts.

"I am glad we have another female in the group. I need someone to have girly chats with since you won't do it, Lei," Annie stated with her smooth Southern belle accent. She looked at Leilani with a smile on her face, blinking really fast.

"I thought that's what I do, Annie?" Reese said as a joke.

"No one could ever take your place, Reese. You are one of a kind," Annie stated as she batted her eyes back at him.

They continued to banter and joke on their journey toward Lau. They each inquired about their new member, starting with what was she like personality-wise and what she had been through while alive.

"*Ua li gumz!*" the brothers howled as they bowed, then walked into the kung fu school. Sifu Lau just rolled his eyes and headed back to the kitchen for another cup of tea before he started their training.

All the Guardians getting ready for training were already in the school, stretching. They were all secretly dreading Lau to begin their vigorous training and exhausting workout. Kinsey was already exhausted, and all she did was stretch and learn basic forms. Lau did spend a little bit of time showing her the form for the swords before the other Guardians came for practice and training. The moment all the Utuas entered into the room, she thought the men were giants, and then she saw Tank. He was easy on the eyes.

Kinsey felt slightly overwhelmed as the brothers came in with their boisterous personalities. The brothers each wore shark teeth around their necks like Leilani, and she kept observing their tribal markings. Almost instantly, she noticed the same sea turtle on their hands like Leilani. When Leilani introduced Kinsey to her brothers, she thought all of their names fit perfectly due to their monstrous sizes. She assumed the names also matched the noises that they made in training.

Jesse Lefler

"Kinsey, this is our group. Meet Big Ben, JoAnne or Annie, Reese, and... Tank." Leilani paused when she said Tank's name because she had never seen the expression on his face. He was studying Kinsey. Kinsey noticed the expression too as she shook each of their hands and slowly reached for his, afraid he might bark at her.

"You ready to dance and earn your wings, Tankerbell?" Poni asked. The question instantly interrupted the group's train of thought and began to antagonize Tank.

"Come on, horse, you really think you are a match for pure muscle and steel? I say nah, bruh," Tank replied, stretching his arms with a smirk. The other brothers laughed and kept nudging each other on.

"Your skill matches your jokes. Lame, bruh! It's a good thing you're already ugly because it won't matter when your face gets smashed in!" Matai stood up and quickly jumped on Tank's back. All the Utua brothers gathered on top of one another in their usual family dog pile. The goal in each of their minds when they began to pile on top of one another was to see who could stay on top the longest. The brothers looked like a ball of yarn that was made from tanned skin and long curly black hair. Tank was the only one who usually made his way straight to the top.

All the other Guardians in the school gathered around the pile, cheering the brothers on. Their cheers added fuel to the brothers' horseplay, and they were completely enjoying the spectacle the Utuas always made of themselves. Not a single person could help but smile when the Utuas were around. They just had an energy to their soul that was of pure light. The boys always made each other laugh, and once they invited someone into the family, that person became like blood. Kinsey took the sight in, and for the first time since she arrived, she thought of her own family and realized her kids were not with her. The thought gave her a small tinge of pain in her heart, and she already missed them so much.

The brothers slammed on top of one another over and over again. She had never seen gigantic men play and not get hurt. Something still stood out about Tank, and she couldn't take her eyes off of him. She had a strange feeling, and she couldn't shake it. It

112

wasn't an attraction but a curiosity. What was it that made him stand out among anyone else she had seen since she arrived? Kinsey had a sinking suspicion that all the members of her group had to have deep and complex pasts. She realized with Leilani's strength, she would have the ability to really fight to help her members survive in such an ugly world. Kinsey secretly wondered what each of them had left behind in the world, especially Tank.

Suddenly, Sifu Lau came out from the little kitchen and yelled out for the students to get in the starting position. The brothers, one by one, slowly climbed off of each other, and at the bottom of the pile was Thud and Thunk, still wrestling with each other.

"Sorry, Sifu, we just get so excited to be here," Thunk said, elbowing his twin in the ribs trying to stand up.

"Yeah, Sifu, we just want to make sure we are good and warmed up for practice," Thud stated.

"Ah, so you want to be the best...at kung fu?" Sifu Lau asked in English.

"Yes!" they both said in unison, thinking they got away with fooling around. They displayed their pearly whites with grins that spread from ear to ear. The twins were both thinking Lau would be impressed with their answers.

"Then go out to the garden and hold your horse stance. You both need to improve on stamina," Lau stated in Cantonese as he began to walk away.

"How long, Sifu?" questioned Thunk.

"Until *my legs* are tired," Lau answered with a smile as he turned to begin another training session.

The twins groaned as they walked out to the garden and both decided they would try to stay out of sight and only get in the stance when Sifu decided to check on them. What they failed to notice was that there was a mirror to help Sifu see into the garden outside the school. Lau waited just a few moments while the other Guardians continued stretching. He knew the twins like the back of his hand and surprised Thud and Thunk when he stormed out to the garden. He kept yelling in Cantonese that the boys needed to keep their honor and continued by saying they would be practicing their splits for the rest of training for that day. Lau was never truly angry, but he loved that his bark had all the bite he really needed.

Kinsey began growing tired but thankful for the few extra minutes provided before she would have to start her forms again. Her eyes were closed when she realized Reese was to her left side and Annie to her right. While they were next to each other stretching, they decided to explain how the dynamic of the group works. Kinsey welcomed the friendly companions for the distraction. She had an overwhelming feeling she would drop to the ground and fall asleep any minute. The warm smiles from the two group members were more than welcome. They were needed.

"So, my new little tulip, how have they been treating you today? Did you get to see your family and learn about the dynamic of becoming a Guardian? Did you get to train with a weapon yet?" Reese asked.

"Well, the two broadswords in the back with the jade handles are mine. Sifu Lau gave them to me today. Most of my time has been spent with him. I saw my family, then Leilani brought me straight here. I noticed each Guardian has a different color they wear. Why is that?" Kinsey asked as she looked to both Reese and Annie.

"Well, the color matches the personality of the person. It's a representation of who you were alive and how you are now," Annie answered.

"My friend, Christina, was in purple, and my aunt wore red. What do those colors represent?" Kinsey asked.

Reese became all too happy to answer because of his adoration for the colors of their gear. "Well, purple is for humility and royalty, so she must have worshiped God with every fiber of her existence. Plus, your friend is a very humble woman. If your aunt has red, then she is excellent with her hands and hardworking. Very alpha female and a leader. Strong to the core," he stated with a smile.

"Yes, that does sound like my aunt. Now that you bring it up, where or how do I find out my color?" Kinsey grew so curious now that she understood why they were dressed the way they were. She had no clue what she would be considered.

Sifu stood in front of all of his students and bowed. The symbolism of bowing is all about respect, and the Guardians respected their master. He then began his usual instruction in Cantonese, and Kinsey was still amazed that she understood him. He explained it was time for them to grapple and spar against other Guardians they had not sparred against before. He began to explain the importance of being prepared. Lau preferred that they not choose someone of the same size and stature.

"Watchers, Tortones, Reeds, and Greater Demons do not play fair. They have no emotion, sympathy, nor compassion. You need to be cunning, quick, and focused. Fighting in kung fu should flow like your heartbeat and form as water. You cannot allow them to gain any advantage over you. Today, you will be fighting against pure strength and power. You have to be able to know how to distract or redirect any attack." Sifu kept talking as he walked up and down the line of his students. "Best way to learn is to just jump in. Let's start with our new student, Kinsey."

Kinsey thought for a minute and didn't realize he called her name until everyone had their eyes on her. Reese finally started nudging her forward. Standing in place, she silently hoped he would change his mind.

"I think it's best I watch so that I can—"

Before she was able to back away and talk her way out, Leilani came pushing up close behind her. She managed to get behind Kinsey without being seen. She pushed Kinsey up to the front of the other Guardians and out loud said, "Nope, I know you too well and I know you need to go first. Just put all of your strength into what you know best."

"So put all my effort into pretty much nothing?" Kinsey asked, slightly laughing. Kinsey thought for a moment and realized that all she knew was sarcasm and redirection. That skill could only be handy if she was grappling with words and not with her body. "Leilani, I will be eaten alive, are you kidding me? I can't go against your brothers!" Kinsey said, pleading with her eyes to head back to Reese and Annie.

"Well, that's good because you're not going against them," Leilani stated.

"Oh, okay, that's good. So is it Reese or Annie since I am a beginner?" Kinsey anxiously asked.

"No. You're going against Tank," Leilani stated matter of fact.

A look of horror spread across Kinsey's face. She looked at the colossal man again and without hesitating said, "*Nope!*"

Sifu grabbed Kinsey's arm and directed her toward the middle of the group. The other Guardians formed a circle and gathered around her and Tank. Kinsey kept thinking to herself that she would just submit the first round and get it over with.

Sifu explained to Kinsey to remember the stances he had shown her and how to put it into practical use. She looked up into Tank's eyes and tried to pretend she wasn't fearful of him laying her down flat. Lau then gave the signal for them to start. As soon as the words left his mouth, Kinsey was straight down on her back. All the Utuas hollered out loud along with the rest of the Guardians for Tank to give Kinsey a chance. She gasped and coughed while she tried to catch her breath. Tank was standing above her, and he put his hand out for her to grab. True to her stubborn nature, she stood up on her own.

Tank looked her in the eye's when he asked, "Are you ready this time?"

Kinsey didn't say a word and decided she would at least try this time. Lau again, gave the signal, and she backed up just enough to slip out of Tank's reach. She knew there was no way she could take him down. She knew, though, if she got a good grip, it could give her an advantage.

Tank moved in, slid his leg behind hers, and as he tried to throw her down again, she pulled down his arm and climbed up on his back and slipped her arm under his chin. She had her left arm around under his neck while the right arm held tightly to the left. The whole school of Guardian's stood up and began yelling and cheering Kinsey on. Thud and Thunk came around the corner, eager to find out what all the noise was about. She kept her arms straight around his neck and applied force. She had a grip so tight that she began to feel Tank start struggling to breathe. In a moment of weakness, she loosened her grip, and the second she did, he flipped her on her back again. Once again, all the "Ooohs" and "Ouches" filled the air from the group. This time, Tank didn't offer her his hand.

The Utuas started yelling, "Hey, bruh, she got the kung fu grip. Crouching Tiger, Hidden Kinsey is gonna take your throne," Matai yelled, and they kept cheering for Kinsey to beat the "Tank."

Sifu indicated this final round determined the winner, and this time, they started on their knees. It was time to grapple. Tank placed his one hand around her neck and his other on her shoulder. He looked at her and waited for her to do the same thing. Leilani yelled out for her to match his hands. Kinsey placed her small hand on Tank's massive neck and felt like she had a grip on a tree. He was solid, and she thought to herself, *I need to try and see what I can do to take him off guard.* Then it hit her. "Would you be so kind as to let me try before you destroy me again?" Tank just looked at her and shrugged.

Sifu Lau gave the signal one more time, and when he hesitated, she made her move. She pulled him in close and kissed him on his lips. While doing so, she felt his body relax and soften. She then made her move and wrapped herself on his back but this time also wrapped her legs on his torso. She wrapped her left arm under his neck again while grabbing with her right. Lau had taught her when the arm was under the neck and the legs on the back of the torso, all she had to do was stretch by pulling up. Doing this movement would make it harder for them to breathe.

His hands kept pulling on her arm to try to get out of her grip around his neck. Tank was starting to turn red, and as he was, everyone kept yelling and cheering Kinsey on. He finally tapped out, and Kinsey let go. When she let go, everyone saw how he pushed back in pure shock and had become completely silent. None of the other Guardians wanted to make a sound. No one had ever beaten Tank. None of the Utuas had ever been able to come against his massive stature and quick skills.

Kinsey wasn't sure what to do since she didn't know him. Tank stood up, looked Kinsey in the eyes, and kept trying to catch his breath. He didn't make eye contact with anyone else in the school and left out the door.

Kinsey still stood in the middle of the school, looking confused, when suddenly she heard the twins yell, "*Ua li Kinsey!* You beat Tank! No one has ever beat Tank!"

"Hey, Poni, we need to make her part of the clan just for that. She gets a turtle just for giving Tankerbell his wings," Cronk said to his brothers, and they all laughed.

"She gave him the kiss of death," Poni replied, laughing.

Kinsey's head started spinning as she stood up. She kept her eyes on Tank as he walked out. Reese, Annie, and all the Utuas charged straight up to her as the others followed. The noise in the school radiated off the walls, and they kept laughing and joking that Tankerbell got his wings. Sifu finally took control again of the school and continued with training. Kinsey went back to the spot she was originally stretching when Reese and Annie gave her the thumbs up and said, "That was awesome!"

Kinsey wasn't sure what to make of what just happened but couldn't deny she felt pretty good in her first win.

EDWARD J. CRIMSON

The Prince of Persia meticulously kept working overtime, manipulating his way through the many groups of radical terrorists. He wanted to make sure that the West would be afraid of anyone who came from the Middle East. It did not matter if an individual person was peaceful, kind, or loving. His job was to cause chaos between the Christians, the Muslims, and those of the Jewish faith. As long as men with corrupt hearts stood upon his sands, the Prince of Persia was in full control.

The whispers through the winds influenced their actions for the god they served. In spiritual reality, they were worshiping the prince. He kept manipulating the men, making sure the black tendrils that Lucifer bound to them would continue to eat away at the mind and spirit. As long as the terrorists or those out to destroy mankind stayed upon the sand, the prince had control to keep the destruction going. Even the women among the east were now fully suffering from the control of male Guardianship and lack of sympathy for their lives. The Prince of Persia kept trying to bring life back to the days of total control. The people inside were slowly dying, begging for God to rescue them from the oppression of corruption. Then there were those who fully became atheists because how could a loving God or Allah allow such chaos and torment upon the innocent for so long?

For thousands of years, the prince remained the driving force behind every slaughter that took place out in the far east deserts. When Moses led the Israelites out of Egypt, Lucifer became vengeful. God chose for them to wander in the desert for forty years because they complained and they didn't obey his commands. Miracle after miracle God performed for them, yet their hearts wouldn't change, making them ungrateful. This was all done by the Prince of Persia in the sands of the desert. Now, in recent years and even recent days, his instructions had been made very clear. He had to make sure the Watchers were torturing and abusing their power. He set out to make sure there would be as much chaos and destruction as possible.

Currently, he was spreading the Watchers and terrorists out throughout Europe, and there was no end in sight. Lucifer stayed pleased with the progress that the prince continually made and mostly left him to work on his own. After all, he had been doing this job for thousands of years. Something was missing, though, and he was trying to pinpoint what else needed to be done and who else he could use to torment those in need.

Unfortunately for Lucifer, he was unable to stay in one location for any major amount of time due to his restraint and limitation of power. He began tracking down every lead given to him, still search-ing for the boy. He wasn't about to give up and he couldn't give up because he knew of the war that was just in sight. He kept asking him-self over and over in his head, how would he find him? What could he do to flush him out while at the same time push the Guardians to slip up and interfere? Lucifer summoned his whole army of dark-ness from all corners of the spiritual world, making his instructions known from his Reeds of Death up to his Greater Demons. They were to interfere in the humans' lives as much as possible. He made it especially clear to cause chaos in front of the Guardians. All it took was one slip-up from the light, and Lucifer would have free rein throughout the world.

The interesting challenge he realized with the Momenti was they only presented themselves in a human life for a brief moment. He decided to order the Tortones to distract the Momenti in any way they could. Anyone receiving help from a Momenti the Tortones had to attack in any way or else they would have to face Lucifer. In doing so, what would normally give the person a glimmer of hope would now turn to an abundance of irritation. The Fruits of the Spirit were mostly children, and if a Watcher even approached the innocent childlike angels, a Guardian had the right to kill on sight. Knowing the rules of the Guardians gave him an advantage in his and God's complex spiritual war.

The whole human world, currently now completely at his disposal, and Lucifer only lusted after this one child. This child would grow up and become a man to give the world false peace. He fully needed to find the boy and destroy not only God's chosen people but everyone. He was going to make it a point to God that the Antichrist would punish and torture all the humans he cared for so much. It would become just like the days of Adolf Hitler, yet worse.

The more the Christians appeared intolerable, the easier it would be to slowly begin his destruction. When the Antichrist became a man, there would be suffering like no one would have ever imagined. His frustration was building because of his full control over an army of darkness, yet he still couldn't flush the boy to the surface. Lucifer would continue to conduct himself above the supernatural law. He was the driving force that created all the chaos and pain, so he couldn't just stop. The hardest hurdle for him to deal with was limitation in his power, and it made his blood boil. To get his hands on the boy, he just needed to find just one Guardian to slip, and it was only a matter of time.

If Lucifer had known where Jesus was when he was born, he would have stopped at nothing to make sure as a baby Jesus, he would have been killed. Lucifer's hierarchy was still in its infancy then, so he could really only count on himself. He tried to find Jesus long before the Son of God became a man. God made sure to blanket his Son with protection and designed him to hide in plain sight until he revealed himself to be the Messiah.

When the spirit led Jesus out to the desert, Lucifer was there, waiting. Jesus had been fasting for forty days and forty nights. He was tired, weak, and hungry. Lucifer then presented himself to the Son of God. He knew that if he turned Jesus against his Father, God would break inside.

Lucifer held several stones in his hand. He leaned in close to Jesus and whispered directly into his ear, "If you are the Son of God, tell these stones to become bread." Suddenly, the rich aroma of freshly cooked bread filled the air, and Jesus's stomach grumbled.

His voice was weak as he lightly responded, "It is written: Man does not live on bread alone but on every word that comes from the mouth of God." As he spoke, the smell of the cooked bread drifted away with the wind.

Lucifer then took him to the holy city, and they stood on the highest point of the temple. He pressed again, this time to quote God's own words to Jesus. "If you are the Son of Yahweh, throw yourself down. For it is written: He will command his angels concerning you, and they will lift you up in their hands so that you will not strike your foot against a stone."

Jesus simply answered him, "It is also written: Do not put the Lord your God to the test."

Then Lucifer, in his anger and agitation, brought Jesus to the highest point of the highest mountain, showing him all the kingdoms of the world with their splendor. "All of this will be yours. I will give it to you. You need only to bow down and worship me."

Jesus replied a final time, "Away from me, Satan. For it is written: Worship the Lord your God and serve him only."

That was the day Lucifer made sure he would seek out for his death. If he had known that the Son of God's death was the key to save the lives of all God's people, he would have kept Jesus alive. It was then he began to build and structure his army of darkness and sharpen their skills against those who followed the Son of God.

This time, the circumstances are completely different. Lucifer would stop at nothing and no one to make sure the boy would be found and rise to power. He could give the world a false sense of protection during the chaos and destroy all of God's creations. Lucifer kept scheming on how to make his desire possible. He decided to start out with an inventory on the newest arrivals, chosen to become Guardians. Their auras would be brighter and their colors would not have been dulled by the interaction with the Watchers.

The blood of his fallen stained the warrior gear that the Guardians proudly wore. The more blood stained on the gear, the more experience a Guardian gained. His instructions to Abaddon and Mott to sniff out as many as possible appeared to be a dead end. He knew the Guardians fought in a group to make them stronger.

The dynamic of a group makes the Guardians quicker, smarter, and adaptable to the Watchers.

Lucifer knew that they were learning more through training. He was constantly creating new Watchers from the slain with new skills to be darker. The more ruthless and stronger, the bigger the destruction. Every generation bred a new level of devastation, and the better his odds became.

Lucifer decided the next step would instruct his Watchers to thoroughly push the seven deadly sins upon all of those who struggled, regardless if they had a belief in God or not. He was successful in making Christians look hypocritical, intolerable, and oftentimes hateful. He loved the reputation given to the Catholic priests over the many years with the numerous accusations. As long as a life was destroyed, the darkness had control. Who else would do such jobs but Morajes and Belial? Belial caused hatred against even the purest of hearts. All it took was a broken heart, and Belial was always at the ready. He made sure to devour anyone in his path and loved to be the driving force in the hatred toward anything pure.

Lucifer designed Belial as a master craftsman, throwing the innocent into the pathways of hate and harm. Morajes had the velvet touch as a seductress, and all it took from her was a gentle blow in the ear to a man, and his sexual desires took over him. Normal interaction sexually would suddenly cease, and the satisfaction and the perversion level would blow out of control. She proudly declared the name her father gave her as the whore of Babylon. It was her source of power. Lucifer was about to start causing major chaos in every country around the world, and he knew the world was going to need some sort of peacemaker. What a better way to destroy the humans that God loved than to destroy them from within? He just needed to find the boy who was destined to do so. He even decided to start a pandemic, just to make himself feel better.

Lucifer was sitting in his home as Morajes entered. "Father?" she called out. "I need to speak with you."

Her high heels kept causing a loud clicking sound across the marble floor as she made her way through the mansion. Her jeans were so tight they looked painted against her skin. All she adorned on top was an animal fur jacket, exposing the sides of her bosom through the opening. Her long luscious hair that she usually kept down was pulled back tightly to the top of her head. The beautiful contour makeup had been done to perfection by her latest favorite pick of the beauty gurus in the makeup world.

She crossed through the fire and found Lucifer sitting in his chair, staring at his accomplishments as they flashed in front of him. Morajes stood behind him and knew better than to interrupt his train of thought. She sat down, playing with her hair, and waited for him to come out of the meditative state he was in.

"Morajes!" he finally broke his silence as his cold dead stare gazed upon her. "You had an epiphany when the generals were all here at our recent meeting. Might I remind you, do not deny what my ears hear and my eyes see," Lucifer said.

"Yes, Father, I did." She paused for a moment, quickly trying to find a way to explain herself. "Father, I have always been suspicious of Legion and Belial's loyalty to you. We are all created from the same darkness, and it's in our design to believe we are greater than others, am I wrong?" she questioned, proud of her answer.

"Yes, you are correct, but what is your intention? And don't lie to me because I will know," Lucifer asked with a clear authoritative voice.

Calling his bluff, she answered. She knew he didn't know. He had said under his breath time and time again when any of the Greater Demons reported to him and left that they "had better not be lying." It was a dead giveaway that he didn't know. She knew his manipulations and tactics and learned them quickly as a child. He raised her to understand body movement, eye contact, and social cues quicker than any of the fallen, and it was to be used against all humans. She was outside of his design because she was not one of the original fallen that fell with him. She had no true loyalty to him, and deep down, she hated him. The truth was she wanted the power and wanted it since she could remember. Lucifer believed he had her true loyalty, and she played up to him. Her loyalty could only be toward herself. He was the master of lies, and he knew it would take only one to break him down in ways he didn't know existed.

"I voiced the best possible statement I could to provoke thoughts out of either one of them. The prince I don't care for, and he is beneath me, no matter how many minions he thinks he has following him. It's only Belial and Legion that I have set out to watch. They have strength and they have brains when the two are combined, yet they lack the knowledge to know together they could try to overthrow you." She sat across from him in a relaxed state and since she knew he was reading her, she wouldn't give any signs to doubt her.

"What makes you think they would even try or that they even could?" Lucifer replied almost as soon as she was done speaking.

"You have raised me to be fast on my feet and to expect the unexpected. You have designed me to be the superspy and the manipulator. I think my way through the maze way faster than any of the fallen within the darkness in any given situation. You have designed a general to fight on your side and to be a spy among spies. Why else wouldn't I think that way?" She finished her statement, proud of her answer. The best part was knowing deep down it was all the truth.

"You are correct, Mora," Lucifer began, "I designed you to be my spy among spies, and you have always reported to me when I asked. Don't think that I don't watch you as well, though. I have watched you play those two against each other. I have seen the subtle touches and glances that you give both of them. I see their looks back to you and I see the desire within their darkness."

"Which leads me to my reason for coming to see you. I have a couple ideas that could help us," Morajes spoke, trying to appeal to her father's curiosity while distracting him from the subject.

"What might that be?" Lucifer asked with his eyes reflecting through the black flames.

"We need to make a little visit to Eddie Crimson. If anyone will know anything, he would be an excellent place to start. I know the Prince of Babylon died along with the Prince of Greece, but what became of the Prince of Rome? You haven't spoken about him in forever or even sought him out. As I recall, you told him to not come out until you summoned him. I believe we need to use all the resources we can. He can control all the chaos that will soon establish throughout the United Kingdom."

Lucifer sat for a minute, deep in thought. He kept debating on whether to send another big demon versus one that could cause chaos like Belial. He even debated if Morajes should go alone or if he should go with her. Without changing his poker face, he spoke, "You are definitely correct about the Prince of Rome. He took the fall of his empire worse than anyone in existence. Let's make Eddie pull him out of hiding. I shall go with you to see Mr. Crimson. He is long overdue for a visit anyway. Where is he hiding these days?" he inquired to see just how much Morajes knew to gauge in order to get the truth out of him.

"I believe right now he is in Paris. He moves every fifty years so he could keep his identity hidden from suspicion," Morajes answered.

Eddie Crimson had been given the gift of immortality and promised everything he wanted. His part of the agreement lay directly in his hands. The request Lucifer wanted in return was Eddie had to cross the sides from the light to the dark, so he joined the fallen after he had been trained as a Guardian. Lucifer knew every aspect of his weaknesses through Morajes and used her knowledge to his advantage when she tempted him to switch sides. The true nature of their relationship indicated that Eddie became Lucifer's snitch. He had to spill all the secrets of the heavenly kingdom and explain the whole structure. Even if Eddie wanted to keep secrets, he could not. Lucifer placed the same black tendrils that he sent to the terrorists inside Eddie's mouth once he switched sides so Eddie would never be able to lie to him nor hide from him.

Eddie was now over a thousand years old and currently was becoming tired of mankind. He was tired of all the darkness in the world, and it was only growing worse. He hated the Internet and he started to become slightly mad throughout the last century. He had lived in just about every country and spoke over fifty languages. Eddie certainly made use of the time since he had plenty of decades at his disposal. Any profession under the sun was given to him as long as he followed Lucifer's demands. The Prince of Darkness had threatened that if he ever tried to hide, he would become a soulless Watcher, and Eddie certainly had no desire to fully cross into darkness. He hated the Watchers because he had the ability to see them, and they terrified him. Eddie saw just how cruel and vicious they could be. He couldn't see the Guardians once he went against God and crossed sides. He ached inside because he felt empty and would give anything to go back to the moment he crossed into darkness.

Over the thousand years of his lifespan, Eddie had the ability to adapt to the changes. In the most recent couple hundred years, he worked as a prep school teacher, a politician, an anthropologist, a romance novelist, an architect, a stockbroker, and finally now a talent agent and comedian. He decided since he was beginning to grow slightly crazy that he wanted to do as little for Lucifer as he possibly could. He didn't care if anyone accepted him as a person anymore because all he had to say to himself was, "They would be dead soon enough anyway."

He stayed by himself mostly now because he was tired of seeing those that he cared for die. The friends, the careers, and most of all, the loss of the only woman he ever loved. Currently living in Paris, Eddie kept traveling throughout Europe on his comedy tour. Laughter was the one thing that took his mind away from the pain, depression, and reality that he would never die. Even if he tried to kill himself, it would just leave him deformed and forever stuck in his state of form.

Eddie consistently took care of his health by exercise, eating right, and always making sure he held onto what was left of the light within his heart. What he called his "spidey senses" always warned him now when Lucifer was approaching. He was on stage at the Theatre Mogador in Paris when suddenly, all the hairs on his arms, legs, and neck stood on end. Eddie knew instantly that Lucifer and one of his Greater Demons were in the audience. He was mindfully looking to see if any of his nasty Watchers were around, and luckily, he didn't see a trace of them. He kept performing without missing a beat, but in the back of his mind, he was curious why they were coming to see him after 1,000 years of dead silence.

He finished his comedy hour and made a fast dash back to his dressing room. He was hoping to change from his wardrobe and get comfortable before he had to speak with his master and monstrous pet with a gnarly disposition. Eddie became deathly afraid of Belial because he had no sense of humor. Legion freaked Eddie out because he would surround him with all the souls that made him a Greater Demon. Every single soul of the fallen engulfed Eddie's comfort zone. They despised him due to his human appearance. From the lowest to highest rank, supernaturally, all the Reeds of Death to the Greater Demons were incredibly deformed. He was the one in centuries who died, became a Guardian, betrayed his father who loved him so much, and the worst part was everyone he ever knew existed had all become a faded memory.

As he was quickly trying to make his way back to his dressing room, he became unpleasantly surprised to walk in on Lucifer and Morajes. Eddie knew deep down not to show fear, but sometimes he wished the surprise of their presence would give him a heart attack and finally end his misery. He was able to hide his fear quickly and always tried to talk his way out of whatever information that Lucifer was looking to have answers to.

"Ahh, the prodigal son, Morning Star, comes to see the low and humble servant, Eddie. To what do I owe the pleasure of this long overdue visit?" Eddie said, and he spoke with a posh British accent since he had spent most of his life in London, England.

"Eddie! Have you missed me?" Morajes asked. Her words danced off her lips like silk in the air. She approached him for a hug and the usual kiss from cheek to cheek.

"How could I not? You're always in my night...dreams." He tried to recover from the comment by smiling sheepishly. He knew, though, that Lucifer caught it.

"Can you possibly guess why we are here Eddie?" Lucifer questioned with his usual flat tone with blank and empty expression. His left eyebrow raised as he was trying to study Eddie.

"Well, one thing I know is it's not for wardrobe advice. You always wear the same suit. Don't you think a touch of color would bring out the black in your eyes?" He paused, looking at both of them. He waited a moment for a response and then continued, "I mean, my dear sweet Mora, you are a stunning and beautiful diamond around this lump of coal. Wouldn't it be nice if he wore an electric blue color? Now that, my friends, would be a sight to see."

Eddie kept trying to stay off course as long as possible. He knew it would do absolutely no good, especially when Lucifer was dead-set on whatever it was he was seeking.

"Eddie, stop stalling. You know why I am here," Lucifer said coldly as the dark mist steamed out of his neck.

"You are right. I know why you are here and I have been expecting you to show up anytime. You already know the boy is born and you want to ask what have I heard? The problem is, and I know that you know this, I can't even hear nor see the Guardians. So explain to me what do you expect from me?" Eddie asked, completely frustrated and exhausted.

Lucifer had a grin spreading across his face, even showing the ashlike lizard skin that gave Eddie the chills. Lucifer snapped his finger, and in came Feassure, Lucifer's super spy. Feassure crawled up on top of Lucifer's lap and glared at Eddie.

"You know I am not big on pets. They are horrible to clean up after, and most of them smell," Eddie said, trying to avoid eye contact.

He knew what would reveal his fear, so he kept running around his dressing room, changing and taking his stage makeup off. Suddenly, Morajes stood in front of him, and Lucifer grabbed Eddie's right arm. Lucifer's dead empty eyes stared straight through him. Eddie knew with just a touch he could find out anything he wanted to know. Lucifer removed his hand from Eddie's arm, and Eddie fell straight to the ground. Not only did Lucifer get the information he wanted, but he drained a good source of Eddie's energy.

Eddie's face instantly became sunken in, and he lost the color in his skin. He felt incredibly dizzy and most of all sleepy. He looked up at Lucifer and decided to just prove his own point. "See! I told you I can't see nor hear the Guardians. I know absolutely nothing and prefer not to."

"Oh, no, no, no, no, Crimson. We are going to give you Feassure as a little gift. He can hide in the natural world as a dog from humans, and he can also hide in the supernatural world so no one on either side can see him or you. He has the ability to keep you hidden so you can see the Guardians and hear the conversations,"

Morajes explained to Eddie in her lightest sweetest voice. "Feassure is going to help you hide along with him. That's one of his many gifts. You're also going to seek out the Prince of Rome, and our little helper here will guide you. Feassure needs to form as a dog so that publicly he can signal when a Guardian is present. The Prince of Rome has been underground for a while, and now we need everyone within the dark to come together.'"

"But I can't bloody understand the little lizard, can I? So how do you suppose I will be able to know what the hell is going on? And not only that, but how do you think I'm supposed to find the bloody Prince of Rome?" Eddie always became so irritable after Lucifer drained his energy. It was downright rude to take his energy, let alone grabbing his arm. Eddie had boundaries, and those boundaries are what made him feel human. It was one of the few things in his lifetime that he still had control of.

Lucifer stood up and looked Eddie dead in the eyes. "You will do whatever it is I will tell you to do. If not, I will make you spend the rest of your life floating somewhere in outer space. Remember who gave you what you wanted and remember who can take it away. This world is about to come to its knees in chaos and pain, and this boy is the one and only way to gain control. You should know by now which side you are on."

Lucifer pulled out a leash for Eddie to direct Feassure. The loyal lizard spy shapeshifted into a rottweiler about the size of a small horse. "Take him out for a walk every day and report on anything you find. I expect you to check in with me on a weekly basis. Begin your search in Rome. That was the last place I allowed him to be seen before he was banished underground from failure," said Lucifer. He began to head toward the door with Morajes and suddenly looked back to Eddie. With the coldest voice, he reminded the immortal, "Don't make me come find you, Eddie. In one week, I expect a report of your findings. The Prince of Rome will be set free when the time is right."

Lucifer walked out with Morajes and slammed the door behind him while Eddie just looked at the giant new pet he held beside him. "Bloody thing better be housetrained."

Feassure responded by growling at Eddie and urinated on his leg.

"Bloody hell. You stupid lizard...dog...creature!" he exclaimed while trying to get out of wet clothes. Eddie realized he would have to cancel the rest of his tour. That was a headache in itself. However, he was more afraid of Lucifer than he was of disappointing his fans. "Well, let's plan a trip for Rome," Eddie said while he tried to clench his clothes. He realized it was only making a bad situation worse. He let out a big sigh because deep down, he knew that trying to find the Prince of Rome was going to be draining and next to impossible. He knew with his recent mission from Lucifer he was going to have to create a new career now and go back into hiding.

Eddie kept mumbling to himself as he traveled to Rome. The train's whistle blew around 3:30 in the morning to notify the passengers they had arrived. Eddie made his mad dash for the city two days after Lucifer graced him with his little visit. He knew that if he didn't leave Paris the moment Lucifer announced his demands, there would be hell to pay. Literally.

Feassure, in the eyes of the humans, took the form of a rottweiler, and Eddie thought it was fitting to name the dog Damien for human appearance. Feassure kept growling anytime someone crossed Eddie's path accompanied with a Guardian. This caused the people to steer clear from the beast and Eddie. For the first time, though, in over a century, Eddie was able to know when Guardians were nearby. He wondered if any of them would recognize him, and he ached slightly inside just by the thought of the group he once had. He would admit only to himself he actually welcomed his new companion. He usually mumbled to himself, but now he had a lizard/dog/friend—a thing.

It was kind of a nice change because he also didn't feel as alone. Still, though, he was unable to date for a long period of time nor build any form of a relationship with anyone because it always ended the same. He would never age and he would have the painstaking task of having those he loved one day die. It had honestly never occurred to him how much he genuinely needed a pet. Feassure was not exactly ideal, but he would do for now. Something was better than nothing.

"*Mi dispiace, signor Crimson. Non sono ammessi animali,*" the woman behind the desk said after he came to check in to his hotel. The train ride was kind of nice because everyone was intimidated by the dog, and it made him laugh.

"What do you mean I don't have a dog with me?" Eddie said smiling as the Feassure disappeared.

She looked back over the desk, and the confusion was noticeable on her face. She knew she saw a massive dog at his side when he walked in. "My apologies, Mr. Crimson. I have your reservation for our finest suite in the hotel. I hope you enjoy your stay. I noticed you have the whole month booked with us. Are you here for business? Would you like any information on places to visit during your stay here in Rome?"

Eddie looked at her for a brief moment then answered, "No, darling, I won't be needing that. I have traveled here many times before." He signed the papers and grabbed his key. He walked straight over to the elevator, and as the doors were about to shut, Feassure made himself appear again. The girl behind the counter had a look of absolute horror on her face. Eddie looked down and couldn't help but giggle at the beast. "Well, at least you have a bloody sense of humor." Feassure lifted his back leg up like he was going to pee on Eddie again, but just as it was about to hit his leg, Eddie moved out of the way.

"Not today, pal. I am onto your tricks." As the trickle hit the elevator floor, smoke arose from the acid excrement that came from the changing beast.

"I don't know where I am supposed to start in this bloody city. What do you say we go to the Vatican and snoop around? I have always wondered what is kept deep within those archives," Eddie said out loud as Feassure changed back into the lizard with the wings. "Good idea. You can fly me in."

Eddie walked into his room and wasn't surprised that the massive suite didn't impress him. After over 1,000 years, it wasn't easy to wow him with anything. He had stayed in castles all over England, Scotland, and Ireland. He once stayed in Buckingham Palace by invitation of Queen Victoria herself, a hundred years prior. He even had a fun encounter with Queen Elizabeth. She was what he called a saucy minx. He was so tired, though, and no amount of sleep would ever suffice.

He often wondered what the lure of immortality actually was at the time it was presented to him. The worst part was he already had it since he was a Guardian. Of course, in his usual way, he didn't think it through. He just got tempted by the money. He was already going to live forever as a Guardian. Eddie could understand why he needed to live forever as a man again. He remembered Morajes and her seductive words. He remembered seeing gold and was told he would live like a king throughout the rest of mankind. He saw images of himself flashing before him in every land and every time frame. People were bowing to him. All he had to do was just reveal the secrets to the Guardian's strength and training.

When Eddie told Lucifer all that he wanted to know, the one thing Lucifer did do was keep his promise. Eddie had an endless supply of money, and he never knew where it came from. In the beginning, the lure was enticing. He could be anyone he wanted and he could certainly do anything he wanted.

After the people he knew and loved around him began to age and pass away, his heart shattered. After he was given immortality, he didn't understand the depth of his loneliness. The first woman he fell in love with, prior to him becoming immortal, made him understand the depth of pain he caused himself. Her name was Annice Benoit from Paris. She was so vibrant and full of life, and he couldn't help but fall deeply in love with her. She even helped him to forget that he was an immortal. She was the only person he shared his secret with. Annice knew she couldn't have any children because if she did, he would outlive them all, and the reality of the situation was tormenting not only his heart but her heart as well.

Her true and selfless heart led him to believe when she passed away, she would become a part of the Momenti. Her gentle nature was unmistakable, and he hoped one day she would reveal herself to him in some kind of way. Then, after the thought of her hit his heart, he realized no angel could ever reveal themselves to him. He was in between worlds and he betrayed the only kingdom that really mattered. He relived the nightmare over and over again in his mind. He silently thought to himself at night, hoping that God would forgive him, and he could see Annice one more time before he was left to perish in eternal fire. He was unable to pray out loud due to the black tendrils that Lucifer jammed down his throat. He would never be able to say the name Jesus, Yeshua, and Yahweh ever again.

The nightmares from the day he betrayed God continuously haunted him. No drug could numb him enough from the pain in his heart nor any alcohol that could drown his sorrows. Once he learned after his final attempt, he decided enough was enough.

His human body was maintained to be incredibly fit, and that was about the only real upside to his existence. He could say, though, that he really lived. He was the best of the best at every sport he tried. Eddie always found it amusing when he would see his own face in history books. That was always good for a giggle when he needed to be cheered up. He fought for the King of England. He was a leader, definitely, but the fighting was always done alongside Eddie. In fact, other than his comedy shows, the last time he was in Rome was with King Arthur. They traveled in one conquest to Bretagne, saving the people from a warlock who was wreaking havoc. The Watchers were always a giveaway for Eddie to see and then warn Arthur who or what was coming.

The hardest part for Eddie to get over in battle was the PTSD. Men in war today had no clue what it was like to be up close and personal to kill a man with just a sword.

Feassure crawled up onto the bed and buried himself under the sheets. Eddie honestly was too tired to care. All he asked was that the animal not pee in the bed. He laid down on the pillow and asked himself, "How am I ever going to find the bloody Prince of Rome?"

HALL OF INFINIUM

Kinsey felt grateful she acclimated to her training and schedule with her group members. Time didn't work the same in the kingdom as it did for those down on earth. So much information was given with each sunrise to sunset. Sometimes she felt her head would explode with so many new discoveries each day. Who knew heaven was way more complicated than what she thought? Then again, what did mankind really know beyond just themselves anyway? Each year that was added to time was another year the dark can gain more control over the world. She was so grateful that she didn't have to hurt, day in and day out anymore. Kinsey loved the peace and calm of no violence, wickedness, drama, or the evil in anyone's heart. She loved that there was no pain holding her down anymore, like an anchor sunk to the bottom of the ocean.

After she became accustomed to her training, she was able to go visit her two children. She missed them so much on earth. Her daughter just graduated college, and fortunately for Kinsey, the two children were together when she descended to see them. Kinsey decided to take a ride in the back seat while listening to Grace and her little brother chitchat. She wanted to let her daughter know that she was with her, but didn't want to startle her to the point she joined her in the afterlife. She decided the best way to let her daughter know she was there was to change the song playing on her daughter's iPod. Kinsey chose the song that she used to play for her daughter when she was a little girl.

One of Kinsey's most painful moments in her life happened when she had to go through a bloodlust custody battle over her daughter. The relationship between her and her ex was incredibly toxic, and the fighting was commonplace. It was a constant struggle with little hope of an end in sight. There was little beauty she could find in the midst of her pain. What little she did find her ex made sure to end the beauty as quickly as he possibly could. Kinsey was in utter turmoil because her ex had tried to obtain full custody of her only child. This was her little girl and her only child, no matter how old she was. So why would he want to destroy her like that? This became one of the few times in her life she fully gave the situation up to God and begged him for the right answer. She loved her daughter more than herself, but she wanted to do what was best for her baby girl.

Kinsey waited for an answer by praying and fasting for two weeks. Morning and night, she read specific verses in her Bible that spoke about facing trials and how God would make everything work out for the best of the situation, even if it wasn't what Kinsey wanted. As long as her heart was in the right place, she would have peace about making the right choice. She sat down with her Bible and wasn't sure how but found verses that all related to her situation. She felt like she went in a trance. There were two verses in particular she held onto the most. When she read in Exodus, "Do not be afraid. Stand firm and you will see the deliverance the Lord will bring you today. The Lord will fight for you, you need only to be still," something struck her like lightning as if that verse was made for her.

The probability of such a situation was completely unheard of, but what she needed was hope, and hope was provided. When she read Luke, "Listen to what the unjust judge says. And will God not bring about justice for his chosen ones, who cry out to him day and night. I tell you he will see that they get justice and quickly," she gained hope she would make the right choice.

At the end of the fast, she was given an answer she never thought possible. The Holy Spirit told her to give her daughter over to her father. She made a stipulation to her ex so she could spend weekends with her. The father would have Grace during the week, but Kinsey would have her every weekend. Kinsey died inside that day, though, yet at the same time knew to be obedient. As much she wanted to fight it, she knew deep down she couldn't. She didn't want to put her daughter through any more hell than necessary. Her love for her daughter was stronger than a need to be hateful. Grace already had enough weighing her down as a child. Grace loved her siblings on both sides but envied the fact that her siblings didn't have to see their parents fight like she did. Kinsey wouldn't find out for another year why God had impressed on her heart to do such a painful task. She was unaware of the upcoming events in her life. All she knew was that she had to be obedient so Grace could be spared from all of Kinsey's future chaos. Kinsey was actually grateful she obeyed and kept Grace from the destruction Kinsey caused.

Kinsey wanted to make sure Grace knew how much she missed her since she had been away. When she had to bring her daughter back to her dad from the weekend, there was a song she always played for Grace. She sang a song where the lyrics allowed her the ability to add her daughter's name. Kinsey made it a habit to always play the tune as she drove her back to her dad's house. She just happened to find the song on her daughter's iPod and hit play. Her daughter didn't seem to notice the pause before the song, and when the melody started to play, Grace turned up the music. Zerek stopped looking out the window and switched his focus toward Kinsey listening intently to the music in his car seat.

"I love this song, Z. Mommy used to sing it to me.," Grace stated. She began to tear up as the words came out of the radio. Zerek's sense of awareness was stronger than anyone realized. Just because he was autistic didn't make him inept to his surroundings. He kept his focus on the words and the tune of the song. Grace and Zerek were both quiet as the song continued, and Grace kept adding her and Zerek's name to the song.

> Ain't no sunshine when she's gone,
> It's not warm when she's away
> Ain't no sunshine when she's gone
> And she's always gone too long
> Any time Grace is away.

Tears streamed down her daughter's face as she kept singing the words to her little brother. "I miss you so much, Mom," she said out loud.

Kinsey was beginning to feel the pain within her daughter, knowing full well the emotions were a part of the package when anyone became a Guardian. Kinsey understood now why family members could only check in and not stay with their loved ones. She would interfere as any mother would to stop a child from pain.

Zerek turned his head toward Kinsey and stared with his big brown eyes. Grace noticed in the rearview mirror his facial expression had changed. "What are you looking at, Z?" she asked, knowing he always had a serious look on his face when he was trying to study and observe anything of interest. He wouldn't take his eyes off his mother, and Kinsey started to think he could actually see her.

"Z-Man, can you see Mommy?" Kinsey asked, looking back at him. She waved her hand and then tried to touch him. Zerek kept staring, and as she approached him gently with her hand, he flinched.

"Baby, I miss you so much," Kinsey said as tears started to fall from her face. She forgot what it felt like to have pain and cry.

Suddenly, Zerek's expression changed and softened as he put his hand out for his mother to touch him.

"Z, what are you doing, bug? What are you trying to grab?" Grace asked as she kept glancing back at her brother.

Kinsey tried to touch the little boy, but her hand went straight through him. Surprisingly, he started laughing as she kept trying to swipe his hand. She loved the sound of her little boy's laugh. It was heartfelt and pure. She smiled at her son and then tried to kiss him on the cheek. He smiled as she got close to his face and tried to grab her. Kinsey whispered to her son, "I love you, Z-Man."

Kinsey then made a shift to the front seat and noticed Grace had placed the song on repeat. Kinsey wanted so badly to tell her that she was right beside her, but she had to be careful in her approach. Strict rules applied to family visits, so Kinsey knew she had to go through the Holy Spirit with what she wanted her daughter to hear, and as the clear formation of a man appeared, he whispered into Grace's ear. Her daughter had to pull over because the tears started to blind her vision. The Holy Spirit signaled to Kinsey it was time to go. Kinsey tried to kiss her daughter and said, "I will be back for you, pretty girl, and I will make sure you are always protected."

Kinsey returned back into heaven and noticed she didn't feel the sadness weighing her down anymore. She never realized how heavy human emotions were. She was grateful that the most dominant feeling she experienced was peace, and peace always meant happiness for her. She had an awesome team and loved the magnetic charm of the Utuas. She absolutely loved Leilani's brothers and enjoyed their banter. She loved how they worked together as a family and could never get over how massive they stood among the other Guardians. Even the Guardians that had the height, like Big Ben, were nothing in comparison to the Utuas. They still made jokes toward Tank about his defeat, and to the present moment, he still had not said a word to Kinsey. She wasn't going to rub it in his face like the others because she was too afraid he would instantly squash her. He was a monster during his practice and sparring against the Utuas and his team members. She was just proud, though. For the first time in her existence, her mouth and her wit helped her in a time of need instead of making it worse.

Just south of the colosseum, everyone throughout the kingdom gathered to eat. The abundance of food overwhelmed the senses with delicacies from all over the world, delicious specialties of all types and every living being in heaven was able to enjoy. The hall was always filled and echoed with family chatter. The children loved the sweets, and the selection looked endless. The ice cream, pies, scones, cakes, chocolate-covered fruits, and cookies tempted every eye that passed by. The long tables automatically grew, the more people wanted to sit together. Kinsey had what felt like an endless taste for Chinese food. She was too afraid during life to try any different foods, but looking at the best of the best, there was no way to turn them down now.

Saige and Jaxon usually took a cruise past the tasty treats last and savored every flavor. The team and Utuas all sat together, and the two children adored, loved, and always sat with Thud and Thunk. More often than not, the two kids crawled all over the brothers. When the twins weren't training, they always kept with little Pomeranian dogs they named Roxy and Hendrix. The dogs only paid attention to the twins when it was time to eat. Since Cronk was never hands-free from food, the sassy dogs followed him everywhere he went. If there was no food in their hands, the dogs would turn and run the other way. It did not matter how many times their names would be called. The two children at every meal asked the twins if they could hold and feed the little dogs. All the brothers made fun of the twins for their choice as a personal pet. Thud and Thunk could have picked any animal born under the sun, and the twins chose the smallest, softest, fluffiest dogs they could bond with.

Thud and Thunk loved Saige and Jaxon as if the two were their own niece and nephew. Kinsey didn't have a big family while she was alive, so she was going to take full advantage of one in the after-life. She loved that her two kids had massive uncles as their personal jungle gym. Several times, the thought crossed her mind Grace and Zerek would love the extended family. Her aunt and grandparents usually sat close by so they could visit and spend time with children.

Jaxon had been scheming with the brothers to ask if he could get the same mark of the turtle on his hand like his "uncles." He got the courage one night at dinner and looked at his mother with sad puppy eyes, begging his mother for the same turtle on his hand. After he asked, Kinsey looked back upward at the table and couldn't believe the sight. All the brothers had stopped eating, except for Cronk, and each had their hands all in the pleading position with big puppy eyes.

"Come on, Ma, let him get his mark so we are officially family," Thunk said to Kinsey.

She looked at each brother individually while they each held a pleading pose and their well-known cheesy smiles. She then returned her focus back to Thud and Thunk. How in heaven would she be able to deny these crazy men? "Does it hurt?" she asked as curiosity overcame her.

"No, no, Ma," Thud replied while pulling out a small wooden pen made of bamboo. He grabbed Jaxon's right hand and began to draw. The mark of the sea turtle was placed in between the thumb and pointer finger on the top side of the right hand. Kinsey was astonished when she saw the drawing penetrate the skin, and the finished design was a blue sea turtle. The marking of the turtle had a bluish sparkle, and Jaxon beamed when Thud was done. "Look, Ma!"

"Mommy, can I get one too? I want one like Aunt Leilani!" Saige begged.

"Well, if you guys are giving the kids one, that means I have to get one too or I will feel left out," Kinsey said with a smile.

"*Ua li*, Kinsey, that's right! Thunk, give her the Utua stamp of approval. Now you're officially family." Thud slowly made the symbol of the sea turtle, and she had chosen pink. Her skin tingled as the mark was made, and then suddenly she became very warm. The mark given by the Utuas was more than just a mark or a creative design on her skin. The mark represented family, and once the feeling rushed through her, Kinsey now had a deep connection and loved them for it.

She and the children now had the Utua family mark of the sea turtle, and the moment felt so natural Kinsey silently praised God for her group. What she had always longed for in a group of friends she now had for eternity in heaven. Big Ben, Annie, and Reese began to get on the twins' case as they were beginning to feel left out.

"I'm the one that gave you the awesome nicknames. I better get a turtle. In fact, I have never wanted a turtle so bad in my entire life," Reese stated with a devious smile on his face.

"Make mine yellow, boys. I need that remarkable design to stand out on my beautiful black skin," JoAnne said with pride as she set out her right hand.

"Make mine dark blue!" stated Big Ben with his hand outstretched.

"Now, boys, mine needs to be light blue like my gear. I can't clash," Reese stated as they drew the turtle on his right hand. That night, everyone in the group became one family with the mark of the sea turtle. This is what life was meant to be, and every ounce of the moment made them closer. The Utuas' approach to life was to be as a sea turtle. Calm, smooth, and just ride the waves.

The following morning, Leilani explained to Kinsey she would be spending the day with Reese. She informed her that there were several places he needed to take her and she would also be getting her color. Kinsey had been wondering what her color would be and was even more curious about where she was going. Every sunrise brought a new discovery, and every sunset, there was a new understanding. Leilani had an assignment she had to take care of with Tank, Annie, and Big Ben, and they wouldn't be back from their assignment until later. Kinsey and Reese were grateful for the extra time they were able to just lay in their beds and not have to rush off to training.

Kinsey and the two children had been switching between staying inside the Utuas' massive home along with the occasional stay at Kinsey's grandparents. It was so beautiful to be with her family and see her relatives young and vibrant instead of aged and frail. Her aunt stopped by occasionally to see the layout of the new home and to visit the children. She was the mechanic of her own group and handcrafted many of the weapons that were laid upon Lau's wall. Her Aunt Judy could make a weapon out of anything. She wasn't the only one who designed the weapons, but it was her master craft. Every design was made in its own unique way. Kinsey was proud that her two broadswords were made by her own family.

The Utua brothers had been building Kinsey's home for her, Jaxon, and Saige. The colossal men were incredibly quick since they were durably strong and worked so well together. They used different types of wood, including bamboo to make sure the house was not only big but strong. The Utuas, Reese, Annie, and Big Ben all had their homes along the shoreline. They asked Kinsey when she first arrived where she wanted to live and what did she wanted to live in. She just wanted a cute little home for her little family out by the ocean with the rest of her group. She was grateful that they offered to help construct her home and became extremely excited because she didn't have to worry about making any house payments.

The day before Kinsey was going to be left with just Reese, she had some free time, and she would head out and explore as much as she could. There was so much to the world she was now in, and she wanted to spend every moment she could to see what it was all about. As she traveled out beyond the colosseum, she was amazed by the beautiful countryside and sporadic little neighborhoods. Animals roamed everywhere, and many herds traveled through the colorful scenery. She kept heading out and came upon a building that caught her eye. The structure was massive and utterly beautiful. The frame seemed to have no end, and the color was an abyss of blues and purples. She walked up to the door and heard music coming from inside.

She was amazed when she walked in and noticed the building had stadium seating with plush purple coverings. It was completely empty except for a single man sitting on a stage strumming his guitar. Inside the building had been designed for a concert. The carpet was so beautiful she felt it was only proper to remove her shoes. She liked the sound the man was creating and decided to walk in and make a new friend. Continuing to listen, she crept up closer and recognized the voice but couldn't figure out from where. This one was distinct. He was dressed in black, and he looked like a rockabilly. His hair was black and slicked back. His voice was deep, slightly raspy, and he wasn't bad looking. The man stopped strumming and singing when he laid eyes on her.

"Hi, sorry. I was…well, I was walking along exploring and heard some awesome music coming from this building. It's huge, and I was kinda shocked I had not seen it yet," Kinsey said.

"Well, you must be new to the neighborhood then, darlin', 'cause this is the Grand Worship Hall," he stated back to her.

"Yes, I am definitely new and I am getting used to training as a Guardian." Kinsey kept walking forward, up the stairs to the stage, and set out her right hand to introduce herself. "Hi. I'm Kinsey."

"Nice to meet you. I'm Johnny. Johnny Cash," he said back.

"Wait…wait…no…are you serious? No way, you're the man in black? I was a huge fan of your songs! Well, I guess I still am." Kinsey couldn't believe it was Johnny Cash.

"Well, thank you. I always appreciate a fan," he said with a smile.

"I never imagined I would meet a celebrity, and I can honestly say this is the coolest moment in my life…well, maybe in my death? I'm not sure how to word that," she stated, laughing at herself, all giddy over the fact that this was the man. "What are you doing in here? I mean, besides singing music at the moment."

"Well, this worship hall runs as it would a church service, but instead of just a Sunday service, there is an everyday service. It's held mostly for the Guardians since they need to be cleansed after they come back from the human world on assignment," Johnny said.

"What do you mean? Why do they need to be cleansed?" Kinsey wondered why no one said anything to her when she came back from visiting her children.

"Have you been back to the world since you passed?" he asked.

"Yes, I didn't go on an assignment, but I did get to visit my kiddos," Kinsey answered, feeling the pang in her heart toward her two children who were still alive.

"How did you feel when you were there?" he asked with pure curiosity.

"Heavy, I guess. I noticed I felt sad because I was with my children, and I began to feel what my daughter was feeling," Kinsey replied, thinking about her daughter crying.

"Well, it's way worse when you are on assignment. Believe me, I know. I am a Guardian too. Every time you are sent down, you will encounter the Watchers. I struggled with them my whole life, so they were nothing new to me, but it changed my whole perception when I saw them. It takes a lot of strength to be around them and even more strength to fight against them." He went back to strumming his guitar and then continued, "After you have a battle with one, you come back and you just don't feel right. Sometimes you will have their blood stained upon your gear and it never washes out. When we come back, we have to clean up and come here. We have to renew our souls and cleanse from everything that lingers and follows us. The music to our God renews the strength, rejuvenates the spirit back to where we are intended to be. Just don't get ahead of yourself and make sure you have been fully trained. It really is dangerous."

"I haven't been in a rush to go back to be, honest. I have completely allowed myself to just take time with everything I am doing. Like this, for example, this Worship Hall. I have never seen anything so comforting and so beautiful. You know I always wanted to be a singer when I was younger. I would drive along and imagine myself as a famous artist and just willed and wished myself internally to be them. You were able to live it, though. Was it worth it?" Kinsey's curiosity kept getting the better of her.

"That depends on your outlook on the choices I made from the life I led," he answered honestly.

Kinsey took his words in and let them soak. She could fully appreciate what he was saying due to her own life experiences. "Well, I need to get going. Thank you for taking the time to talk to me. I find it ironic that in life, you were known as the man in black and you were assigned black as your color."

Johnny smiled at her words, and she headed back off to do some more exploring.

Kinsey took the journey back to meet Reese at the shoreline. She took a quick nap, and after she got out of bed, dressed herself in her usual sweats and tennis shoes. She was excited she was finally going to get her color.

"Hello, bright eyes!" Reese said as Kinsey approached.

"Hello, darling," she replied.

"Are you ready to conquer the rest of the day?" Reese asked with a gentle smile.

"Yes, let's do this," Kinsey replied as they began to walk along the shoreline.

They passed the Utuas working on her home and stopped and waved as they did.

"*Ua li gumz!*" they howled at the two.

"They never cease to amaze and entertain me," Kinsey said to Reese.

"They can be a hoot. Anyway, how are you feeling lately?" Reese asked as they continued to walk.

"Well, I am sore, but this is a different type of sore. It doesn't feel the same as if I had not worked out in years, which by the way I had not done. It's a good sore, like I know I have a different purpose to be strong or healthy. It's not just for myself. The reason goes beyond my own existence, and the training is made for others. This is for the love of God toward his people, so in the end, it's all worth it. Does that make sense?" Kinsey asked.

Reese stopped and faced the waves coming onto the shore. His eyes got lost in the blue abyss in front of him. Kinsey suddenly noticed he wasn't walking alongside her anymore. She turned to face him and didn't want to ask but curiosity overcame her. "Reese, you okay?"

"Yes, dear, I'm always good, but today… I am taking you somewhere you would never expect. Somewhere off the beaten path." Reese kept his focus on the water, and his eyes reflected the calming scenery.

"Oh, really? Should I stretch before I go? Because every time one of you brings me somewhere new, I end up working out with a whole new level of pain," Kinsey stated with a smile.

"Well, dear, do you have that item that either Michael or Gabriel gave you in the colosseum?" Reese asked.

"Yeah, I have carried it with me this whole time. No one ever explained what it was, and I just kind of assumed it was like a good luck charm," Kinsey said, trying to make eye contact. "Why, what is it?"

"It's called a Makirus, and where we are headed, you are going to need it." Reese looked back at Kinsey in the eyes with full sincerity and continued, "My dear, this next step is one of the hardest you will have to experience. It can be slightly painful."

"I am not too fond of the painful part, but then again, I haven't completely felt normal with no pain in my current existence," Kinsey responded to Reese. "Chaos is not unknown to me.

Reese turned from the shoreline and signaled her to follow him up the flower-covered hill. Kinsey waved to the brothers and told the two children not to be too much trouble. She didn't want the two kids to drive the Utuas crazy, and she stressed to the children to go play if they got bored. It was a strange feeling to be able to leave a child at any time with anyone. Everyone was always safe, and Kinsey loved that a child could play all day with no worry.

Kinsey caught up to Reese and noticed that his demeanor changed. This was the first time she had ever seen him look serious. He was always upbeat, carefree, and even silly, but his expression turned somber. He kept looking down while deep in thought. Reese braced himself before he spoke again as he was struggling to find the right words. He wasn't walking fast, and she began to wonder about this new mystery place and why they had never even mentioned it to her before.

"It's called the Hall of Infinium," Reese finally broke his silence and stated as he stopped dead in his tracks.

Kinsey was unsure if she should ask or just wait to see what was ahead of her. In the middle of her mindful debate, Reese broke her train of thought.

"The Hall of Infinium is incredible. Every moment recorded in history, and I mean *every* moment for every country and even every person. All of the major events throughout human history. The good, the bad, and ugly, my friend. It's all there and it's all recorded. That odd little item you have kept with you is holding all of the moments recorded in your life. So in a way, it's like a hard drive." Reese studied Kinsey's face as he spoke. Her expression didn't change as she pulled out the trinket that was handed to her by the Archangel. It was smooth, colorful, and had a small hole in the middle.

"I had more bad moments in my life than good, Reese. I honestly don't know how I feel about seeing all my ugly decisions and heartbreaks."

"Those moments are honestly not the easiest to watch, but believe me, when you can see spiritually what was happening, it will give you a whole new perspective. You will understand more now why the painful experiences in your life happened the way they did." Reese paused as his mind took him off into a far distant place again.

Kinsey didn't want to distract him but at the same time really wanted more information about this place. She didn't want to admit there was fear inside her. It was now odd and out of place to have a sense of fear. She was afraid of seeing her bad choices and even more concerned about seeing the Watchers' effect on her life. Little by little, she was taught how complex each side worked within the light and the dark. It was scary in a way because each level gradually becomes more complex than the next, yet all of them were equally important. She had yet to go on an assignment or a mission since she was still learning the basics. The Guardians needed to be trained killers, and she was just barely scratching the surface on her skill and kill level. She knew that each person in her group had a talent known to be beneficial in war. She became deeply curious about her specific talent. She loved her swords and the fact that when she held them, she felt like they were an extension of her own body.

Reese turned and began to walk again. Kinsey walked alongside him, trying to remember her past that once came so easily but was now clouded and blurry. She attributed that to the bloodstained pages of her mistakes that Christ had sacrificed for everyone. Once she passed through the gate, beyond Ray and Mittens, it was all gone. A far distant forgotten life.

They continued in silence through the various gardens and waterfalls, passed the noisy and bountiful marketplace, across the courtyard, and into the colosseum. Kinsey always had to stare at the majestic horsemen carved and created so delicately upon the marble frame. As they entered into the colosseum, Kinsey was expecting to see the obstacle courses that the Guardians practiced through daily or even the welcoming parties for those recently passed, but not today. It was silent, eerily silent as their steps upon the sand echoed around them. Just before they reached the other side, another archway appeared for them to enter. As she and Reese kept walking, she noticed there was limited visibility. Kinsey didn't know what compelled her, but when she turned to look behind her, the first archway they entered through closed, and then the second. It was completely dark for a few moments, and Kinsey held onto Reese's arm to make sure she didn't run into anything.

Suddenly, light started to appear through a final archway that led to a beautiful water garden. Water was flowing in all directions—up, down, sideways, diagonally—and as they stepped out, they stepped on top of the water. The water that was shooting and spraying from all directions went straight through them and filled them with a pure sense of peace. The miracles never seemed to have an end in Kinsey's eyes. She could tell that Reese was unfazed by the aquatic performance, but Kinsey was going to soak up the new scenery as much as she could.

"Do you know why this is a water garden?" Reese asked

"Not a clue," she stated without really thinking.

"Well, with God, we need to be as water. If the water goes in a bowl, it fills the bowl. If it is poured into a cup, it fills the cup. Water doesn't discriminate by age, color, or creed. Water is flexible and pure, and this water is to remind you that before you look back over your life to be open to everything you *will* see," Reese stated.

Not far off in the distance, a white marble structure similar to the Roman colosseum design was standing before them. The difference with this building was that it was square with a solid gold roof. Kinsey and Reese stopped just before the steps that lead up into the building. Kinsey looked up and noticed just above the door was an infinity symbol with a small light continuously in motion. She kept her eyes on the small hypnotic light, tracing the design. Reese held Kinsey's hand and gently asked, "Are you ready to remember, dear?"

The words lingered in the air as Kinsey questioned for a moment if she even wanted to look back over her life. She squeezed onto the odd object in her other hand and as hard as she tried to remember, even the good moments, she couldn't. She looked down, took a deep breath, and lifted her eyes to Reese. "I am as ready as I could ever be, my friend."

Reese took the first step, and Kinsey numbly followed. The outside of the structure was handcrafted with beautiful designs of men and women throughout history, godly men and women who spent their lives serving the Lord and not the world. They reached the double doors adorned with golden handles that had been decorated with beautiful emeralds and rubies. Reese opened the door, and a blinding light came from inside. Kinsey grabbed the other door, and tears swelled her eyes as soon as she saw the magnificent scenery. People were everywhere. They surrounded numerous platforms and podiums, and as they gathered around each podium, huge spheres made of light brightly lit up the room.

"This is incredible, Reese, what are these?" Kinsey asked. She instantly charged toward one of the platforms with the magnificent golden spheres. They radiated in light, and just below them were labels. Inside the first sphere was the creation of the world, and below it was a gold-plated description. Kinsey looked up and noticed around her people were touching the different spheres and instantly kept disappearing. Her eyes widened, and she began to look at every sphere while reading the golden plates neatly placed below. She kept scanning quickly through the descriptions, searching for a specific moment in time. The first one she wanted to see was when Noah built the ark. As she was looking at all the different platforms of the spheres, she finally found the one she was looking for. The excitement was noticeable in her voice when she asked Reese, "Can I touch it?"

Reese smiled and stood next to her. He formed his hand so that only his middle and pointer finger stood out and as Kinsey mimicked his hand, they slowly both touched the sphere.

Her stomach tickled and felt like she was on a roller coaster while they were whisked back to the time of Noah and the ark. There were thousands of her fellow angels around her, watching the same moment in time. She listened intently as God spoke to the only man on earth that was righteous and walked blameless in his eyes.

The voice sounded like thunder, yet majestic at the same time. "I am going to put an end to all people, for the earth is filled with violence because of them. I am surely going to destroy both them and the earth. Make yourself an ark of cypress wood; make rooms in it and coat it with pitch, inside and out. This is how you are to build it: The ark is to be 450 feet long, seventy-five feet wide, and forty-five feet high. Make a roof for it and finish the ark to within eighteen inches of the top. Put a door in the side of the ark and maker lower, middle and upper decks. I am going to bring floodwaters on the earth to destroy all life under the heavens, every creature that has the breath, every creature that has the breath of life in it. Everything on earth will perish. I will establish my covenant with you, and you will enter the ark. You and your sons and your wife and your sons' wives with you."

It played like a movie, and she watched him obey every command he was given toward the massive boat. They began gathering the animals and food for storage. The predators were walking alongside the prey, and they would not eat. Kinsey was in awe as the Guardians with Noah's family kept the wild animals tame. She was shocked to see how horribly others treated Noah, calling him crazy and insane.

"I can't imagine how he must have felt when everyone treated him like he was a basket case," Kinsey stated, keeping her eyes focused on the real-life movie playing in front of her.

Reese took a deep breath. He found it ironic that Kinsey specifically wanted to see the time of Noah when she herself had been living in the world of a modern-day Noah. People in the current day's world are so focused on themselves with all the social media sites that they rarely try to be selfless instead of selfish. Reese decided the moment was a good time to explain the irony of her choice. "Kinsey, I want you to notice something."

Kinsey was distracted instantly as a thunderstorm began to build and massive raindrops fell from the sky onto the world. Water was exploding from within the earth, and lightning kept dashing across the heavens. People came running toward Noah. All the people on the outside of the ark were pounding, screaming, and begging to be let in. People from everywhere came running toward the massive ship. She grabbed Reese's hand in shock as they continued to watch Noah on the deck of the ark. He was looking down at his neighbors, strangers, and even those that he once called friends. She could tell by his expression that he was hurting, and his body language was restless. He kept debating on whether or not he should let anyone in. God had Noah shut the door so no one could enter, but he debated on dropping down a rope because he didn't want to see anyone drown or suffer. Even the ones who made fun of him publicly, calling him crazy, he still had compassion toward them. He began to cry since he didn't want to get hurt. His heart broke as he watched women and children crying out to him.

Kinsey noticed something that she had never thought of before. She knew that the fallen, who were also called the sons of God, found the women of man to be beautiful and attractive. When they took a wife or bore a child with the human, their children were known as the Nephilim. They were half fallen, half human. The offspring of the combination created a whole world of curiosity and confusion. Women gave birth to some children that grew up to thirty-six feet tall. Others could be born with only one eye, six fingers, and two rows of teeth. Kinsey instantly suddenly realized this is where Greek mythology originated. The Titans were real, just born from the fallen angels.

She began to see actual giants coming toward the massive ark. They were doing their best to look innocent. They were trying to persuade Noah, just so they could survive. Just as Noah was about to get a rope to help the small few he could, Kinsey watched as his Guardian whispered in his ear. She couldn't hear what was being said, but she could tell by Noah's body language that he had to walk back into the ark and not come out. Noah's Guardian, along with the family's Guardians, took their place outside the ship to protect the family from any harm. Kinsey became mystified because there was no verse in the Bible that talked about his emotions and feelings once the water began to rise.

"Kinsey, look toward the mountainside off to the left," Reese stated, pointing in the direction.

It was a man or what she thought was a man. He was wearing black and dressed in modern-day clothing. Wait…was that who she thought it was? "Reese, is that Lucifer?" she asked, completely shocked.

Reese nodded his head yes, and suddenly, they noticed him walking toward the top of the mountain where Kinsey assumed he would try to stay safe as long as possible. She looked back up toward the sphere and noticed people were touching it again. Kinsey signaled to Reese, and she put her fingers back into the sphere, and Reese followed behind.

"That was incredible to see, and there are so many more! What do you want to see next? What to choose? What to choose?" Kinsey stated as she began searching around all the podiums.

"Kinsey, hold on for a minute. We need to go turn in your Makirus with the history of your life first so they can be officially stored. Every life is connected to another like a giant puzzle and if you don't turn it in, the picture will never be complete. The other reason this is important is because you can visit anyone else's memories that you are in. Every piece is as important as the next," Reese stated as he began to direct Kinsey from the platforms.

The words were still buzzing in Kinsey's head as Reese grabbed her hand and brought her to an upper level of the Hall of Infinium and straight into the House of Memories. They walked down several long hallways, and as they passed the different podiums, Kinsey kept trying to read the gold labels. At the end of the long hallway, they turned right, but she just happened to notice to the left, the spheres were gray. "Why are those different?"

Reese looked at Kinsey without stopping and explained, "You are about to find out why in a minute, my dear."

Kinsey didn't like the sound of his answer. As they continued to walk down the hallway, it was lined with doors leading into separate rooms. The hallways reminded her of being in a luxury hotel. She was half tempted to open and sneak her way in one of the rooms. As she kept looking all around at the different spheres, Reese tapped her shoulder, and they turned down yet another hallway. There was a man standing all the way at the end with just a wall behind him. He looked as if he was expecting them, and the closer they got, Kinsey realized who the man was. "Hey, Ray?"

Ray smiled as they approached. "Kinsey, what's new, girl? How have you been? And how is the training going? What's going down, Reese?"

"Good to see you, Ray." Ray and Reese did some weird hand-shake that took a few minutes, and Kinsey finally made a noise to remind them she was still there.

"Where's Mittens? What are you doing here?" Kinsey was imag-ining the giant lion sitting at the gate, purring.

"Mittens is guarding the gate, and because I am responsible for the Book of Life, I am also in charge of taking care of the House of Memories. Remember, I know all the good, the bad, and the ugly, baby girl. Do you have your Makirus with you?" Ray asked, holding his hand out.

Kinsey placed the odd object into his hand. He turned to face the wall behind him and placed the Makirus on top of a small spoke that fit into a hole in the middle. Suddenly, the wall shook, causing

Kinsey to jump. Reese and Ray just watched as the wall crumbled and a new door appeared.

"Ah, look at that! A door! That's cool. Is this, like, a key?" Kinsey inquired. She turned to look back at the other doors and noticed that each of the doors were missing the odd-looking item for the handle.

"All right, baby girl, you just turn that knob, and Reese will show you the rest. I got other doors to open and need to get Mittens his lunch. He gets a little moody if I am late," Ray said as he kept walking away from the two.

"Thanks, Ray, it's good to see you again!" Kinsey said.

Kinsey faced the door and hesitated. She wasn't sure what was holding her back.

"Open it, Kins, it's okay," Reese stated, looking at Kinsey.

Kinsey braced herself as she turned the Makirus. Little sparkling and twinkling lights appeared as she looked inside and saw hundreds and hundreds of spheres. The spheres were delicately placed upon shelves that filled up along the wall. They were only a quarter of the size as the big ones in the main hall. On one side, the spheres were gold, and on the other they were gray. She noticed more gray spheres than gold. She approached the first sphere directly in front of her and read the plate that stated "Birth: 1-21-81." She slowly walked past the gold spheres, reading each of the labels. Some of them she suddenly remembered and smiled. As she continued to look at all the different images of her life, memories came flooding back to her.

Reese stayed at the door and watched as she looked over each individual moment and memory from her life.

"Can I touch them like the ones in the main hall and see my past?" Kinsey asked with tears that began to swell in her eyes.

"Yes, you can," Reese answered

"Do I really...want to?" Kinsey had a pleading yet saddened look in her eyes. It was by that same look she was trying to ask Reese if she really wanted to see her life.

"Depends on what you want to remember," he answered honestly.

"What did you do?" Kinsey asked while continuing to look around.

Reese took a deep breath as he met Kinsey's eyes, and she felt as though they were burning through her. "I would go slowly. If you spend too much time here, you can get overwhelmed. You honestly have eternity to look back and watch your life's experiences. Some people open their doors and never come back. Others come when they are missing a loved one that currently doesn't live here and then look at the memories with them." He looked at her with a halfhearted smile, and it was visible on his face, the reflection of his own memories.

Kinsey pondered this for a moment, and then a label caught her eyes. It read "1-20-17 Zerek and a Feather." Suddenly, Kinsey's heart pounded harder in her chest. She couldn't help but to touch the sphere without thinking of forcing Reese to join her. Once again, she touched the sphere as Reese had shown her and was whisked back in time.

There she was, looking at herself and her son. She felt a small pang on her heart because she missed her little boy so much. Zerek was fascinated because he just happened to find a tiny feather, and he brought it to Kinsey. Kinsey smiled and placed the feather in the palm of her hand and lightly blew on it. The tiny feather went straight up and slowly fell to the ground. Zerek had the brightest smile, and he giggled as he placed the feather back into her hand. Several times, she repeated the motions with the feather. Kinsey even went as far as to place the feather in Zerek's hand, and he tried to blow on it.

Kinsey was standing and watching this memory she once treasured so deeply. A tiny tear dropped from her eye. Such a simple moment filled with peace and the joy of a child's discovery. Suddenly, she was curious if a Guardian was nearby. Kinsey looked around and then saw Leilani coming and walked straight through her. Even in heaven, they weren't able to walk through another person. However, because this was a memory, Leilani wouldn't see her.

Kinsey was ready to leave the memory when she then saw herself holding her son, giving him a big hug and tickled him. She touched the gold sphere and came back into the room of her memories. "Sorry, Reese, I knew the memory instantly and just had to see it."

"Not a problem at all. I figured if you took too long, I would come in get you," he said with a smile.

Kinsey then saw four menacing black spheres in the corner, and compared to the gold, they made the room look dark. "Wait…what are those?"

Reese didn't answer right away, and the truth was, he just couldn't. As much as he wanted to tell her, he didn't want to. His eyes and expression softened because he had only seen one other black sphere, and it was in his own memories. He knew what it was, but he didn't quite know how to explain to her the significance of the pain she was pointing at. It just happened to be the darkest moment any person could emotionally handle and the impact from choices that caused a tidal wave in a person's life.

"Well, dear, those are your most painful memories from your life. The ones that linger and affect you tremendously, those moments that never quite leave you the same."

Kinsey soaked in the information and slowly backed away. She knew exactly what moments he was talking about, and she started to feel almost terrified. "I think I will pass for now. I spent too many years living in pain and just want to remember good moments. Is it weird if I want to leave?"

"No, not at all. In fact, follow me. I'm going to take you to a place I know you will find interesting." Reese reached out his hand toward Kinsey for her grasp, and as she did, he gently squeezed it. It gave her a sense of comfort before she closed the door and removed her Makirus off the little door spoke.

"Where are we off to now?" Kinsey inquired as they began to head back out through the different hallways.

"I am going to take you to a place that not many angels know about. It's called the Hall of Mirrors, just the opposite side from the House of Memories," Reese answered.

"Why do only a few know about it?" Kinsey was genuinely curious how only a few angels would know, considering all the people throughout time that had lived and died.

"Well, to be honest, when I got to have my time with Christ, there were questions I desperately needed answers to. So when he answered, he brought me to the room I am about to show you."

"Reese, I have been wondering why haven't I seen him yet. I mean, isn't that the first person we are supposed to see? Don't get me wrong, I thought it was cool to meet a blind man named Ray with a massive lion he named Mittens, but I was told to expect to see him."

Reese smiled and replied, "Kinsey, God provided a key or map with the Bible. These are the directions to follow, and when you get lost or confused, you are supposed to use your key. Unfortunately, what it's not going to do is reveal all the wonders of his majesty. Have you ever heard the phrase, 'I had my come to Jesus meeting?'"

Kinsey smiled and giggled. "Yes, of course."

"Well, that's where it comes from. Every person who enters the kingdom gets their own 'Come to Jesus' meeting. I had mine early on when I arrived because he knew I desperately needed some questions answered."

"I haven't had mine yet. Why is that?" Kinsey stopped and wanted to look Reese in the eye.

"I honestly can't answer that because I don't know, Kinsey," Reese replied. "It's always when the soul really needs the encounter the most is what I was told. Since we know his timing is never off, I assume your time will come at the perfect hour. The only difference between Jesus and midnight is 11:59," he said with a chuckle.

Reese began walking again and linked his arm through Kinsey's. She rested her head on his arm, and they both remained silent as they passed through the different hallways. They entered into a red hallway with black doors. A somber feeling crept over Kinsey as she kept walking, and she noticed that the doors were all missing knobs. Reese turned and stopped at the last door to the left. He pulled out his Makirus, similar to Kinsey's, except his was green and oddly shaped. He placed it on the door, and they heard it unlock. Reese passed through the door first, and Kinsey followed, looking absolutely confused. Inside the room, she was face-to-face with hundreds of mirrors. Some mirrors faced to the west, and some were facing to the east, but in all, the mirrors faced the center of the room. Kinsey walked up to one of the mirrors, and all she saw was darkness and absolutely no reflection. She passed to the next mirror and the one after that, and it was all the same.

"Why can't I see my—" Her voice trailed off as she noticed Reese was several rows back and tenderly kept looking into one particular mirror. Each mirror was unique in shape, size, and design, but inside, it was all black. Kinsey walked over to Reese, and he was staring deeply into a mirror, and suddenly, she was able to make out a person. It was a man in complete darkness, but he was asleep. It was as if he was sleeping in water, yet alone in deep space. His hair, arms, and legs were just drifting in the darkness with his eyes closed. Kinsey noticed that Reese had his hand upon the frame of the mirror, looking intently at the man.

"I assume"—Kinsey paused and debated on asking but decided to just continue—"this is someone you really cared about?" Kinsey questioned delicately.

"My best friend, my partner in crime, my morning and evening star—Mark. He was an amazing man. He provided light in the darkest of moments in my life. As I struggled to understand and learn who I was, he was always there to help guide and love me for me. Even when it felt like the world turned its back on me, Mark never did. I know you can't tell right now, but his smile could brighten a room. His laugh was contagious, and he saw the humor and beauty in everyday situations. He could people watch all day at a mall if he wanted." Reese stopped for a moment and began laughing to himself before he continued, "One day, just to cheer me up, he bought me some ice cream, a goofy pair of sunglasses, and made me sit on a bench, and we people watched until I was laughing and in a better mood. He was so selfless and changed my whole world." As Reese finished speaking, a tear slowly dropped from his eye.

Kinsey wasn't sure how to ask why Mark was in the mirror. She knew the situation was delicate, so she decided to take a sensitive approach to get the answer. "Reese, why do these mirrors have people in them? I am trying to understand. What is this place?"

Reese took in a deep breath and then methodically spoke, "Mark didn't choose to trust God and ask him into his heart, so he sleeps until Jesus returns." Kinsey noticed how tender Reese was touching the mirror, and when he touched the glass, it made a ripple in the darkness Mark was in.

Kinsey suddenly realized that Reese loved this man once upon a time. Mark was the love of his life, and she could see the passion in Reese's eyes. She looked at Reese and gently asked, "Reese, did you love him?"

"Yes, I did. I love him now, but it's a love without sin. It's pure, like a best friend." Reese paused for a moment and looked at Kinsey. "I am sure you weren't expecting to find out in my life that I was gay, right? Well, believe it or not, I was raised in a Christian home." The words buzzed in Kinsey's head as she continued to study the man in the mirror. She waited for Reese to continue because she suddenly realized there was little she really understood about such an incredible afterlife.

Reese began to pour his soul to his new friend so she could get a better understanding of him as a man while he was alive. "Kinsey, I was born in 1961 and grew up in a small town in Germany. I was very fortunate, having such a well-ordered life where old traditions were kept and life was slower paced. My father was a master craftsman and even took care of the renovations for our church."

"What was it like to feel different than everyone else and having to hide it? I mean, I am sure it had to be difficult to hide such a lonely secret." Kinsey looked intently at her friend with sympathetic eyes.

Reese sighed and then replied, "I think the hardest part for people to grasp was the fact that I didn't choose the affliction. Why would a five-year-old child want a life of pure rejection and hatred? I certainly didn't. I prayed every night for God to take these feelings away from me. Over and over again, I begged God to take the affliction from me. I didn't choose to be that way. I begged God because it was a true thorn in my side. The response I always received was that God's grace was sufficient enough, and I did my best to live as a moral and righteous man. Nothing from the beginning was easy for me." Reese paused.

"What do you mean?" Kinsey asked.

"Well, first, I was diagnosed with Crohn's disease at age nine, and I had a hard time with the cortisone treatments. I was miserable and had panic attacks every time I ate. It was hard to handle because I was picked on by kids for having to be delicate or a sissy boy as they called it with my illness. The treatments were to try and help me with the disease, but in reality, it stalled and stunted my growth. My voice didn't even change until I was seventeen. If that wasn't bad enough, I noticed at a very young age I had an attraction to boys which I knew was not okay. My parents were religious, and I tried my best to conform to what was acceptable. I couldn't understand. If I was being raised in a godly home, why would I have not only the illness but have an attraction to men? I read all the verses that talked about what I was, and I was afraid no one would accept me if they knew."

Kinsey waited for him to continue, and she dared not to interrupt because it had never crossed her mind, not even once, what all the Guardian's "sins" were. God sent his only Son, and everyone was forgiven with his blood. That included everyone, no exceptions. If she was forgiven for terminating two pregnancies, then this man she had grown to love as a brother was forgiven too. She realized how many people throughout life liked to cherry-pick the verses in the Bible that suited them. Sin was sin. Pride is considered worse than murder. She knew no one ever liked to ever hear that argument, but fact...is fact.

Since she first met him, Reese was always laughing, joking, and it was very rare that he wasn't in his playful demeanor. She was fascinated about his story and here he was baring his soul. She didn't think any less of him; in fact, she loved him more. He remembered his pain; he was revealing his scars, and he had no fear to do so. Deep down, she truly admired him. Every time she tried, the judgment was quickly followed. It wasn't even the fact of her past; it was the fact she shared. The people she knew all thought it was about attention. It became exhausting mentally. Then the thought popped up as curiosity got the best of her when she decided to ask, "Did you ever tell your parents?"

Many parents, especially in the generation Reese grew up in, disowned their children when they confessed to being gay.

"Well, when I was fifteen, I was so broken inside. I was tired from the illness and just being different. I had no one around me to understand. I mean, kids who have been treated differently for their skin color or religion can at least turn to their parents. But when you are gay, who would understand? I didn't even know that there was a word for being gay. How sad is that? I didn't even have a name or title to what I *was*." Reese paused for a moment, debating on whether he wanted to just bare the rest of his soul or hold back. He decided to just share everything and lay it all out on the table.

"We had a barn on our property, and I had finally decided that I wanted to end my life. I didn't want to ever tell anyone my feelings and was so tired from trying to pretend to be normal. I went out to the barn, and there was a rope through a pulley hanging in front of me, like it had been left there just for me. It was the only thing my eyes focused on. I grabbed a bucket and was able to basically make the rope a noose. I cried and prayed for a moment, asking God to forgive me for what I was about to do. All the while I was praying, I kept explaining to God why I wanted my life to end."

Another small tear dropped from his eye as he continued, "I put the rope around my neck, and just as I was about to knock the bucket down, my father came into the barn. He ran straight up to me with so much fear in his eyes. I cried in his arms for a few minutes as he held onto me, asking me again and again, why? He had tears in his eyes, trying to understand what could make his only son want to take his own life. It took me several minutes to calm down, and when I was finally able to get my composure, I explained what was going on. My father told me that I was his only son and he would love me no matter what. That's when I fully understood God's love. He loves us, and *nothing* can separate us from his love. Not death nor life. Sin is sin across the board, and people try to put me into a category that my sin is the worst? You would think it was a murder? No, it's me being a man and being kind to people and reliable to friends."

Reese wiped the tear from his eye and looked down. Kinsey grabbed his hand and lightly squeezed. She understood his feelings of an existence so lonely and broken inside. Her heart pounded as she thought of the black spheres and knew eventually her curiosity would overcome her, and she would eventually go back to watch what happened.

Reese looked back up at Mark in the mirror and then back at Kinsey and continued, "As I grew up and became a man, I still hid from most of the small world I knew. I even had a couple girlfriends. I didn't want my family to feel the shame from the affliction that was over me. The day I met Mark was the day my life changed. I was working in a small restaurant, and one day, ten men came in to eat lunch, and they were all incredibly attractive. The funny part was they all worked for one of the airlines. Mark grabbed my attention, and we began to joke and flirt. It was the first time in my life I felt free, and I was free with a man who was just like me. He stayed a couple extra days and even met my family.

"My mother and father saw the chains that weighed me down break. My father said he had never seen me so happy. Mark asked me to come to the States with him, and crazy enough, my family supported the idea. So I headed for the US, and we ended up in West Hollywood, California. Of course, you and I both know the city is absolutely fabulous, and that is where I became a professional interior designer. Mark always supported my dreams, and he was the most amazing man. You never quite get over your first love, and Mark was mine. We were together for nineteen years, and I enjoyed every moment with him."

All her life, Kinsey longed for a love like Reese had. She was trying to hide her own tears as she asked. The pang in her heart was starting to become overwhelming, and she decided to ask more. "So what happens to all these people in the mirrors? How do they get here?"

"Well, do you remember when you first arrived and you met Ray and Mittens?" Reese fixed his posture, standing firm again.

Kinsey smiled. "Of course."

"Well, when those who never accepted Christ as their Savior arrive at the gate, Ray directs them to a waiting room. By the way, I designed the room. There is a comfortable couch, so plush and soft they can't help but sit on it. Oddly enough, there is a TV in the room.

When their Guardian leaves, within a few moments, the person falls asleep, and this is where they end up: the Hall of Mirrors."

"So even the people who were incredibly evil get to stay in a place of permanent rest?" Kinsey questioned with a discouraged face.

"No, dear, they don't. Let me take you back to the hallway with the gray spheres." Reese took one more look at Mark before he headed back through the maze of doors and hallways. As Kinsey and Reese passed the gray spheres, the walkway that led to the new set of doors was completely different. It seemed cold and unwelcoming.

"I think this door is where he is," Reese stated as he used his Makirus to open the door.

Kinsey walked inside, and she instantly felt different. It was a similar room with the mirrors, but each one was facing the walls and not the center. She could also hear voices coming from within the room, but she wasn't sure from where. Reese guided her to the last mirror in the far corner, and she couldn't believe her eyes. She was looking at Adolf Hitler, but he wasn't sleeping. He was in outer space. His eyes were sunken in, and he was pale. He was panting and panicking. Then Kinsey heard growling noises, and like lightning, a creature darted in front of Adolf, knocking him around. Another creature screamed and howled and clawed him in the face. The creature was so fast it made Kinsey jump. She turned to look, and she saw all kinds of people in agony and crying as they aimlessly were floating in vast darkness. "How long do they stay in there?" Kinsey asked.

"It's the same as before. When Christ returns, they will definitely face what they have done. No one gets away with anything because it is all seen and it is all recorded. All the horrible things these people did, they will be held accountable. Every knee shall bow, and I believe when Hitler bows, he will have a lot of explaining to do. He makes me sick, and I was so ashamed of my countrymen. He will be in charge of toilets in hell for the rest of his existence since we both know what a piece he is!" Reese paused as he looked again at the man yelling in the mirror. "Well, let's go. We need to get you your color today. I believe after this, you get to train with Big Ben and Annie. That will be hard work, so make sure your muscles are warm and ready."

Kinsey followed Reese out of the Hall of Mirrors, through the House of Memories, and into the main room in the Hall of Infinium. There were angels of all ages on the platforms, still looking at the different podiums. She saw a whole family enter into the hall, and it looked as though they were taking a mini vacation. They set out as a group to go throughout the different historic moments in the world. It was a cool thought. Instead of Hawaii for a week, she would tell her kids, "Hey, let's go visit the building of the pyramids, and while we're at it, try to find the lost city of Atlantis." Now those would be some fun vacations.

As soon as they were out of the hall, it was quiet again. Kinsey took a deep breath as her head felt dizzy. She stopped for a moment and watched the water coming and going from all directions. "That was definitely interesting, to say the least, and I will eventually come back and check out some of the memories."

"All in good time, no need to rush. Are you ready to get your color?" Reese asked with excitement in his voice.

"I am, actually. I have been wondering since the day I saw the different colors because I have no clue what I would be considered," Kinsey answered honestly.

"Off to the marketplace we go then, my dear!" Reese stated as he hooked his arm again through Kinsey's. "We are actually going to see my personal favorite seamstress in the whole market. She is utterly incredible and has an eye for fashion and flair, if you know what I mean. So she is one of a small select few who hands out the color for her assigned Guardians. She doesn't do the Fruits of the Spirit as most are children along with the Momenti because they change form when they go to visit the living anyway."

"So getting your color is like finally completing a probation period on a new job?" Kinsey asked with a smile. She had been through way more of those than she cared to admit. Her bipolar disorder was truly her downfall. She always made the statement all things would work out until she couldn't pretend anymore. That included everything: boyfriends, employment, and unfortunately, some friendships.

"Something like that," Reese responded.

They walked back out of the colosseum, but this time, as they walked out, all the obstacle courses were filled inside the arena. Kinsey did a quick scan to see if she could see anyone from her group, forgetting they were on a mission. They continued walking out of the colosseum, back underneath the four horsemen, and across the courtyard. As they approached the children's playground, Reese and Kinsey scanned for Jaxon and Saige. As sure as the sun rises in the east, the two kids were putting on a play for their friends, enjoying their innocence as children were meant to do. Kinsey and Reese smiled and waved at the two children.

"We are going to my favorite tailor and personal friend, Debbie. Debbie is absolutely incredible with any fabric. I came to her to help with my home as we both have a flare for design. I believe we would have worked together if she was alive during the time of disco instead of the Romans. She was given the newest Guardian's color that had been sent straight from the top. Each outfit is made with a unique design to best flatter our attributes, and the color is based on personality and skill. She also designs our gear to fit our personal weapons. She has an eye for design." Reese smiled.

They continued through the marketplace, eyes wandering through all the women, singing, and laughing. Kinsey had repaid the woman who gave her the chocolate-covered strawberry by helping her sell the juicy sweets for a day. She had such a great time watching all the people come through the market. Kinsey could even spot the new arrivals by their awed expressions and slow movements. She couldn't take the smile off of her face the whole day she stayed. The kind woman had told her she didn't need to stay, but Kinsey really wanted to experience the joy of the interaction with all the different people. She smiled the whole day and loved the encounters with some incredible people.

"Ah, here we go," Reese said as they arrived at Debbie's location. "Hello, my dear friend," Reese stated as they kissed cheeks upon arrival. "This is my new partner in fighting crime, Kinsey."

Kinsey and Debbie skipped the casual hello, kissed on the cheek, and Debbie instantly spoke, "My dear, you have been an absolute struggle for me to figure out. I know you have many hours of training and have been staying with the Utuas. I love that family, but you, my dear, are particularly unique," she said in one breath.

Kinsey realized Debbie had a knack for saying as much as she possibly could in one breath. "Okay, so what did I get? And what is the meaning?" she asked.

"Believe it or not, you are black, and... I have added a dash of silver," she said with a smile. "Since all the Utuas are black as well, I thought you needed a feminine touch," Debbie stated while she pulled out several of the outfits she had already made for Kinsey.

Reese's jaw dropped, and Kinsey didn't know what to make of the two colors. She assumed most people who received their uniforms from Debbie would each have a specialized touch. Kinsey slowly grabbed the black top lined with silver and held it out in front of her. "So... I know that each color represents something. So what do each of the colors mean?" Kinsey asked, looking toward both Reese and Debbie, waiting for an answer.

Reese and Debbie looked toward one another, and Reese, after touching the soft black material, stated clearly, "I honestly don't know what silver represents. But I assume you know. Right, Debbie?"

"All I know is these are the two that came down the line." She didn't know why she added the silver, other than the color added a feminine touch to the masculine black uniform.

After Kinsey's triumph against Tank, she didn't even want to think about how Tank might respond to her new color. Her assumption was that he wasn't going to be happy she received the same color that represented him and all of the Utua brothers. The other side was she had not seen anyone with a double color before.

Reese knew what each of the colors meant. Black he knew backward and front, but silver he had never seen. "Well, dear, I don't know either. I know what black is, of course, but have you ever done double color before, Debbie?" Reese asked in all seriousness toward Debbie.

Debbie thought for a minute, and she then remembered. "Yeah, actually I have. Now that I think about it, it was ages ago. I mean, literally, ages. It was a man. Oh, what was his name? Eddie something! Oddly enough, though, I haven't seen him in, well"—she paused a minute, trying to remember the only other Guardian she provided a double color to—"it was…about a thousand years ago, if I remember correctly."

Kinsey instantly became curious about the only other person. There was someone that was once assigned a color with a dash of individualism like hers. She wasn't sure, but if she went by the odds in her life, she knew it would be something bad. Nothing good came out of being different. On top of that, Kinsey wanted to see how much Debbie could actually say in one breath.

Reese took in the information and let it stew for a moment. He didn't know who Eddie was, and he certainly would have noticed someone running around with a double color.

Kinsey wasn't sure how to feel but decided to just ask about the color they both knew. "Okay. Well, then, what does black mean?" Kinsey kept looking back and forth between Reese and Debbie and waited for an answer.

Reese began to slowly answer and was still slightly confused why the double color concerned him. "Well, black represents strength, honor, loyalty, and flexibility. It also coincides with a background of tragedy and near death." He kept looking at the combination of the two colors while running his fingers over the fabric.

Suddenly, in almost a shout, Debbie broke Reese's train of thought by saying, "Crimson was his name, and his colors were red and silver! It was the talk of the market for several weeks and almost as soon as he received it, he disappeared. Then no one ever discussed it again. It was incredibly odd, but then again, when you live in this heavenly realm, anything and everything is possible." Debbie stared at both Kinsey and Reese, waiting for one of them to speak.

"Well, come on, dear, let's go. We have had a long day learning about new places and, of course, a woman's best friend is shopping. Let's get back and join the group for dinner," Reese stated with a wink. "Goodbye, Debbie, I am sure I will see you again soon."

"Just don't fall in anymore swamps!" Debbie yelled back as Kinsey and Reese walked off.

"Should I call you Swamp Thing from now on?" Kinsey asked, giggling at the thought of Reese sloshing and gurgling around in mud.

"I am the one who makes the nicknames, doll face, so only in private may you call me that!" Reese stated with a wink as he looked at Kinsey.

The aroma of food began tingling both of their senses, and they instantly both realized it was definitely time to eat together for dinner. Kinsey wondered if her group would be back yet from their mission, and most importantly, would she be ready when it came time for her first mission? Kinsey decided to bring her uniforms home and surprise them the following morning with her color. "How do you think Tank and the Utuas will respond to my color?" Kinsey asked after several moments of silence between her and Reese.

"The brothers will love it. Tank, on the other hand, well, let's just hope he doesn't have his weapon in his hand when he sees you," Reese said with a wink.

"Yeah, you know what? I think you are right. I think I will surprise them in the morning," Kinsey said with a smile.

The Internal
Battle Ends

Kinsey woke up the following morning, feeling so incredibly drained after the previous day's adventure. The visions from the Hall of Infinium kept flashing in her mind. The vivid scenery into the past and watching Noah building the ark was utterly incredible. The giant offspring from the fallen or Nephilim was captivating and utterly mesmerizing. When Reese explained the correlation between the end of man's time on earth and that it would be the modern-day Noah, it made her grateful that her time was already done on earth.

She was also grateful for the day of rest from physical training because she knew that today she spent time with Big Ben and Annie. It should be serious business. If the choice came down between the two, she would hands down choose physical training because at least she knew what to expect. Emotional journeys were not her forte. She knew deep down the real test would come when she would be sent down for her first mission. Kinsey wasn't ready to face any of the Watchers, and she was honest with herself about it.

She was fighting with herself internally, debating on if she wanted to get out of the most comfortable bed she had ever rested on in her entire existence. "No, not really," she said out loud to absolutely no one. "I think I am going to stay right here until Reese or Annie come to get me."

The Utuas had finished the foundation and structure to her home, and all that was left was now the decorating. She certainly planned on having Reese help her create the perfect home for her and the two children. She stayed with her grandparents for the night to catch up and spend time with her aunt. She was enjoying the family time and was thankful that she could sleep in just a little longer since she wasn't on the shoreline with the rest of her group.

Almost as soon as the thoughts entered and left her mind, she noticed a clicking sound. It was coming from the bedroom window. Kinsey slid out of bed and stretched as she walked over to the window. She pushed the window up and open, and as she slid her head through, a pebble hit her dead center in her forehead. She looked down, and all the brothers and her group members were dressed up ready to go. They all laughed since it was Big Ben who got her dead center.

Surprise, surprise, she thought to herself. Laughing, yet slightly annoyed, Kinsey called out the window to her group, "So check it out, I have a front door, and all you had to do was knock!"

"What's the fun in that?" Thud yelled back up to Kinsey. "Come on, girl, time to get up and face the day. Literally, with lots of faces."

"Okay! I will be right down. Did Reese tell you what my color is?" Kinsey asked, hoping that she would get to surprise them.

"No, no, Ma, come down and show us," Matai replied.

Kinsey instantly had butterflies in her stomach as she dressed herself. She stood in the mirror and flexed because she felt hardcore. It was the first time she realized she looked at the mirror and realized she didn't look the same. Same face but not the same face. She felt she looked like she was a part of a SWAT team. Reese was definitely right, though. Debbie had a flare for design. Kinsey always loved to wear tube tops in her life, and she definitely loved how slender she looked with the military style pants and her awesome stomping boots. She noticed two bracelets that had been placed with the several sets of her new military-style gear. One was black, and one was silver. Kinsey found the accessories interesting, considering that throughout her life, she always wore thick bracelets to cover the scars on her wrists. The scars were gone now, but Kinsey found herself occasionally rubbing her fingers over her right wrist as was her habit when she was deep in thought. She snapped the two accessories on her wrist with the black on the right and the silver on the left and gave herself one more look over.

"Get 'em killer," she said to herself in the mirror, and suddenly the instinct cut in that she should check her armpits. Yup, they were good, and she headed out to greet her group.

She took a deep breath and opened the door. The moment she walked outside, all of their eyes fell upon her. The silence was deafening. The brothers didn't even joke. Thud and Thunk both had the same confused expressions. Mongo's left eyebrow raised. Grunt grunted. Matai stiffened while Cronk kept chewing on a chicken leg. Ben and Annie slightly shifted back. Reese and Leilani kept a straight face, and in unison, they all shifted their gaze to Tank.

Tank didn't change his poker face. He slowly approached Kinsey, and the rest of the group held their breaths. He had never explained his reactions from the day of his takedown and when he stormed out nor the time they all received their mark of the sea turtle.

Kinsey didn't realize she was holding her breath as he approached her and jumped when he lifted his right hand to her. A smirk crossed his face and, with a smooth romantic voice, surprised Kinsey when he said, "Welcome to the family."

The brothers and the group were all stunned. The twins looked at each other and, in sync, yelled as loud as they could, "*Ua li Kinsey!*"

The group jumped as they were broken from their train of thought and laughed. Cronk dropped the chicken leg that he had been gnawing on. He bent down, picked it up, wiped the dirt off, and continued his usual habit of chewing.

"Well, let's get going over to Sifu. He is waiting for us, and Kinsey has a complicated day ahead of her," Leilani said as she began walking toward the kung fu school.

Tank gave Kinsey a look that took her by surprise. It was welcoming and warm versus the stone-cold face he usually gave her and signaled for them to walk together. "So were you afraid I was going to bite or what?" he asked.

"Well, to be honest, I was afraid you might slice me in half with that ax of yours," Kinsey answered.

"Nah, I would never slice you in half, but I might nick a finger or two," Tank said with a smile and a wink.

"Okay, so... I have to ask and I really need to know. Why were you always so angry when I came around? Was it...because... I beat you grappling?" Kinsey asked, trying not to sound cocky, but couldn't help but feel a sense of pride that she once, and only once, took down the unbeatable.

"The truth is...the moment I saw you, you reminded me of someone. She was the only person in my life, other than my sister, who wanted to be my friend. She wanted to just love without any hidden intention. She just wanted to love me without any motive other than loving me. I don't mean just romantically, though. I mean, she saw through layers of a broken man and was the first person in my life to just show me kindness. I saw you, and you look just like her. I was conflicted inside because I had to make sure that you weren't her."

Kinsey was stunned silent. She had been thinking this whole time his emotion toward her was anger and realized how foolish that seemed now. His emotion was fear. It seemed odd and out of place that a man as huge as Tank would even have fear.

Tank remained silent for a couple minutes and then finally continued, "After you beat me grappling, I finally had my moment with Christ. Until recently, I had not gone to visit her in the Hall of Mirrors and had only checked in on my sister." Tank kept looking ahead. After another moment of silence, he then continued, "Kinsey, I am sorry if I seemed cold or even acted like a jerk. I'm sure you have figured it out, but we still have free will, and some human attributes die hard, especially when I was a man who never had a reason to ever trust anyone. I was honestly impressed the day you got me to tap out. Everyone had always been trying to take me down with strength and never with smarts or distraction. Let me say, though, you nailed it! I walked out of the school right after the takedown because I saw Christ standing just outside the school, and he was signaling me. Sifu saw him, so he knew that it was my time to have some long overdue and much-needed answers."

Kinsey's mind was utterly blown. This guy just said more in the last five minutes than he had said in the past few months. She let the words simmer in her mind. She wondered what kind of life he could have lived where *no one had* shown him any real kindness. Kinsey experienced many years of loneliness and pain, but she at least had friends throughout her life. She realized by his words, along with the heartfelt truth from Reese the previous day, her whole group had come from some serious dark places. She could appreciate in her heart, whatever it was, what they all had in common. She had a hunch on what exactly that was but decided to wait and see if she was right. After all, what was the hurry? She had an eternity to find out more about them.

"Well, that definitely explains a lot. I am glad that you had your moment with him. I'm sure you know that I haven't had mine yet, and I am really curious when that will happen," Kinsey said, reflecting on her own words.

"Honestly, the world we are in now is so outside of mankind's time, you could have met with him the same time I did. It's always right when the soul needs it the most," Tank replied.

Those were the same words Reese said to her the day before. She realized that she may have to wait a while before she got to see Jesus's face. She didn't have a deep need at the present time, and she was sure she would appreciate more of a surprise encounter versus an on demand one.

"Tank, may I ask your real name?" Kinsey asked.

"Sam. Samuel Corona," he answered.

"Can I ask where you got the nickname?" she asked.

"Prison," he stated matter-of-factly.

Just as she was about to ask more, Matai pulled Tank to the side to discuss a new mission that was just handed to them personally.

He doesn't get away that easy, she thought to herself. She decided she was going to make sure that she would sit him down and ask about what his life was like. To Kinsey, that was not a comment a person makes and just walks away. Now it made complete sense when he said that no one ever just cared about him without any underlying intention. The one thing she could confirm right in that moment was he was definitely built like a tank.

The group passed through the marketplace and had to keep Cronk from going to get more food. He happened to swipe some chocolate-covered pineapple pieces from his favorite food vendor and, while munching, told the woman, "I'll be berk letter to trud." Apparently, the woman understood the garbled words he said and waved him off.

They continued past the children's playground and waved at the kids that were playing with Saige and Jaxon. Kinsey's kids came running through each of the group members while laughing and then headed back to one of the many castles and raced toward the slides. Kinsey smiled and blew them a kiss as they ran off. Saige reached up in the air and grabbed the kiss and placed it in her pocket. The two kids were so adorable, and Kinsey's heart panged slightly at the thought that she didn't let them live. She reminded herself, though, the kids never had to experience pain and they lived in a wonderful world of love, happiness, and make-believe.

The group passed the colosseum and the dining hall and headed to the right toward Lau's ancient bamboo garden. The front of the kung fu school welcomed the group with the ancient Chinese design of the curled-up sides with the gold and red structure. The group entered through the open doors, removed their boots, and bowed as they stepped out upon the mat. Sifu Lau came out in his usual calm fashion with his hands crossed behind his back and bowed back to the students.

"So I see our newest member…just received her color," Lau said as he was observing Kinsey's black color. Lau spoke in English because he knew how important receiving a color was for a Guardian. Obtaining an assigned color was as important in heaven as it was on earth to obtain a driver's license at sixteen. He slowly circled her and suddenly observed the silver that was threaded through the black. He had never seen a double color before. He did, though, remember a story about one other Guardian that had been assigned a double color.

Lau never trained the other Guardian due to the time frame that Lau was born. He did remember, though, through the archangels there had been a man who once existed and who was once given red and silver. The archangels explained how Eddie had been marked by the colors to complete an almost impossibly discouraging task. He was meant to stand out so Lucifer would mark him and entice Eddie to switch sides. Lau then suddenly realized there might be a reason to be concerned with the new double color. It had meaning. Nothing was just by chance, and the fact that Itherial told him recently the boy had been born meant her colors had meaning. This was the time they had all been waiting for. This was serious.

"Well, what do you think, Sifu?" Kinsey asked with hopeful eyes. She could read his face, and instantly, her stomach dropped.

Lau answered back in Cantonese that she looked tiny compared to the Utuas, but then again, the Utuas were a bunch of big sissy girls.

The brothers all heard the comment and decided to stiffen up, thinking it would prove their manhood next to one another. Thud elbowed Thunk, Thunk smacked Cronk in the back of the head. Cronk smacked Thunk back in the front of his head. The next thing they all knew, there was a whole dog pile of Samoans in full effect. Reese, Annie, Big Ben, Leilani, and Tank just sat by, completely unfazed as the brothers continually fumbled around one another.

Lau continued to stay distracted by the reality of the double color. He knew he was going to have to visit Michael, Gabriel, and Itherial to ask about the double color. This was something that he knew he couldn't just sit on and at the same time knew that the day's training was particularly important.

Today, Kinsey was going to end the voice in her head that was full of doubt and any remaining negativity from her human life. Until the time of man actually ended, all Guardians who visited earth would continue to face vulnerability to feel what the humans felt. She would be going against each one of her team members while sparring with their weapons. This made the sparring extremely complicated because they each earned a weapon that was made best for them for battling against the Watchers. Each was designed to match their personality from when they were alive. He asked Kinsey to gather her swords and display her form that she had been practicing on.

Slowly, she swayed to her own heartbeat, swinging the swords gently to each movement. The swords had become a part of her from her shoulder to her arm, arm to hand, and hand to sword. She even closed her eyes, and as her heart began to speed up, she sped up. Suddenly, she felt someone standing close behind her, and her first initial instinct was to swing the swords around to make contact with whatever or whoever approached her. She heard the clink of the weapons making contact and opened her eyes to see Big Ben standing behind her.

"Good," he stated matter-of-factly. "That is the first test of your skills. Can you sense what is around you? Some of the Watchers can remain hidden, even to our eyes. You have to be able to sense your surroundings and not just see but sense and feel."

Annie then spoke behind Kinsey and slowly circled around her. "There is a reason why Ben and I train as we do. You need to be able to hit your mark no matter where you are. You have to be quick-thinking, no matter who or what you come up against. The Watchers don't play fair. They shift, they change, they sting, they bite, they stab, they strangle, and the most dangerous ability they have is to deceive." Annie kept walking around Kinsey as she was explaining more about the darkness.

The group was dead silent as they listened to their words, and Lau stayed perfectly still as two of his best students spoke. It was almost as if they were in a trance, holding their breaths, hanging on to the explanation that was coming from Big Ben and Annie.

Lau slowly approached to Kinsey and, with the softest voice, spoke. "Kinsey, you have trained vigorously, and today is the biggest test to your true martial arts skill. Your demonstration right now will be a window to your ability against the Watchers. You will now need to face the things you were most afraid of in your life. Your deepest pain. None of us know what will walk in from the garden into the school, and it could be man or beast, friend or foe…or even yourself. You are now going to fight each one of your members as you try to shut out the traces of darkness still left within you. Remember, you are strong, you are worthy, and you are loved. Don't believe the lies that the enemy whispers to you when you are weak and worn down. The Watchers will try to gain any entry point they can to make you weak. This will be the closest simulation to what you will experience." Slowly, Lau backed up to stand with her group and the brothers.

Everyone stiffened when instantly a black and white mist enveloped the entryway. A distinct smell of roses and blood filled the room. Through the white mist entered in a beautiful woman. She wore white high heels with white leather pants. Her shirt glistened in the light like glitter, and her skin was as smooth as ivory. Her face was gentle and kind with a smile that could warm any heart. Her hair was short, white, and full of curls which surrounded her face and shoulders. She took her place to the right of Kinsey and smiled. Kinsey wasn't sure what to make of her. The woman was beautiful, but Kinsey couldn't help but to ask herself if she was facing deception. What would she have to fear from her? Maybe that was the trick since Kinsey didn't trust anyone so easily while alive.

Kinsey's focus was then taken off the woman when a black fog became more distinct in the entryway. Another woman appeared in the entryway, and she was the exact opposite as the first woman. She had long black boots that went up to her knees with pants that had been ripped and tattered. She had a red tube top on with a black leather vest, just barely covering her large bosom. Her left arm was covered in tattoos that kept moving and morphing into different symbols and objects. On her right wrist was a bandage, and on the lower side was showing a small hint of blood. Her hair was black, straight, and long. Her red lips were full and eyebrows distinct. When she walked in, she took her place to Kinsey's left side. Her left eyebrow raised as she looked directly into Kinsey's eyes, and Kinsey noticed she could see her own reflection in the woman's eyes. She wondered if this was the monster inside her all those years she struggled with her pain.

The bandage on her wrist made Kinsey remember the day in the bathtub. She had to be the one who tried to destroy her all those years she lived in pain. The two women were the supernatural manifestation of the voices that had long tried to destroy her and also keep her going.

Lau indicated for Reese to take his place in front of Kinsey. She turned to look at Big Ben and Annie, pleading to know if she was really ready to fight her own internal demons. "Remember all that you have learned and use the wit you used to defeat Tank. Know who you really are," Big Ben answered as if he knew her thoughts.

Lau made the signal for them to begin, and Reese's sword met with hers. The two women, solid and stoic at her side, stayed completely still as she and Reese began to gain the advantage over one another with their skill and weapons. Suddenly, both women at the same time spoke in her ears. Kinsey couldn't tell which one said what, but the words both affected her.

"Do you really think you can do this?" one said while the other whispered, "Remember all the pain you have overcome!"

Kinsey turned to strike at Reese, and suddenly, they were in her ears again. They moved so quickly she couldn't tell which one was for her and which one was against her.

"You can't defeat anyone."

"Ignore her, she knows nothing of your strength."

Over and over again, she kept trying to come at Reese with all the force and skill she could physically build. Everything she had gained with her training didn't seem to prevail through any of her attempts toward Reese. The more the two women spoke, the harder it was to gain any kind of advantage over him. Kinsey never realized how fast Reese truly was when he became deep in concentration. He became a light blue blur in his element, and the more she tried to keep up with him, the further behind she fell. His strikes hit her each time like lightning, crippling her defenses, and the more the women distracted her by speaking in her ear, the more confidence she kept losing. After numerous attempts which kept ending in failure, her time against Reese was over. Kinsey felt so defeated. She didn't understand why she wouldn't be successful if she was putting all her training to use. Her discouragement was getting the best of her.

Up next came Annie. Kinsey tried to catch her breath before she had to go against the next team member, but she wasn't going to go easy on Kinsey. She and Annie took their places facing one another, and Kinsey let out a huge sigh. She was out of breath, and she knew how incredibly quick Annie was, and Kinsey felt internally that she wouldn't be able to go another round. Kinsey's thoughts were apparent on her face that she wanted to quit. Right before Lau signaled for them to begin, the two women were in her ears again.

"Do you really think you can do this?"

"You can do all things through Christ who has always strengthened you."

Annie made the first and hardest blow, making sure she showed no mercy toward Kinsey. Her three-ended metal and lead bow staff was all about the ability to think and act two steps ahead of any opponent. Annie was known for being and what Leilani called "The Maze Runner." Quick, stealthy, intelligent, and deadly. For every strike Kinsey made, Annie already had many counterstrikes back. Kinsey couldn't understand how anyone in any existence could bare such tenacity and skill. Annie was always sure she was ready and by knowing where and how to strike while at the same time keeping herself two steps ahead of any movement that had just been made. Her dark skin made the yellow uniform appear as if she had fire dancing upon her body. Whether Kinsey struck from above or below, Annie kept redirecting her swords, and Kinsey was beginning to struggle, grasping for breath by trying to simply and quickly keep up. The two ends of the metal staff kept trapping her swords, and she was able to knock them out of her hands many, many times.

After the last strike, as the swords fell to the ground, Annie stopped. She knew it was a cue for her to ease off of Kinsey. Without missing a beat, the two women, speeding past her, spoke again.

"You could never do this, and what makes you think you ever could?"

"You are a daughter to the greatest of Kings, and he will never fail you. Believe, Kinsey, and keep believing."

"Who are you to think you belong to a King? You are nothing but a slave. The dog of a slave. Even a flea on the dog has more value than you do."

"You can choose to believe the lies or you can choose to hold every thought captive and quiet her out."

Both voices were getting louder, one more vicious and the other more comforting. Which voice belonged to who? And how was she going to be able to tell the difference between the two? The hardest part for her to figure out was what to do once she figured out which voice was the dark one. Did they represent the darkness and the light both together? Were they both meant to be deceiving? Then why would one comfort her at all? Maybe she was just thinking too deeply into it. Maybe that was it? She had to not let it distract her any further.

Big Ben walked out and stepped in front of her. Kinsey felt like her arms were about to fall off and did not believe she was going to be able to keep moving forward. With the two women, whatever they could be considered, deep in her ears and the fast pace against one of the best in her group, fighting felt utterly impossible.

"Can you give me just a minute to catch my breath?" Kinsey begged.

Big Ben looked at her, full of compassion, and then spoke, "I don't know if you really want to do that. You can't stop because you are tired. You can only stop when you are done."

Kinsey, barely audible to anyone's ears, pleaded, "Please" as a single tear rolled down her cheek.

As Ben stood in front of her, it was as if a hornet's nest had just been thrown right at her. The two voices passed around her faster, more intense, and would not stop.

"Of course you need to quit because you are pathetic."

"Breathe for a moment and then push through. She will have no power if you keep pushing."

"I will always have power because you have always given me power. That's not about to change. It will never be any different because we are one."

"It will change. It will change today, but you have to keep fighting. Don't let her in."

"What does she know? She couldn't stop me all the years of your life, and that isn't about to start now."

"Kinsey, remember everything good in your life and focus on the power of right now. Look at the amazing talent it takes to fight off a physical person and the manifestation of an attack."

"Manifestation? I will never leave you. You will never get rid of me because I am a part of you, no matter where you are."

"She lies."

Kinsey held her hands to her head. She looked up at Ben and asked, "They aren't going to stop, are they?"

"No. They get worse when you stop. You have to keep fighting because once you get your second wind, you will start to see the true deception," Ben stated as he got ready with his spear.

He took his stance, and Kinsey got ready. Instantly, the minute Kinsey got ready, one of the voices got louder, shouting in her ears, *"Give up now, you are a failure!"*

Kinsey screamed and charged toward Big Ben. The two swords met with his spear and made almost no impact. No matter what way she tried to come at him, his counterstrikes were twice as strong and caused her twice as much pain. Several times, he was able to use the staff to slide against the back of her legs and knock her down. She closed her eyes for a brief moment, and surprisingly, when she opened them, she was able to see one of the women. She kept circling her like a shark, waiting to devour its prey. One drop of blood, and it would turn into a feeding frenzy, yet the one she saw didn't speak.

At that exact moment, she heard from the other, "Get up no matter how many times you are knocked down."

She slowly willed herself back up, silently begging God to give her the strength of a true warrior that she had been training all this time for. She now knew which manifestation was lying to her. It was almost as if she was struck by lightning because now she knew what Big Ben meant. She received her second wind, and it was time to fully face her biggest enemy. It was her own mind. It had always been her own mind. All those years she spent holding on to the past was due to the Watcher who tried to keep her living in the past. The Watcher knew what made her the weakest. All those years, she hated herself for the many and repeated mistakes she continuously made. All the years she held onto pain and did not allow herself to forgive the ones who hurt her most, drowning her to a point of no return. All the years of being alive now came down to silencing that evil demon who wanted nothing other than to take her out.

She turned from Big Ben and was able to fully grab on to the woman with white hair and held her sword up to her neck. Kinsey was ready for the slaughter. She gripped on to the woman tighter than the day she beat Tank and had no intentions of letting this beast go.

Sifu slightly moved forward and realized that he could not make this decision for her. He was not allowed to warn her because this was her choice. If she made the wrong one, then she wouldn't be able to go down for her first mission until a much later time, and she was stronger. The group all looked at Kinsey, bruised and beaten with a fire in her eyes that could not be mistaken. She had made her choice.

Big Ben stood in front of her, unsure of what to say. The other woman that had been circling her stopped and had the same smirk on her face. The woman backed up toward the group and turned to face them all. "Do you think she has made the right decision? Or would I be the right one to kill?" she asked.

The same woman kept looking at the whole group, individually one by one. As her eyes met each person, they all turned away. Her stare was so intense they felt like they were children who had been in trouble. It appeared as though Tank was the only one who really didn't seem worried. Kinsey looked at every single one of the Utuas, then group members slowly and finally stopped at Tank. He was the only one who gave her a look that she had made the right choice. He slowly nodded, and Kinsey gripped tighter.

"I made my choice," Kinsey stated. She began breathing heavily and without warning sliced the throat of the woman in her arms. The whole group held their breath and then released as the black blood of the Watcher began to stain her gear and fill the ground.

Sifu stood motionless and then was startled by Thud and Thunk yelling the Utua stamp of approval, "*Ua li Kinsey!* You had us worried there for a minute."

Big Ben and Annie approached Kinsey along with Reese, Leilani, and Tank. They all told her she fought well and that they completely understood how hard the fight was. They were also impressed because each one of them had to fight against one of the Utuas before they knew which voice to silence.

"Hey, you know you didn't do bad at all, right?" Matai asked.

"I don't see how that is even possible. I was barely able to keep my footing. In fact, with Annie, I didn't have feet," Kinsey said.

"That's the whole point. They have to come at you as hard as they possibly can, and through your test of skills, they can tell what needs to be worked on. It's actually a good thing," Matai replied.

Kinsey noticed the other woman was still in the room. The woman slowly approached and smiled at Kinsey. "I have tried to help you fight your whole life, and all I ever wanted was to see you succeed. Now that I know you have the fight of a true warrior inside you, I can go get some rest."

The black fog filled the entryway again, and she disappeared through the smoke.

"This was the most exhausting day of my life...my death." Kinsey still wasn't quite sure how to express her existence since she died. All she knew now was that she wanted a nap.

"Well, we have something special planned for you tonight. Every single person gets a celebration when they pass the test of fighting their inner demons. Since yours was particularly draining, we have a fun night ahead. Even Sifu is coming, isn't that right?" Leilani asked, looking in Sifu's direction.

He slowly nodded his head toward them and then bowed to the rest of the group. He needed time himself to pray before the festivities because this whole issue with the double color had his attention gripped. He realized it had to be an incredibly important meaning, and he wanted to find out what it was.

All the Utuas, including Tank and Kinsey's group, walked out of Lau's school with her. She was so tired but at the same time felt so energized. She just conquered her inner demon that had tortured her for many, many years. It was incredibly exhilarating to win against a manifestation in human form of a creature that had always tormented her. Kinsey began wondering, *How could a Watcher have the ability to enter the kingdom?*

Reese could see by the perplexed expression on Kinsey's face she was trying to figure something out. "What are you thinking?"

"Okay, so how did the Watcher get in and why did it take human form?" Kinsey asked, completely confused.

"Well, it's a little tricky, my dear. The Watchers that have been breaking the rules get captured and are taken into captivity, just outside the gate near Ray and Mittens. They are blindfolded and are only allowed on a certain path for protection purposes. Now I know sometimes there are certain Watchers that can hide even from Guardians. The Guardians who have the same gift I do can still see them. Hiding in the spiritual world gives you a whole new view of life after death. If the Watcher you fought against did gain the advantage over you, she would instantly be bound and unable to move any further," Reese answered. He smiled at Kinsey to show her he was so proud of her. He appreciated her tenacity and was ready to celebrate she overcame her biggest enemy.

"That is wicked cool. No pun intended. So how does your gift work when you hide?" Kinsey asked.

"Well, the only time I can see them all is when I am hidden as well. We blend into the background and become a part of the current scenery, like a chameleon. I have to focus, but eventually, I can spot them all," Reese said.

"So how do you communicate to the group if they can't see you?' Kinsey asked.

"Well, each Guardian has a sound they use to notify their group members that a Watcher is close by. I also use my signal to let our group members know I am following a Watcher who doesn't know I'm there," Reese answered.

They began heading to the marketplace, and Reese decided to surprise Kinsey for her hard work. "Are you hungry or thirsty for anything? It's my treat."

They were startled to find out Cronk had approached them from behind them like a ninja and answered for Kinsey as he pushed his way through. "I'll take some strawberries with chocolate and whatever the lady wants," he stated with a cheesy smile.

"I wouldn't expect any less," Reese laughed.

"I think I am with Cronk on this one. Some of those incredible strawberries sound like mouthwatering deliciousness to me," Kinsey answered.

Reese took the two of them over to Kinsey's favorite merchant. "How did you do today?" she sweetly asked with her Indian accent.

"How did you know about that?" Kinsey asked.

"Mr. Cronk is my best customer, and of course, he told me. I assume you did well since you and Mr. Cronk are here," she stated.

Before Kinsey had a chance to answer, Reese broke in, "She did incredible. She fought against three of us. I am actually really proud because she gave it her all. She had to silence a Watcher, and some of us weren't sure she made the right decision. Then it was as if you could feel the power in the room, and she conquered." He lifted his fist in the air.

"Congratulations! That is a huge accomplishment. I will be bringing the largest and juiciest of my strawberries tonight for the celebration," the woman stated with the warmest smile.

"Thank you so much, and I can't wait to see what you have in store for me," Kinsey said. She could feel herself start to get excited as if she was a child about to go to Disneyland.

"Well, my dear, let's get you cleaned up and ready. Wear another set of your gear, and tonight you get to show off your color." Reese winked at Kinsey as he handed Cronk his fruit. He then placed his arm around Kinsey as they proceeded out of the marketplace.

Kinsey didn't see Jaxon and Saige playing in the children's paradise and assumed that they were off with her family. She was grateful she was going to celebrate the small success of the day but felt her heart sink a little at the thought of Grace and Zerek not celebrating with her. She became excited again and actually proud of herself. Feeling a sense of pride, regardless of being in heaven, felt foreign to her. There were very few moments in time where Kinsey could be proud of the decisions she made. Today definitely became one of them, and to her, it felt exhilarating.

As the sun was beginning to set over the beach horizon, Kinsey found herself welcomed with tiki torches and flower decorations. Tables had been set up with incredible delicacies from the different countries around the world. Kinsey always got a kick out of seeing her newly met friends dressed from the different time periods. Kinsey made a conscious decision to let the moment carry her as long as the celebration lasted.

She did a walkthrough of her new home, and to her surprise and pleasure, Reese had already done most of the work decorating her home. The living room and master bedroom did not display as many items as the rest of the home. Reese approached her from behind and explained that every throne needs to be decorated by the king or queen of the castle themselves. She decided she would gather the items from her grandparents' home and Utuas' the following day after the celebration. Then to her amazement, Reese walked over to the dresser and displayed all of her gear and other items.

"Is there nothing you didn't think of?" Kinsey asked as she gave Reese a hug.

"I'm a perfectionist when it comes to decorating my sweet friend," he said with a smile.

"And what did you do for work while you were alive?" Kinsey asked.

"Honey, can't you tell?" he stated with a huge smile.

"Really? I didn't strike you as a man with a talent for decorating such extravagant rooms," she said sarcastically.

From the commotion outside, Kinsey could hear her name being called. Leilani was beckoning her out to the beach. She walked out on the sand and was blown away by the beautiful display. Everyone had assembled to make this day incredibly special. Hundreds of people had gathered together for the celebration, and Kinsey noticed there were even jugs of wine. It was the first time she had seen wine since she arrived. She smiled and laughed when she saw Ray pouring himself a grail of wine for him and Mittens.

Leilani and her brothers were dressed in the traditional Polynesian warrior ensemble. She had a spear in her hand and yelled out in a foreign language, and everyone took their seats on the sand. Leilani and several other women demonstrated a traditional Polynesian dance, also known as a haka, and everyone in attendance enjoyed the quick pounding of the drums by the Utuas. The brothers would yell out and bang down on what sounded like loud sticks clanking in a rapid motion.

Leilani looked like a woman in charge, and she did her heritage proud. The performance lasted a good half hour, and even the brothers had their own display of heritage they wanted to exhibit. Their faces were painted, and their haka was incredible. Instead of the goofy group of brothers who bounced around one another, these were men claiming their ancestry, and everyone in attendance enjoyed their tribal dance.

The next to stand in front of the group was Sifu Lau. This was definitely new. Lau rarely had shown any of his students his forms, let alone practiced in front of any of them. Itherial made his appearance and came to watch his best friend and his unique skill. Just before the celebration, Lau spoke with Itherial about the double color, and Itherial just happened to agree that this was something of significance. They had both decided to visit Michael and Gabriel to find out what specifically happened in the past with the man who once had the red and silver. Itherial had a hard time looking at Kinsey, knowing she was the girl in the bathtub he helped save. He wanted nothing more than to tell her he was there and he was with her. She wasn't alone, but he just couldn't bring himself to do so. *Maybe one day when the time is right.*

Several beautiful Asian women took their place on the sand close by where Lau was standing, ready to show his forms. They had beautiful blue and gold oriental dresses on, each with a different colored dragon woven throughout the fabric. They gathered traditional musical instruments that were made in China and began to set up a little performance with music to match his movements. The whole audience, sitting upon the sand, couldn't wait to see the skills of the man who mastered his style of kung fu.

Hundreds of Guardians, Kinsey's group members, patiently waited to see what Lau was truly capable of. The music began gently flowing, and Lau's arms glided through the air. Everyone watched in awe as he could shape his body into positions that seemed utterly impossible. The strength in his legs was undeniable, the flexibility unmistakable, the beauty remarkable and breathtaking. Lau was so incredibly fast, and all his students realized he would tear them to pieces. Even Itherial didn't know the full extent of Lau's ability. When he was finished, everyone on the sand was silent. After a moment of silent adoration, they all cheered as loud as they possibly could, giving him a standing ovation. Lau was so humbled and honored by their approval since it was the very first time he had ever let them see what he was truly capable of.

Little by little, people from all over the world performed dances for Kinsey's achievement. The celebration was also about the completion of training so she could officially go on her first mission. The woman she helped sell the amazing chocolate-covered strawberries for wanted to sing for the celebration, and Kinsey cheered as loud as she possibly could. Kinsey felt humbled and honored all these people would do this for her. Tears filled her eyes because she never imagined how incredibly fun heaven would be. She realized no one ever mentioned anything about parties, celebrations, and they certainly never said anything about wine!

The party lasted for several hours, and everyone in attendance danced to the different styles of music. Saige and Jaxon were joined by numerous children, and they kept trying to mimic the Utuas' dance from earlier. Kinsey felt so much peace watching the children and while sitting with her grandparents and aunt, her excitement was beginning to wind down. All the food provided by the guests was considered a gift for Kinsey and her new home. She knew the children would eat all of the sweets before she had a chance to even smell them. The joy of being a child was slightly missed in her eyes. Her grandparents and her aunt told her over and over how proud of her they were that Kinsey had overcome such exhausting adversity.

"Today's accomplishment is no small thing," her Aunt Judy said. "I had three myself, and while two of them were my own Watchers, one was the voice of my first husband. His voice was the one that made me the weakest. My love for Dale and my hatred was the reason I ran from God for so long. Dale was my reason I was so angry for the majority of my life. He was the reason my heart stayed broken for so long. I was grateful that I was given a second chance in my life, no matter how old I was. I felt free when I finally moved forward. We have all deserved it. It's just a matter of if we take it or even recognize it."

Kinsey let the words sink in. "I think that was my biggest problem too. I couldn't recognize the opportunity when it was right in front of me. I just let it eat away at me."

"That's the Watcher's job! They are responsible for your anguish and heartache. If they don't succeed, they get severely punished. So they will do whatever it takes and throw the nastiest punches to make a person angry with God. Have you ever noticed people who don't believe in God don't get attacked the way believers do?" Judy asked.

"All the time. My friends would always say they couldn't understand how I managed to experience all the loss I did," Kinsey replied.

"That's because the Watchers go after the families with the most faith. Pastors have targets on their back more than anyone else. If someone doesn't believe, the Watchers have them right where they want them. So there is no need to attack. The minute they begin to inquire or start to learn about God, they wreak havoc everywhere and anywhere they can in that family's life," Kinsey's grandmother said.

"That makes so much sense now. I remember on several occasions, someone would ask me, how could I still choose to believe in God and have faith with all the pain in my life? How could I say there is a God and kids get cancer? It was simple to me because it was all I ever had. If I lost faith, then I lost hope. That scared me more than anything else. On top of that, it was all I knew. I couldn't imagine my life without any belief," Kinsey said.

Kinsey's grandfather placed his hand on hers and gently said, "Today's victory over your spiritual accomplishment is deserving of this celebration. Everyone deserves a celebration. The pain and the Watcher who tried to keep you held in bondage throughout life has now been defeated in the afterlife."

Kinsey smiled at her family and thanked them for being a part of the celebration. So many words could describe the peace and happiness in her heart, yet none would do justice. "I love having you guys around right now and I can't wait until the rest of us will all be together again."

Kinsey noticed Judy's eyes averting off in the distance and asked, "Who is that?"

The minute Kinsey locked her eyes on the person, without saying a word, she left the table and ran up to Johnny. "Wow! They said anyone I had interacted with would be here, but I never imagined you would come," she stated with pure excitement.

"You might be surprised we have a lot in common, and tonight is a celebration. Is it true you love music as much as I do?" Johnny asked with a wink.

"Are you serious? Oh, no way! Please do. I don't even care if you play the same chord over and over again. Yes, come play for us all!" Kinsey begged.

Johnny walked through the crowd, and everyone went silent again. Lau even wanted to see what had caused the loudest group he knew to become mute. Johnny walked up to the front of the crowd. He placed his guitar in his hands, and his captive audience listened intently as he said, "I just happen to notice that most of Kinsey's group has the color black, and since some people may know what my nickname is, I thought I would sing a song that could represent us all."

Everyone, including the children, sat once again and grew just as excited as they were when Lau had performed. Slowly, Johnny strummed his guitar, and Kinsey noticed something interesting. Every single person, including herself, began to find themselves in a soft trance. The music hypnotized their senses. It wasn't just his words. Every chord had meaning, and their heartbeats lined up with the tempo. He was singing about strength, pushing through life, trusting God, and the best part of all, making Lucifer run. Kinsey wasn't sure why, but it dawned on her that she now knew his gift in battle. His music put the Watchers in a trance. He had the ability to hypnotize anyone with his music, and it all depended on his lyrics.

When Johnny was done, everyone gave him the same excited standing ovation they had given Lau. He slowly bowed, thanked the guests, and began to make his way out. Just as he was about to pass between the Utua home and Kinsey's, she tapped him on the shoulder. "Thank you. Thank you so much. There is nothing more precious in this afterlife than a gift of song. Well, to me anyway. I always *felt* music instead of listening to it."

Johnny looked deep into Kinsey's genuine eyes, then for reasons he was unsure of, he happened to take a closer look at the black gear she was wearing. He had not realized before when he first arrived at the celebration that there was silver color woven through her gear. "What's that supposed to mean?"

Kinsey's focus shifted to her clothes. "I am not sure. The woman who made it for me just happened to add silver."

"Interesting," he said with a weird expression on his face. "Well, kiddo, enjoy the rest of the evening. I'm glad I came. You have a great group and look very loved," he stated with a smile.

"Thank you," Kinsey stated as she waved him off and turned back toward the celebration. Little by little, everyone in attendance began to slowly return to their homes. The two children were finally winding down, and everyone was ready for a great night's sleep. This day had to have been the best day of her life...death—she was never going to figure out how to correctly say it. The point, though, was that it was awesome. She looked upward at the night sky and saw a star that was twinkling, just slightly more than the others. "Lord, what I have longed for my whole life I now have, and I couldn't be happier. You are an awesome God, and I thank you that even in an afterlife filled with people, you still acknowledge me." A small tear rolled down her cheek and Kinsey went to gather the two children. She was truly in paradise, and nothing but nothing could take her peace away ever again.

THE PRINCE OF ROME

"All right, you gnarly little demon, where do we begin, eh?" Eddie asked the lizard as he sipped on his coffee, looking out the window over the city. The beautiful view made Eddie wish he could just stay in Rome and disappear. In fact, all he ever wanted was the ability to hide from Lucifer for the rest of his existence. He kept wondering if Feassure could hide from Lucifer. As the thought crossed his mind, he tossed the sausage from his plate down toward the little demon. Eddie was beginning to like the idea of having a companion, even if the creature was ugly as all get out.

"All right, you bloody lizard," Eddie said as he bit down on a green apple. He set it down then asked, "Where do we begin?"

Feassure watched Eddie place the green apple down on the table. The lizard spat it's tongue out toward the apple, and Eddie assumed the motion from Feassure was trying to ask about the apple.

"Well, if you must know," Eddie started to say as he stood up, "it's my way of reminding myself why I am here day after day. As Eve and Adam ate the apple from the tree of knowledge, I too took from that same tree when Morajes and Lucifer found me. I have hated myself every day since."

Eddie continued to enjoy the view from his penthouse suite, chewing his remaining bites of the apple in his mouth. It did not matter how many times he made his way to Rome; the city was frozen, locked in time, and every visit always took his breath away. Unfortunately, the beauty of the city was buried by several millennia with wicked secrets of torture and death. "I only take one bite to remind me, if I ever get a chance to go back and become a Guardian,

I will have already eaten my apple, and no evil temptation will consume me and take my second chance away."

Eddie then tossed the fruit to Feassure who hissed through his razor-sharp teeth and backed away.

"Don't like fruit either? What is it that you eat?" Eddie asked as he leaned down by the giant reptile.

The sound of two men distracted both of their trains of thought as they heard the men loudly storming the hallways outside the door. The men sounded like they had been out all night, drinking. Feassure instantly stood straight up and disappeared. The lizard began to climb up the wall, opened the door with its tail and made his way out toward the two men.

"Bloody hell, where are you going?" Eddie yelled out to Feassure.

The two men at the end of the hall, staggering with one another, turned toward Eddie and gave him the bird. They laughed as they opened their room, and Feassure followed in behind them. It stunned Eddie because he literally, in a thousand years, never saw a Watcher prey upon the living to eat. The Watchers were known to attach themselves to men and women everywhere, but no one was ever eaten in front of Eddie. Almost as soon as the thought crossed his mind, Feassure opened the door to the room he was just in and made his way back to Eddie.

"Well, what the bloody hell was that all about?" Eddie asked. The lizard looked up and smiled with his razor-sharp teeth filled with blood. The view of the blood in Feassure's mouth made Eddie cringe.

"Did you kill them?" he asked, horrified and intrigued at the same time.

Feassure just looked up at Eddie and shook his head no.

"Ah, so you *can* understand me?" Eddie asked with a smile.

Feassure nodded his head.

"Sooo…they were about to die and you can tell? I assume because you are a nasty little Watcher, they were either overdosing or killing themselves with an addiction? Is that one of your…talents?" Eddie asked.

Feassure again nodded his head yes.

"So you can form into a dog in front of humans. You can spy on the Guardians in the spiritual world, and you can tell when a person is about to die? Are there any other talents I should know about?" Eddie asked, completely baffled.

Feassure crept up to the window with the view of the city and sat down. His body was facing the direction they needed to go to find the Prince of Rome. On cue, Eddie walked up beside Feassure and very lightly said, "Piazza del Colosseo. So he is down beneath the Colosseum, is he?"

Feassure took his form as a dog just for the humans while Eddie finished getting himself ready. He usually only wore clothes that were either black or gray. Today, he decided on black pants and a gray cashmere sweater. "All right, let's give it a go," Eddie stated as he grabbed his wallet and key for the room.

Eddie placed a leash around Feassure, and they left the hotel. The demon would growl from time to time, signaling a Guardian was close by. For the first time in a thousand years, Eddie knew the Guardians were around him. His excitement was visible on his face since he could not stop smiling. He also noticed that there was a scent or smell in the air he once took for granted. The Guardians each give off a scent, and this particular scent had a combination of roses and honey. All those years ago when he crossed sides, those beautiful, sweet, soft, powdery smells were instantly taken from him. No perfume could ever compare to the smell of the Guardians nor any angel in heaven, for that matter.

After crossing a few blocks, Eddie and Feassure found themselves outside the giant Colosseum constructed from the days of the Roman empire. Tour guides kept coming and going from every direction, fully distracting Eddie from where his focus needed to stay. Guardians kept passing by with the humans. They were on assignment, and Feassure kept growling, notifying Eddie that the Guardians he had once trained to fight with were currently around him.

People kept coming from all directions and taking pictures. Their starstruck eyes kept trying to imagine what the structure looked like when the Colosseum was first built. Eddie had visited this place so many times; it was nothing special anymore. The exception was he knew the world would not be the same once he released the Prince of Rome. He wasn't ignorant to the fact that the Greater Demon had been underground for centuries and, once released, could possibly be responsible for the loss of thousands of lives. The potential for a Greater Demon to consume like a vicious wildfire, devouring everything in its path was far greater than not.

Fear began giving him anxiety, just thinking how crazy and reckless the Prince of Rome could be. Eddie was starting to lose his mind, and he wasn't banished underground. The demon would now be so hungry for destruction after thousands of years, and even Feassure seemed to be hesitant to lead them where they needed to go. The exception for Feassure was his fear of Lucifer was stronger than any other demon out there.

Suddenly, Feassure took off on the leash, and Eddie began to chase after him. "Slow down you bloody…thing!" he yelled.

Feassure quickly turned into a dark corner. Eddie had almost passed him, then suddenly he realized Feassure was no longer a dog but back to the shape of the lizard. When Eddie approached, they both became like a canvas, painted onto the background of the walls surrounding them. Eddie realized no one could see him anymore, and to his surprise, he noticed three Guardians pass him by. Eddie wanted to grab them and hold them. He took in the sweet aroma and wanted more than anything to follow them. He desperately wanted to ask if they knew anything about the only Guardian who traded the secrets to the greatest kingdom in existence. He was so desperate to find if he would ever get a second chance.

Unfortunately, Feassure pulled back on the leash and made Eddie go in through a hallway. The darkened access granted them the ability to be hidden from everyone who could possibly see them. They passed all the tourists, and Eddie noticed the sweet smell of the Guardians became overwhelmed with the stench of death. Eddie knew the aroma undeniably, only because of his interaction with the other Greater Demons. The further Feassure led Eddie down a series of corridors, the stronger the smell became. The scent was suffocating and thick. The voices above, with all the tourists, guides, and employees, grew completely silent.

Feassure stopped at an old wooden door. In a slow rhythmic motion, he noticed a draft kept slowly seeping out and back out every ten seconds. Eddie froze in place. He wasn't sure if he should knock since just opening up the door and introducing himself sounded reckless. Nothing sounded normal for him in this situation, but then again, he realized his whole existence wasn't exactly normal.

"Stranger things have happened," he said quietly to himself. He looked down at the lizard and waited for some sort of signal or clue on how to approach his current situation. Feassure gave no indication. He ended up crawling behind Eddie and sat as far back as he could.

"Bloody lizard," Eddie said, looking annoyed toward Feassure. "All right, then, let's press forward, shall we?"

Feassure shook his head no.

"Bloody coward," Eddie replied.

Eddie braced himself before he pulled on the iron rod connected to the door. His heart had not raced this fast in his entire life span. He was anxious and incredibly afraid. He had encountered Belial, Legion, Morajes, and even the Prince of Persia. He learned over his thousand-year existence how to approach each one of them in a precise and meticulous way. So how would he know to react around a demon, a Greater Demon, who had been locked up since the fall of the Roman empire? "Well, only one way to find out," he said under his breath.

He pulled the door open and became blasted by a gust of air that smelled so stale he began to dry-heave. The air felt so thick he could actually taste it. It took him a few minutes to debate his entry, gain composure, and fight his fear before he could pass through the corridor. Complete darkness surrounded him, and Eddie had to feel along the wall as he continued his way down a circular stairway to God only knew where. A small light came from the distance, and the gusts of air kept blowing his way as the stench grew stronger with each step.

Feassure did not follow Eddie down the dark path but placed himself like a statue, solid in his stance, outside the door. Eddie was hoping that Feassure would help keep anyone away if they came his direction. From the look of the actual hallway, it didn't appear to be a frequently visited door.

As the light grew brighter, Eddie found himself in a masculine arena. He thought to himself this had to be the location where the gladiators were enslaved and practiced to fight for their life. Directly in front of him appeared as though to be a giant curtain. The cloth had faded in color, and if Eddie looked just right, he could see that the fabric was once purple with some red along the bottom. Thousands of webs spread across the tapestry, and as Eddie grew closer, he realized the Prince of Roam, breathing, was directly under the enormous cloak. He slowly crouched down and made his way around the giant beast beneath the surface. Just as Eddie was about to get to the other side, a booming voice with heavy vibration came from under the cloak.

"Has the master finally summoned me?" he asked.

Eddie froze. His legs would not and could not move. Eddie hated Belial because he didn't have a sense of humor and couldn't help but wonder, would this beast be any different? He secretly hoped they both would kill each other.

"*Well?*" the voice rumbled, causing Eddie to fall back. The voice had such depth the dirt began to fall from overhead in the enlarged area. Eddie began to feel dirt clots and dust particles fall on top of his hair and shoulders.

He began dusting himself off as he replied, "I...uh...my name is Eddie. And... I have been sent to...to release you," he tried to say, hoping it would let the Prince of Rome know they were on the same side.

The beast under the cloak began to move, and the colosseum shook directly under Eddie's feet. Eddie jumped from shock when felt Feassure attach himself at his side. The little frightened demon was so scared he almost knocked Eddie down. "Ah, so you're back, huh? Thanks," he said, looking down toward Feassure. The action by the demon made Eddie feel even more anxious than he already was. He had to ask himself, if Feassure was afraid, what should he be?

The Greater Demon grew taller and taller, rising to the height of the room. As he stood completely up, his body barely fit the underground arena. His presence left little space for Eddie to see anything other than the Prince's lower half of his body. Feassure grew a death grip while he crawled up onto Eddie's back, holding on for dear life. He realized, though, that the Prince of Rome was massive, and Belial wouldn't stand a chance against him, which Was perfect because he wanted him to be taken out. He would have to find a way to antagonize this Greater Demon to the point he cut his head off.

"Who...sent...you?" the Prince of Rome asked with the same base vibrating the walls in the room.

"Well, erm"—he cough—"I...well...my name is Eddie, and good old Lucifer sent me down, you know...to, well...release you," Eddie stated after he debated on running away or not.

"Ah, so the Prince of Darkness...needs me once again?" the Prince of Rome asked. The Greater Demon began to lean down to get a closer look at Eddie. He had not seen another mortal for thousands of years. He didn't look much different except Eddie's clothes looked ridiculous.

The Prince of Rome resembled every stereotype Eddie imagined from the height of the Roman Empire. His handsome face was utterly chiseled to perfection. Eddie noticed the incredible muscles showing through the tattered cloak, and his throat suddenly dropped to his stomach. *This* was the demon he was releasing, and he knew that chaos was about to be released to destroy Europe. Eddie hesitated before he answered. He knew Lucifer would punish him if he didn't release the Greater Demon. "The truth is...the boy...the one Lucifer has been waiting for since Christ died—"

"*Don't say his name to me!*" the Prince of Rome thundered. "His resurrection was the reason my beautiful empire fell. My brothers, Babylon and Greece, fell before me, but I was supposed to last. I should have been the ruler over all the men in my region"

"Is the Prince of Persia still around?" a voice suddenly asked from behind Eddie and Feassure.

"I recognize that lizard."

Eddie spun around and noticed a man who appeared similar to himself. They were similar in stature and looks, and Eddie had never seen him before.

"A thousand pardons. I was with The prince of Rome when Lucifer banished us," the man said.

"Us? Who the bloody hell are you?" Eddie asked, beginning to panic.

"My name is Gatticus. I was a Roman officer who made sure to cover Christ's burial tomb to ensure he wouldn't get out. Just before I was asked, Lucifer offered me everlasting life if I did all I could to ensure "the son of God" didn't escape. I am going to assume you are smart enough to know that didn't happen. When Lucifer found out that Jesus had left the tomb, the Prince of Rome and I were banished. Since we were cast underground, we obviously became friends."

"Wait, you mean you have been alive all this time down here?" Eddie asked, surprised by the fact that someone else had also been offered eternal life.

"Yes, I have," Gatticus answered.

Eddie stood, stunned that another person had eternal life just like he did. Maybe he could possibly have a friend now? Someone to pal around with until the end finally came? After thinking for a moment, he decided to share his own story. "Well, I was offered eternal life as well, except I ended up becoming a fallen angel. I have regretted the choice ever since," Eddie said in all honesty. The minute the words left his mouth, he began to regret his moment of vulnerability.

The Prince of Rome glared down at him. Feassure crawled off Eddie's back and stood in front of Gatticus. Gatticus smirked. "How could you say such words against our master?"

"What do you mean? You have been down here all this time. Life has completely passed you by, and you aren't angry?" Eddie questioned, completely baffled.

"He said he would come for us and, look, he has," Gatticus answered.

Eddie realized he did not want this man with him to pal around with. Gatticus had to be utterly mad. Eddie wondered how could anyone stay underground for centuries and not regret making such a decision.

"Well, I guess you are free to go," Eddie said plainly and annoyed.

"Since you have been given eternal life...have you traveled the world?" Gatticus asked.

"Yes," Eddie answered, feeling defeated. Suddenly, all of his hairs stood on end. Eddie instantly knew Lucifer was approaching behind him.

"Feassure, come," Lucifer called to the lizard. As Feassure made his way over to Lucifer, he gently stroked the top of his head. "You did well. I knew you would find him."

The Prince of Rome got down on one knee, as did Gatticus. Lucifer approached both of them, and they each kissed his hand. Eddie thought the Prince of Rome looked ridiculous with his massive body kissing Lucifer's tiny hand. Eddie made a half attempt with a curtsy. He didn't want to get chewed out for not showing respect, which he didn't deserve.

"Eddie! I knew you wouldn't let us down," Morajes said from behind Eddie. She kissed him on the cheek and left a red kiss mark on his face.

Eddie didn't even bother to wipe the lipstick off his cheek. He simply couldn't because he felt paralyzed. Surrounded by evil, he felt he would never have peace in his heart again.

"Well, boys, are you ready to worship me once again?" Lucifer asked as his demeanor changed.

"Yes," they both answered in unison.

The Prince of Rome and Gatticus stood up and noticed Morajes.

"Morajes, you look beautiful as always," Gatticus said while he kissed her on both cheeks.

"You don't look so bad yourself, lover. I think you and I have ancient history to catch up on. Let's get you both out of here and get some sun on that skin of yours. You look horrible, and I simply can't sleep with you looking like that," Morajes said.

"Eddie!" Lucifer snapped, waking Eddie out of his trance.

"Yes?" was all he could say.

"Where is your favorite place to live? I mean, in your whole existence, what country or even city have you loved the most?" Lucifer asked with a smile.

Eddie didn't look up, completely missing Lucifer's smile. If he had caught it, he would have been able to tell good old Lucifer wasn't just asking for his opinion. Lucifer never did anything without underlying intentions. If Eddie wasn't so defeated, he would have been more astute to his surroundings. Unfortunately, he didn't think twice about his answer. Standing still in front of the others, he didn't look up as he answered softly, "Paris."

"Excellent. What do you think, Roman? Should we have your welcome home party in Paris? I have a need for explosives and mass destruction," Lucifer said.

Eddie instantly looked up and couldn't believe what Lucifer just said. Eddie learned the hard way in his thousand-year life span never to trust Lucifer with anything he cared about. He consistently remained careful with his answers, and now, he officially just screwed up. Now the city he loved was about to be under devastating chaos and mass destruction. How could he ever forgive himself for walk straight into Lucifer's hands?

As soon as the thought left Eddie, the ground began to shake. Lucifer snapped his finger, and the Prince of Rome had a fresh wreath on his head with green and gold leaves. His robe transformed into vibrant purple with silver trim. The Prince of Rome shot straight through the roof. All the people in the direct area each became shocked and stunned the moment they felt the vibrations. The groups of tourists began screaming and ran out from the Colosseum. All of the people that had been visiting the historical landmark all made their way out, stunned due to the fact they never felt earthquakes before.

"Gatticus, let's get you into some new clothes. Some of the best places to shop are near here," Morajes said as she hooked her arm into his, and they escorted one another out through the door.

Lucifer approached Eddie with Feassure at his side. "Excellent job, Eddie. It's time for the real fun to begin." He then passed him, and Feassure stayed at Eddie's side. Lucifer took notice that the giant lizard was no longer following him. "Well, let's make sure you don't regret your next thousand years. You can keep the lizard for now. It's pathetic how badly you need a partner."

Eddie looked down at Feassure, completely confused. "Bloody hell, lizard, why would you want to stay with me?"

Feassure took the form of the dog and lifted his leg.

"Great, go ahead and pee on me. It couldn't possibly make my day any worse," Eddie said as he rolled his eyes.

Feassure then put his leg down and rubbed at Eddie's side.

"Oh, you were joking?" Eddie asked with a smile.

Feassure barked. That was the only answered Eddie needed. "I kinda like having you around, but just know I might get you back and pee on you while you sleep."

Feassure growled at Eddie and barked as loud as he possibly could.

Eddie chuckled at his new buddy's reaction. "All right, let's go back and watch the news. I'm sure we will see some sort of chaos in Paris soon," Eddie said with a lump in his throat.

The two made their way back into their hotel room when Feassure found himself another tasty meal. He quickly feasted off two young women that had a high level of cocaine in their system. The hotel staff were already in an uproar from the two murders earlier in the day. The police began questioning all the guests on Eddie's floor, and he grew nervous, hoping Feassure left no evidence linking his room to their crime.

Eddie, feeling sick to his stomach as he sat down on the bed and turned on the news. There it was. All the chaos and destruction Eddie never wanted to witness. He failed to realize the date was Friday the thirteenth. The city of Paris was being attacked by gunmen and suicide bombers, leaving 130 dead and hundreds wounded.

"The attacks were described as an act of war against the French people by the Islamic State militant group," the woman on the television news said.

Eddie knew in the pit of his stomach that Lucifer had the Prince of Persia work with the Prince of Rome. He debated on if he should even keep listening, but he had to know all the details from the attack.

"The first of three explosions occurred outside the Stade de France stadium on the northern side of Paris where France was playing against Germany in an international football game. A man wearing a suicide belt was prevented from entering the stadium after a routine security check detected the explosives. The man apparently backed away and then detonated the explosives he had attached to his body," the woman on the TV announced.

Eddie kept feeling himself get sick. He was trying to hold back the pain in his heart and found himself throwing up as the news reporter spoke on. "The game was attended by President Francois Hollande. Then, a second man detonated his suicide vest outside a different stadium entrance at 9:30, and the president was rushed to safety. A third suicide bomber detonated his explosives shortly after."

Feassure looked at Eddie. Eddie couldn't speak. The report went on to explain several other shootings had taken place in an area known for its fun and beautiful nightlife. He finally hated Lucifer with every blood vessel pumping in his body. He didn't care anymore and began to try to pray, hoping God would hear him and show some form of mercy. Unfortunately, the words couldn't leave his mouth. The harder he tried, the more his body clenched and tightened up. Out of frustration, he started to cry, and the only word he could get to leave his mouth was, "Why?"

He turned off the TV, ran into the bathroom, and began to vomit blood. He felt a slimy lump stuck in the back of his throat. He heaved, over and over again, trying to get whatever it was out of his mouth. It began choking him, and Eddie thought for the first time in his existence he was about to die. Just before he didn't think he could handle anymore, the slimy lump flew out of his mouth. It took him a couple minutes gasping for air before he could look into the toilet and see what was choking him.

As he looked into the toilet, he couldn't believe what he was seeing. It was one of the tendrils Lucifer forced down his throat when he betrayed the kingdom. The tendril wasn't moving, and he grew thankful it was dead. Eddie sat in between the toilet and the bathtub and as he wiped his forehead said, "Thank you, God, thank you."

It took a few minutes for him to realize the words he just spoke, and tears fell from his eyes. His thoughts then flooded his mind and began to wonder maybe he would get his second chance after all. Maybe—just maybe—this could be a sign that he would one day return to heaven. All he wanted, since the moment he bit the apple, was to go back home and be with his group and all the friends he knew. He was thankful that he got to say the word *God* when before he couldn't, due to fear from Lucifer and the restrictions from the slimy sludges he placed in his mouth. He was going to do all he could to remove the rest of them and possibly use Feassure to help him find a Guardian. He had to at least try. He couldn't stop because of fear or because he was tired. He could only stop when he tried everything he possibly could.

THE UTUA CLAN
AND TANK

Several weeks had passed since the celebration, and all of the Guardian groups were back to business as usual. Numerous new students joined every day, and Kinsey enjoyed the chance to meet as many people as she possibly could. Every day of training, every accomplishment made, she seized the chance to grow closer to her group and really learn to know herself.

Kinsey made her way through several simulators in the colosseum with Big Ben and Annie multiple times. The first time she tried to make her way through one, she had to face monkey bars. She had not been on them since she was a kid, so when she tried to make her way across, she slipped off the second bar and landed straight on her face into the mud. She laughed so hard she cried. She kept getting stronger, and her stamina improved drastically the more she worked out. She realized conditions would never be perfect on earth, so it was best to give herself the hardest challenges.

Secretly, she hoped that each time Leilani was handed an assignment, she would be able to go. Kinsey felt she was ready. Each time a group member left, though, she was generally accompanied with at least one other group member. Leilani kept needing Reese more and more because of his talent to completely hide from the Watchers.

One morning, Kinsey was woken by Saige and Jaxon because they were ready to go play. They woke her up from a beautiful sleep, and Kinsey decided to see Lau to practice and maybe train with a new weapon. She didn't like to just sit around and do nothing. She was wondering why she wasn't ready to go with her group members but decided to just wait. Besides, what was the hurry? So she kissed both the children as she left and requested that they check in every couple hours.

Kinsey walked her usual path toward Lau, past the marketplace, and couldn't resist a chocolate-covered strawberry from the same woman who gave her one the first day she arrived. She made her way into the school and noticed Matai, the eldest of the Utua brothers, waiting for her. She found it slightly odd it was just him, considering she never saw him without his brothers or Tank.

"Hey, Matai, why are you on the lonesome?" Kinsey asked.

"Well, let's just say it's my turn to hang out with you today," he replied.

"New babysitter. Awesome! I'm down for whatever you want to do today. I have been feeling kinda antsy and want something new and fun," Kinsey told him honestly.

"Something fun, huh? Are you sure you can handle it?" he asked with a big cheesy smile.

"I took down Tank...do I really need to answer?" she asked, trying to flex muscles she didn't have.

"Okay, we are going to head out toward the beach," Matai stated as he picked up both of their gear.

"Sweet!" Kinsey said as she followed him out. They took the usual route, and as they passed the children's area, Saige and Jaxon came running toward Matai and Kinsey.

"Hey, do you guys want to go play in the water with Mommy and Matai?" she asked as she crouched down to look at them both in their twinkling eyes.

"Heck yeah, man! Let's do this," Jaxon said and tried to flex.

Matai couldn't contain his laughter. "Wow, like mother like child. I think you guys have been hanging out with Thud and Think too much."

Kinsey never really noticed before this moment, but she thought Matai was very handsome. It wasn't a sexual attraction, though, more like a pure notice to his good looks. She admired his perfect teeth and bright smile, his smooth tanned skin with the markings on his body neatly placed, and she was amazed that his sea turtle, decorated on his massive hand, caused Kinsey's to look more like her sea turtle just hatched.

Matai placed Saige on his shoulders, and Jaxon grabbed Kinsey's hand as they continued to walk back to their homes. As they reached the flower-covered hill, the two children began to race toward the shoreline.

"Well, get your swimsuits on and meet me back out here. Even the kids will love it," Matai said as he walked toward his front door.

After a few minutes of quickly changing, they all met back up, and Matai walked into the water. Kinsey waited for a minute, unsure if he wanted to follow her with the children. The crystal-clear water displayed various breeds of fish cruising by, and the waves didn't crash down on the shoreline but slowly rocked back and forth. The breeze from the water filled her senses with a salty yet sweet smell. She could see off in the distance a giant whale slowly rose up, then back down with his tail smashing against water. Kinsey smiled to herself as her children pointed toward a family of dolphins jumping out in the distance. Kinsey had grown to appreciate that the world she was in now could not be ruined by man's selfish desires. No major cities could be surrounded by smog and no oil spilling into the ocean. No more coral reefs dying little by little. She loved this beautiful, serene, and warm world.

"Well, you guys coming or what?" Matai yelled out, breaking Kinsey from her trance.

"Let's go," Kinsey said, and the three of them began swimming out toward Matai. Kinsey didn't realize how fast her kids could swim, and if she was honest with herself, they were better in the water than she was. Kinsey loved the ocean, and she was going to soak up as much as she could in the sun and water. She loved playing with her children, and secretly inside, she wished her other two kids were with her playing in the water too.

"How far out are we going, man?" Kinsey yelled from behind Matai.

"What? Don't tell me you are getting tired. Come on, don't be such an old lady! Besides, we just need to swim around these rocks because we are heading into a cove," he yelled back.

They continued to swim and finally reached the cove. Kinsey's eyes widened at the sight of hundreds of sea turtles completely covering the beach. The two children squealed with excitement and started to swim faster. Kinsey felt the same level of enthusiasm as her children and couldn't seem to remove the smile from her face. The four of them walked up onto the sand, and Kinsey couldn't help but pick a baby turtle up and hold it.

"This is beautiful, Matai, thank you for bringing us here. Are these the turtles you and your brothers take care of?" Kinsey asked.

"Yup, it's one of our trades," Matai answered as he laid down into the sand.

"Saige and Jaxon will never want to leave now. You know that, right? You've seen how they are with the twins' dogs," Kinsey said, still holding the turtle. "You know, I have to admit you and your brothers are hilarious. I genuinely consider myself lucky to be included as your family. I didn't have a big family in life and always wished my sister and I would get close. I always wanted a special bond with her, but it wasn't until just before I died that we were able to let our differences go. I am thankful, though, that I didn't go to the grave with no forgiveness from and toward her," Kinsey stated.

"Something like that doesn't register with me. All I ever relied on was my siblings because they were pretty much all I had. The most important rule we all decided to keep was to be respectful of each family member and nothing comes before family, ever." Matai went into the water to clean off some of the sand from his upper body. He quickly dunked himself in and gradually began to walk back up toward Saige and Jaxon. "So...what was the reason you guys didn't get along? Were you too close in age?"

Kinsey thought for a minute, then answered, "Well, we were nine years apart, and growing up, she always said she couldn't relate to me. That was the answer she gave my mom, anyway. I also know I was a weird kid anyway. The biggest issue I recognized was we expressed our love for each other differently, and we both couldn't catch when the other was trying to express it. I idolized her as a kid, but I think I spent way more time with my parents than she did. So I was kinda needy. I spent a lot of time with my dad at car shows, and we would go out to the Salton Sea for the day and put money on the railroad tracks and try to find the coins after the train passed."

"I can't imagine how that could feel," Matai said.

"It hurt. I hated it. I would watch my friends and their siblings interact, and deep down, I wished we could be friends as sisters. Don't get me wrong, there were times when we were close, but when my life spiraled out of control, she just couldn't understand the pain and chaos," Kinsey replied.

"Why do you think she kept her distance from you? Do you think that was the main reason because of the chaos?" Matai asked.

"Probably. My bet would be yes. Please understand I am not putting all of it on her. I was a daddy's girl and a mommy do girl. I always went to church with my mom. I needed affection. I think my sister struggled with me because I was so much younger and was interested in completely different things. I needed more time and attention from my parents than she did." Kinsey began picking up different turtles to hold before she continued. "In all honesty, the only reason I received more attention was because of my poor decisions. Most of them were made due to a lovely condition called bipolar disorder. My sister was very independent and had made all the right decisions. She married her high school sweetheart, she earned her master's degree, and lived in the house with the white picket fence. My sister is beautiful, incredibly smart, and extremely hard working. Ironically, I can see clearly now, why she couldn't relate to me." The sudden epiphany made Kinsey lightly laugh to herself.

Kinsey knew she was rambling, yet she realized she had never been able to express the way she felt toward her older sibling. She was rarely able to talk about it with her immediate family because everyone became defensive. Kinsey looked to Matai, hoping for some outside wisdom before she continued. "We did have good years too. I still love her more than anything and can't wait until I see her again. I am sure she will be so grateful and thankful that I have no more chaos." Kinsey giggled for a second and continued, "At one point in time, we lived close to each other, and she had just recently given birth to my second nephew, Aidan. When he was six months old, I remember going to her house, grabbing everything Aidan would need for the evening, and just telling her that I was taking him for the night. I told my sister that her husband should take her out." Kinsey paused to look back at the sea. A smile crossed Kinsey's face just picturing Aidan as the cute little six-month-old baby and the ridiculous lobster costume he wore for his first Halloween.

She looked back at Matai and continued, "Don't get me wrong, I fully appreciated when my sister and I had our great moments and how much she did for my daughter over the years. I was jealous when she and her husband took Grace across Europe. I would have shaped myself in a suitcase just to go. So it was things like that, which are huge things, that showed her love." A single teardrop fell from her cheek, and Kinsey turned her head away from Matai. She wiped off her face and decided to play with the kids, building a little sand castle.

"Man… I'm sorry. I can understand the pain from my family. In our lives, our upbringing wasn't so great," Matai said. "You may have had a small family, but at least you had your parents. Can you imagine how it could have felt to lose your mom and dad or never have them in your life? My brothers, Leilani and I, all grew up in separate homes. We were raised by our aunts and uncles because our mother was so addicted to meth and whatever drug she could get her hands on. What made it worse is she found herself swimming in the bottom of a bottle…when she couldn't get her hands on the drugs," Matai said.

"That is a situation I don't think I could have handled. My parents were my everything. They still are along with my kids. I can't wait until they get here and get to meet Saige and Jaxon," Kinsey replied.

"That's why we were and still are so important to each other. None of us ever knew who our real fathers were. Missing a father feels like an empty hole in your chest along with feeling completely abandoned. Add insult to injury with a meth-addicted mother, and it made us feel unworthy," Matai said as he lowered his head to face the sand.

"It breaks my heart to hear you say that. I hated seeing kids suffer, even when I was a kid myself." Kinsey replied.

"Our aunts and uncles tried their best to help break down who may share the same father. We realized Grunt and I share the same dad because we look so much alike and we are the oldest. Mongo and Cronk share the same dad, and obviously, Thud and Thunk have the same. We had no clue who Leilani's dad was. Unfortunately, since I am the oldest, I had to witness the majority of her destructive melt-downs. It finally broke me inside when Leilani was born because I never trusted any of the men my mother kept around," Matai said.

"How did it feel each time she got pregnant since you are the oldest?" Kinsey asked.

"Each time, she swore up and down that she would clean up from her addiction. I believe she meant it, but she just didn't have the strength to do it. When I saw Leilani for the first time in the hospital, I knew I officially had to become the family protector. In my eyes, there is something precious in the heart of a little girl. I was so grateful that the aunt who was raising Grunt and I took Leilani away from her. My mother died of an overdose shortly after, and it's sad to admit, but I am glad she was gone. I believe deep down all my aunt and uncles were relieved as well because the cycle was finally over. They were tired of hurting since she couldn't get her act together," Matai said.

Kinsey turned to look toward her own children and couldn't imagine them so lost in a system made of nothing more than a vortex of utter despair. Matai's words echoed in her thoughts, and she kept trying to imagine all the Utuas as children. The most difficult thing to imagine was all of the brothers separated and dispersed among different family members. She felt compassion for their mother, knowing how difficult an addiction can truly be.

"We were no angels toward our aunts and uncles. Fortunately for us, though, they vowed to never allow us into a horrible system. They would do whatever it took to keep us all together. The hardest part for our relatives was my brothers and I became so angry. We felt shattered from watching our mother care more about the drugs than any of us. Our aunts and uncles tried to help and keep us all in line by going to church every Sunday," Matai said as he began playing with Jaxon and Saige in the sand.

"Did you guys hate going as a kid? I know I did because I wanted to stay home and watch cartoons," Kinsey replied.

"Oddly enough, we didn't mind going. We looked forward to the youth group because it was our time alone with each other. Those bonding moments gave us the peace we desperately needed. Each one of us grew addicted to the laughter, and we just brought out the best in each other," Matai said.

"How did Leilani feel about being the only girl amongst you monsters?" Kinsey asked.

"She loved it. She was and still is the baby. She had a separate class than the rest of us because of her age, so in church, she wasn't distracted by us morons," Matai said with a huge smile. "Man, you should have seen Thud and Thunk as kids. They are nothing now compared to what they were then. Our laughter was our source of comfort and escape."

"So how did you guys finally get the healing you all needed? How did Leilani do as the only girl?" Kinsey asked.

Matai kept building the sandcastle with the kids as he replied, "The good thing about her being the only girl and the youngest, she took everything she learned seriously. She always had a fire inside her that the rest of us didn't comprehend. I remember she was about ten, and she said to all of us she would die for her faith."

"She said that at ten?" Kinsey asked, completely shocked.

"Yeah, she did. Interestingly enough, we could all tell she meant it. Leilani was the first one of all us kids to truly believe and understand what it meant to have a belief in God. Growing up, it wasn't just us kids from my mom. We each lived with our cousins, and the total number of kids was sixteen."

"Holy Lord, your family didn't mess around when it comes to kids," Kinsey teased.

"I know, right? Well, actually, they did mess around if you think about it," Matai laughed and replied. "Anyway," he continued,

"Leilani genuinely believed and acted as though she was an adult when it came down to her faith and belief in God. One Sunday, after we were headed to the traditional lunch after church, she asked all of us out loud if we believe that God had a Son, and his Son died for all of us."

"Yes!" Saige and Jaxon said in unison.

"Silly kiddos, that's what his sister asked him!" Kinsey said with a wide smile.

"We know," Saige said. "We just wanted to make sure you two knew."

Matai and Kinsey looked at one another, and both were a little shocked at her response.

Matai smiled at the two kids, then continued, "My aunt who was raising Grunt, Leilani, and I turned around, completely stunned that the youngest actually took church seriously. Leilani went on to say that she had asked God into her heart that day and she didn't think it was too much to ask if God sent his only Son to die for us. My family and I were stunned silent. Grunt and I realized not to make fun of her and asked her why she believed so much in the Bible. The only answer she said was, 'I know it in my heart, like I know my own name.'

"One by one, each of us, including my cousins, accepted Christ into our hearts and began to heal from all the agony our mother caused. There was something about her spark for the Lord that my brothers and I wanted to feel. We wanted the same peace our sister felt." Matai stopped talking and continued helping the kids build a larger sandcastle for all the baby turtles to live in.

"So I am curious...did you guys all get here at the same time?" Kinsey hoped the question wasn't too morbid.

"Yeah, my siblings and I died in a car crash. We were all in the same car, and I was driving. I was taking everyone home from school, and we never made it. I don't remember what happened, exactly, and it's not recorded in the House of Memories," Matai said, plain and simple.

"So...how did Tank get to become a part of you guys?" Kinsey asked, trying to look Matai in the eyes.

"Tank's life was worse than ours, if you can believe that. He had no one up until his early thirties," Matai answered, looking up from his little sandcastle.

"How did Leilani get picked to be his Guardian? I assume you guys all went on missions together?" Kinsey asked.

"Truth be told, we saw Christ the minute we got here. He comes at the deepest moment a soul needs him," Matai said.

"Yeah… I have been told that a time or two. Still haven't had mine. So what was it that you guys needed to know?" Kinsey asked, remembering Reese had said he desperately needed answers about Mark. She assumed it was the same type of situation.

"We wanted to know if our mother was here, and he took us to the Hall of Mirrors. I don't know if Reese has shown you the room or if you know what it is, but she was asleep in the mirror. She looked beautiful and at peace. All the years of drugs and running the streets was officially removed from her body and face. We all just held on to each other, allowing the tears to flush all those years of agony, torment, and pain away. We told Jesus that we had to stay together. We were not going to be separated anymore. He honored our request, and from that moment on, we all function as one unit. He chose to have Leilani be a team leader because of her ability to discern situations, and she is a natural born leader. She can read between the lines faster than any of us," Matai said.

"Sounds like Annie." Kinsey said.

"Who do you think trained and sparred with Annie, besides Lau and Big Ben? She was the first, even before there was an official group. Leilani can kick some serious Wu Tang, if you know what I mean," he said with a smile.

"So with that said, how did you get assigned to Tank?" Kinsey asked as she sat down next to the castle and the baby sea turtles. "He told me he was in prison but didn't say anything beyond that. Was it hard to be a Guardian in a place filled with so much evil?"

"Tank was our first assignment, and yes, he needed all of us at one time. When we first met him, he was in solitary confinement, serving his sixth out of eight years. None of us could understand how he had the ability to survive in that kind of solitude. Men all around him began losing their minds, and it was easy to understand why. To keep his mind from utter despair, he gave himself a routine or a schedule to pass time. In doing that, it kept him from losing his sanity. All of us ached as we watched over him." Matai had stopped playing in the sand and was looking back at Kinsey. "You want to know more about his life in prison, don't you?"

"Yeah, from the minute he said the word *prison*, I had about a thousand questions," she answered honestly.

"Well, his childhood was similar to ours, unfortunately, and I believe that's why God sent us to him. A random person who knows nothing about how it feels to have an absent parent, let alone two, would be able to relate to a man like him. On top of that, his mom had an addiction, like our mom," Matai said.

Kinsey nodded her head and answered, "I see what you mean. Someone like me wouldn't know how to comfort or give hope to a man like him."

"Exactly," said Matai. "He needed Guardians with strength and power to survive a life sentence that started when he was just sixteen years old." Matai stood up and slowly walked back into the warm sea water. He kept letting the gentle waves tickle his feet before he continued.

"His life in prison started at sixteen? Wow. I can't imagine how awful he must have felt," Kinsey said as she kept trying to picture Tank as a teenager. "How devastating it must have been to be locked away for life and completely forgotten about."

"Christ had us look over his past in the House of Memories. You know, in the Hall of Infinium?" Matai asked.

Kinsey nodded her head yes.

"Christ wanted us to fully appreciate and understand Tank's childhood so we could grasp his thought process when he grew into a man. How else would we be able to relate unless we saw his memories and knew his past? Most of all, he wanted all of us to realize even a person locked away in prison is still worthy of God's love and acceptance. Tank didn't have an understanding of what a normal family is supposed to look like," Matai said.

The two children began making little mud patties in the sand and, shortly after, started playing splash tag in the crystal-clear beach water. Matai and Kinsey jumped into the water and decided to play, boys against girls. Matai kept grabbing both of the kids and threw them out as far as they could fly into the water. Saige and Jaxon screamed at the top of their lungs, begging for more. Finally, Matai's arms grew tired, and they all walked back to lay on the beach.

"Okay, now where were we?" Kinsey asked with anticipation. "You were saying something about how Tank didn't have an understanding of a normal life?" Kinsey reminded Matai.

"Right. Okay, so life went wrong because his mother was a severe alcoholic. Now, don't get me wrong, he had his own choices to make, but given his circumstances, his decisions were based on all he knew. I mean, he really didn't stand a chance. My brothers and I definitely understand and empathize with him. Our mother was just as broken as his mother, but her afflictions were caused by some type of abuse. She only had two ways of coping with the demons of her past—overzealous Christianity or stupid, belligerent, and incoherent drunkenness. Those two extremes never mix well. The results of those moments led to many visits from Social Services since he rarely went to school. Over and over again, Tank was taken from her and placed in boys' homes." Matai stopped speaking for a minute, allowing his face to reflect Tank's life.

He laid back down on the sand to soak up the sun. He closed his eyes, and Kinsey went to sit beside him in the sand while continuing to build the sandcastle with the children. It took Matai a minute before he spoke again.

"I believe the saddest memory I saw that affected all of us, and I mean all of us, made us cry. Tank was about twelve, and his brother, Josiah, and sister, Alyssa, had just been taken away to go live with their dads. His mother was not taking care of herself or the three kids. There was no food, they were dirty, and none of them had been to school. Tank never knew who his father was, so all he had was his mother. When his siblings were taken away to be raised by their dads, something broke in him. To see the Watcher influenced his mother to drink the way she did was incredible. She drank one fifth of whiskey every single day. Can you imagine how much alcohol that is?" Matai opened his eyes to look at Kinsey.

"I know my grandfather was an alcoholic. I never met him, though, because he basically killed himself drinking long before I was ever born. My mom rarely ever spoke of him, but since I have died and become a part of this beautiful kingdom, it's hard for me to imagine the man I see now drunk," Kinsey said.

"Well, think about it. A fifth a day is fifty-two gallons consumed a year. It took three years to actually kill her." Matai continued, "Anyway, Social Services had just made its grand entrance, and Tank was somehow left alone with his mother. He felt like the walls seemed to be closing in on them in the small apartment, and his mother's only reaction was to drink more. That's when Tank snapped. He was only twelve years old at the time, and he asked himself, how could she betray his other siblings so quickly? That bottle was the reason he didn't have the mother he needed and deserved. That bottle was the reason horrible men took advantage and abused her. Tank couldn't take the loneliness anymore, and he was tired of catching his mother passed out with lit cigarettes and almost burning herself."

"It breaks my heart to imagine any child living the way Tank did," Kinsey replied.

"It only got worse when Tank swiped the whiskey bottle from her hands and began screaming at her from the top of his lungs as he ran down the street. His mom chased after him, begging for him to give her back the bottle. She looked so disheveled with a ponytail half falling down to her shoulders and makeup smeared all over her eyes and lips. She had on only one sock, a tank top, and just her underwear. It reminded all of us of our mother. Tank suddenly stopped in the middle of the street and turned to face his mother with tears falling from his dirty face. There was a fire burning in his eyes as he began screaming at her from the top of his lungs, '*Why?* Why do you need this? This is the reason they take us away. *This...stupid... bottle* is the reason those men hurt you and then they leave you! Why, Mom? Why aren't we important to you?'"

Matai paused, remembering the moment as if he was still there, and continued, "His mother slowly approached him and got down on one knee. She looked into Tank's eyes, pleading to God for him to understand a woman's pain that a boy his age should never need to know. A neighbor nearby, walking their dog, couldn't remove their eyes from the tormenting scene. His mother tried to pretend the person didn't exist while she slowly and delicately placed her fragile hands on his shoulders. Tears were streaming down her face as she spoke, 'Baby, my precious boy. Samuel, I wish I had a good enough answer for you, but I... I just don't know if you could understand how deep my pain goes. You are my special guy, and Mommy is just...just so broken inside. You are my whole world. I know deep down you are the only man who will never leave nor hurt me. I know it's hard to understand why. I promise, though, I will make it right. Okay? We will get Alyssa and Josiah back. We will be a whole family again. I know we can do it. You and me. I promise, Nathan, but please...please give the bottle back to me.'"

Matai's eyes had begun welling up. It took him a second before he could finish the story. Kinsey's heart melted inside, knowing Matai understood Tank's pain. Matai, as the oldest, felt the same responsibility for all of his brothers and sister. She let him take his time before he spoke again.

"Tank looked so defeated as his shoulders just slumped, and he slowly handed her the bottle. His mother wrapped her arms around him, and she began to sob uncontrollably, and not even the great Tank could fight his own tears that day in his mother's arms."

Kinsey's heart shattered for Tank, and she noticed that even her two children were listening. Saige and Jaxon's facial expressions appeared as though they understood the feelings and emotions Tank experienced.

"I can't even imagine. I may have had a small family, but I had a great childhood. What did he do to end up in prison, though? Especially with a life sentence as a kid?" Kinsey asked.

"His mother never did get Alyssa and Josiah back and hurled herself into a deeper and darker depression. They lived in Colorado where the state followed the three-strike law. Since his mother never made him go to school, he had a truancy warrant out for him, and that became his first strike. Not his mom but him, a kid who didn't know better. Social Services would eventually catch up to him and place him in some kind of boys' home. Every time they did, though, he would run away at the first chance he got and always ran straight back to his mom.

"She wasn't about to rat on her own son. His caseworker would consistently stop by to try and catch him, but his mom would just hide him. One day, in juvenile court, the judge asked him if he was just going to run back to his mom again." Matai stopped for a minute to watch Saige and Jaxon. "He told the judge honestly yes, he would, and to add insult to injury, they kept trying to call his mom to come pick him up. They couldn't get a hold of her!"

Kinsey's mind began spinning. How was that possible? Their lives were so painful. No wonder they all had the same color she did. She began observing her children along with him. After a few moments of silence, she finally said, "Nothing was ever more important than my babies. I may not have always made the greatest decisions in the men I dated, but my kiddos were my world. I feel sorry for his mom, though. An addiction isn't so easy to give up, and those who never suffered from one can understand. They think it's so simple to just drop the one thing that takes the pain away. The addiction always took...takes the pain away."

Matai realized that Kinsey had corrected herself. He knew she had not been back to the Hall of Infinium to go over her memories and also knew some raw emotion would come out when she did. He decided to continue discussing Tank's childhood. "Exactly," Matai continued, "he did understand from an early age, though, that he needed to take care of his mom because she literally didn't even know how to take care of herself. With his experiences, he quickly learned the only way for him to survive was to hustle on the streets. He got caught on several occasions trying to steal food when him and his sister were hungry as their mother lay passed out on the couch. After catching him on several attempts, the store owner finally called the police to make him learn a lesson. That became strike two, believe it or not, because they knew his mom and they were tired of her not taking care of him."

"Wait, what?" Kinsey asked. "You would think if each time he was caught stealing food to make a sandwich and not candy, the store owner would take the hint the kid was hungry."

"Sad how some people are so clueless, isn't it?" Matai replied. "Anyway, because of that moron, Tank turned to the men and so-called friends his mother surrounded herself with. He noticed they always had money, so he began watching them. Though he was young, he was wise for his age. He learned from them selling drugs is a quick way to earn money. Regardless of her affliction with alcohol, she and him were very close, so he felt he needed to take care of the family. She was all he really had and all he knew.

"Unfortunately, though, his last strike came, and it was for the most ridiculous reason ever. After everything the poor kid went through, he received no mercy. He still wasn't an adult yet, so they placed him in another boys' home until he could face the judge, but like he always did, he ran back to his mom. The problem, though, it appeared like it was just a regular home with no bars or fences. Tank, at the first opportunity, just walked straight out the door. Unfortunately for him, it was then considered an escape, and that was the nail in the coffin because it had then become a felony. Poor kid barely had a chance."

Kinsey felt overwhelmed by Tank's story. It made complete sense now when she defeated him on the mat why that kiss distracted him as much as it did. "So what happened to him after he was sentenced?"

"This just adds insult to injury. It was close to Thanksgiving, and his mom came to visit him at the newest youth center he was being held in. Due to his track record, they put him in lockdown and kept him in chains. He had been in a fight that day, and his eye was swelling up when they told him his mom had come to see him for a visit. We all sat, and our hearts sank when they embraced because we knew what was about to take place. She was sitting at the table, and they were allowed to hug for less than thirty seconds due to his restrictions. He could smell the alcohol on her breath, and she began swaying slightly in front of him."

Matai stopped and looked out over the horizon, sighed, and then continued, "She gently touched his swollen eye, ran her fingers through his hair, and tried to hold onto him as long as she could. When the guard told the two their time was up, she didn't want to let go and stayed with her arms tightly wrapped around him. Finally, she kissed his head, told him she loved him, and left. As if it couldn't have been any worse, it was the last time he saw her. She died the following morning."

"I... I... There are no words, are there? I can see now why you consider him family." The look on Kinsey's face represented the broken heart she felt for her team member. All this time, Tank appeared as this monster of a man, a dangerous beast with a battle ax. Yet his true nature represented a boy sent away for life to fight against the nastiest monsters that were known to mankind. Tank had been sent to live with what most people considered the waste and trash from society. A boy of sixteen forced to become a man and live a life of not knowing who to trust, racial hatred, and never a chance to be free again.

"No, there really aren't any words to describe him or his upbringing that would do any justice," Matai answered.

Saige and Jaxon made Matai and Kinsey realize they had been in the sea turtle bay for the entire day. With the lowering of the sun, they needed to head back and get ready for dinner. The fellowship of friends and family along with the Grand Worship Hall had been designed from the beginning of time as a recharging for the soul. The bonding of souls throughout the kingdom kept families and friends close and mutually healthy.

"Well, let's swim back. The turtles need to rest, so let's let them sleep. Okay, kiddos?" Kinsey said as they each began to swim back to the shore toward their homes. "Thank you again, Matai, for today. Every sunrise has brought me new surprises, and I can't get enough of it." Kinsey paused for a minute, then from behind him, swimming, she said with a smile, "It's also pretty awesome to be able to call you my brother."

Matai looked back to her and smiled, making sure all of his pearly whites were brightly showing. "This is what family is for."

DOUBLE COLOR...
DOUBLE CONCERN

Lau had been unable to keep his mind off the double color since Kinsey came in to present herself before him in her new gear. Since Lau was a problem-solver by nature, deep down in the pit of his stomach, he knew this was no minor coincidence. He had been hearing random whispers among the elder Guardians. He heard about a previous Guardian who went missing shortly after his first mission and was never seen again. Lau never gave the whispers a second thought at first. After all, if the double color had any serious significance, Itherial would have surely mentioned it to him.

Lau felt determined to find Itherial, though, wherever he may be. The situation felt concerning enough that when he came to visit him about the boy, there would have been something mentioned about a different Guardian assigned with a double color. Lau ran their conversation through his head over and over again, and every single time, he came to the same conclusion. Itherial never hinted to anything about a new Guardian with a double color.

"Sifu... Sifu...can I speak with you?" Leilani called out. She entered into the school with all her brothers and everyone in the group with the exception of Tank and Kinsey. They barged in quickly, distracting Lau from these thoughts. "I really need to speak with you," she said with a pleading look in her eyes.

"I assume...you wish to discuss your newest member's color?" Lau asked in English, knowing his slow pace would allow Leilani to calm down.

"Yes! No one has explained anything to us. We have heard someone was presented a double color years and years ago. Our problem is, we don't know who it was or where they are now. Do you know anything about this?" Leilani asked with desperation.

Lau looked into her eyes, and the truth was, he had no answers. "I heard of a double color years and years ago but never gave it much thought." Lau turned to Reese and then spoke, "When she received her color, what was said? Who gave it to her?"

"I know about as much as both of you do. I saw the color, and...and... Debbie and I were both just as shocked. She said she had done red and silver gear about a thousand years ago." Reese felt guilty he didn't ask more questions and wished he had more answers for them. "I'm sorry, Lau, I... I have no answers either."

Lau looked into each one of their eyes and decided it was time to go speak with the archangels. "Why don't we all go and meet with Itherial, Gabriel, and Michael? I believe they would be able to give all of us an explanation," Lau said as he slowly turned and began walking out toward the colosseum.

Everyone looked toward one another, and then to Leilani. She agreed and followed Lau out of the school toward the colosseum. Every single one of them knew the archangels would be there, welcoming the new arrivals, enjoying the family reunions, and assigning the new people their responsibilities within the complicated structure. The group continued in silence, each one of them secretly hoping that Tank could occupy Kinsey's attention long enough so she would not try to look for anyone.

Matai revealed to Tank that he had spoken of Tank's early years and what brought him to prison. "Take her to the turtle bay and talk about prison. Oddly enough, she is incredibly interested. I am guessing Kinsey never knew anyone with macabre stories that only you can tell, brother."

Tank took note, and just like every other Guardian, his memories hovered in his mind like a thick dense fog. He would have to take a quick visit to the Hall of Infinium and try to remember some stories that could take time to distract Kinsey. He decided to take her back to turtle bay as she requested and hoped the group would fill him in when they all returned.

Thud and Thunk explained to Saige and Jaxon why their mother would be spending the day with Tank. The twins told the children if their mother came back too early, it was up to them to complete her distraction. That way, she would look for the children and be occupied with them before she would find the members of her team. The twins figured it would help the group out and promised the children that if they distracted their mother before everyone got back, Saige and Jaxon would be able to keep the two dogs, Roxy and Hendrix, overnight. The children pinky swore to keep the promise.

Tank surprised Kinsey when he knocked on her door first thing that morning. She was half awake, assuming she would be greeted with Reese's cheerful early morning face but instead found herself gazing at Mr. Serious himself.

"Uh, hi," was all Kinsey could say.

"Morning. Wanna come help me with the turtles today? It's my turn to make sure they have everything they need," Tank said.

"Sure, let me just get Saige and Jaxon and—"

"They are with the twins. Thud and Thunk took them out to play with the little dogs, so it's just you and I today," Tank interrupted.

Kinsey thought it was incredibly odd she would be alone with Tank. Unusual moments happened all the time, but this moment seemed to really capture every last bit of her attention. "Okay. Well, then…give me a few minutes, and I'll be back out," she replied.

Kinsey got herself ready to go back into the warm ocean water and felt herself excited and curious. Why was it just her and Tank today?

Walking out of her door to meet Tank at the water's edge, she realized there was no point in questioning this new life anymore. Everything would work out as it was supposed to, even if she was left completely in the dark.

Kinsey approached Tank with her biggest smile and asked, "Ready?"

"Always," he answered.

Swimming in the water, Kinsey's pace was slow but steady. She felt the situation seemed odd because Tank was never alone. Never! The silence between the two of them became deafening, so she decided to start her version of "small talk."

"So they gave you the day off? That seems slightly odd, considering you are never without any of the Utuas," Kinsey observed with one eyebrow raised toward Tank.

They reached the turtle bay and, in unison, lay in the sand and began soaking up the sun.

"It's my turn to entertain you, I guess," Tank replied flatly without looking back to Kinsey.

"Don't you mean it's your turn to distract me? I may be the newest, but I am certainly not dumb," Kinsey said with a smile. "Tank, they never leave you behind, so just tell me, are they all weirded out because of my color? I ask because I am weirded out by it too," Kinsey said, cutting straight to the point. She knew when Leilani mentioned the previous day they all had a so-called "mission" but decided to leave Tank behind. It had to just be a facade. "All right, spill it, and don't leave any juicy details out. What's going on, Sir Tank?" Kinsey asked.

Tank finally looked at her and sat up. As he sat beside her in the sand, he gently grabbed one of the turtles to hold, and his expression looked as though he was deep in thought. He didn't say anything for a couple minutes, then decided to go with, "So... Matai told you about my past?"

Kinsey knew he was killing time, and she knew she would get her answers eventually, so she decided to follow his lead. "Yes, he did. He also said that his past was somewhat similar to yours, growing up in a less than stable environment. I mean, I assume it had to be heartbreaking?"

Tank hesitated. He thought back to the memories he had to see from the Hall of Infinium and responded, "I don't know if I can agree with that statement because to me...the unstable was stable and normal. Going to school, doing homework, playing baseball and following the rules was not normal to me. Running away from boys' homes and helping my mom get up out of bed after a night of binge drinking is what I knew as normal."

"So how long did you spend in prison?" Kinsey asked, trying to get Tank to look her in the eyes.

He kept his face forward toward the water, and it took him a few minutes before he finally decided he wanted to continue to discuss the subject.

"We don't have to talk about it if you don't want to. I don't mean to dig in an area of your life that you don't care to discuss. Believe me, I completely understand." Kinsey felt she had pressured him too quickly, and since she didn't even want to see her own past in the Hall of Infinium, she understood that it really wasn't fair to force him to share his.

"I remember the first time I saw a man murdered," Tank said out of a dead silence.

It took Kinsey a minute to register the words he had just spoken. Then the shock and interest overwhelmed her curiosity.

"I hadn't even been in prison a week." He paused. "I was in a ruthless prison that was considered a thunder dome. Two men enter, one man leaves." As Tank spoke, he kept his eyes focused on the water.

All Kinsey could do was stare at him. She had chills the moment the words left his mouth and silently prayed he wouldn't end the story abruptly. She was far too interested to see where this story could go.

"There was this oddly shaped area in the prison where no cops would go and no cameras could see. It was far back behind a stairway. The other prisoners and guards knew what went on, and they just let it happen. Our lives didn't have value to the guards or anyone else, for that matter. Everyone knew what it meant when two men would start walking toward those stairs. That was everyone else's cue to start walking away. We didn't see anything and we didn't hear anything. Even if we saw it all, no one said a word. That is prison 101. No one wants to be a rat because that can get you killed." Tank paused as he looked to Kinsey, and her eyes were studying him.

"Anyway, it was even worse if a group of men headed back there because someone was about to be killed. When an order came down from the leader or head of a group to punish or kill, it didn't matter the race nor age. No one got involved."

Kinsey's mouth dropped. She never knew anyone who went to prison, and deep down, her biggest fear was being trapped in a situation she couldn't get out of. She stayed perfectly still and quiet as he continued.

"It was my first day in prison after I was transferred from the county jail. I didn't know not to watch or get involved. I mean, after all, I was only sixteen. Out of nowhere, an old-timer came and pulled me aside. He took me to his cell, and there stood several guys waiting for me. For a minute, I thought I was about to fight for my own life, but thankfully, the old-timer was head of the group, and he asked if I had family on the outside to take care of me. My mom had just died while I was in the county, and I didn't have anyone other than my younger siblings. So he gave me a starter kit to help take care of myself. It was a bag filled with some hygiene products, coffee, soups, snacks, and a shank. They said I had to hold onto it and try to keep it hidden. They also said I was going to have to start working out if I was going to survive."

Kinsey found herself even more captivated by his story than the day before with Matai. She thought to herself and was trying to imagine going into prison alone with no family to help her survive. She had been through hell in her life, but it was her own personal hell. She wasn't forced into a world known for survival of the fittest. She felt like her life was completely minor compared to living like an animal in a cage.

"There were many times I was forced to do. Things—" Tank stopped for a minute, debating on if he really wanted to tell Kinsey all about the horrible choices and fights he was forced to do in prison. Things he knew that he could be hated for. "I can remember the names and the exact days when I was forced to kill someone."

Kinsey's back stiffened. That woke her up and got her attention. "How many did you have to kill? That had to have been horrible."

It took Tank a good minute before he could answer. Then finally, he replied, "The first time I was ordered to, I was twenty-three. The guy had messed up in our group. He had snitched on one of the guys in charge and got him locked down in solitary. Order came in and was given to me. Thankfully, by then, I had grown another foot and gained another fifty pounds from working out and building muscle. They chose me because I was close to his cell, and we usually worked out together. You would think it would have bothered me to do it, but unfortunately, I was so brainwashed by then, so most of my humanity was long gone. I had been doing drugs and was doing anything I could to numb the pain from the loss of my mom," Tank said.

Kinsey didn't want to move. She didn't want to miss a single word he said. This was serious stuff.

"I can't imagine what that must have been like for you."

"When you're numb, you don't care. When you don't care, you get dangerous," Tank replied.

"So what happened? How did it go down?" Kinsey asked.

"I had to learn where he was and what he did throughout the day; meaning where he went and what time it usually was. So we started hanging around each other more. I was told to take my time. Don't rush. Learn when each guard was coming and going, and pay attention to where they went. We had different guards at different times, so I needed to learn which guard would be easy to distract and which guard would need something serious to leave the area they worked in. I took small notes. I learned about his family and his interests. I took a good six months learning all of the information I needed to make my move," Tank said.

Kinsey didn't move. Her heart began to thump inside her neck. She sat in awe of a man who could act so cavalier under those circumstances. It didn't come as a surprise, though, given his surroundings during that time. "So what happened the day you did it?" she asked.

"I had been sending information down to the guy who wanted him taken down. Based on that information, he told me what to do with the guards who were easily distracted and those who would need something bigger. The morning of, our group didn't even know what was going on because any one of them could slip up and end up ruining the whole thing. The guy in solitary was trying to make a point. You don't rat on your own group.

"I had given a couple guys some drugs in a form of payment to help with the distraction. One guy, I had him start a fire in the kitchen. In fact, he started three fires. Two other guys, I had them start a fight with anyone they could separately. I gave them the time, and during that time, the guy I was working out with would be far from view. As soon as those things happened, I took the guy out with an X-Acto knife to the throat," Tank said flatly.

"How did you feel after you did it?" Kinsey asked.

"I had apathy. I felt nothing. That kill got me eight years in solitary," Tank replied. "I know I am saying this with no emotion behind it. I am well aware of that. It's just something I haven't talked about with anyone until today. The next guy I killed came at me because I had grown to become one of those leaders after earning my stripes the whole time I was there. He didn't stand a chance. The guards knew about it, oddly enough. They knew and they did nothing to stop it. I know that because they didn't put me back in solitary. They told me they didn't think it was going to happen. This is who I was supposed to trust my life with? No thanks.

"The third guy I killed was during a riot. Every man for himself type thing. It was after that I met that girl I said you looked like. She was dying of cancer and decided to write to me from a website set up to help prisoners make new friends or find love. She was dying and just wanted someone to talk to. She was so sweet. She was what changed me. She was the one who taught me about God. I told her God wanted nothing to do with a man like me. That's when she asked me, 'How do you think I came to find you?'

"One day, I gave in and asked and ended up becoming a Christian, and yes, I felt like a hypocrite. I was just so broken and needed to know there was hope. Christ changed me, though. I fully embraced God after that because I didn't want to become a monster deep down. I had to gain what little hope I could keep. I am grateful for her." Tank finally had no more to say.

Kinsey noticed a small tear drop from his eye. She decided not to bring it up and sat quietly.

As Kinsey and Tank continued talking at the turtle cove, Gabriel and Michael had been expecting Leilani and her group to arrive. Itherial greeted them at the colosseum opening and stayed by Lau's side. Since Itherial knew his best friend, he instantly began talking with him and explained, "I know just about as much as you do. God told me to meet you all here, and I am really curious to know what this is all about."

"We have been expecting you," Michael the archangel said as they arrived. "We know you have a lot of questions, and we also know your concerns."

"Okay, so why don't you tell us about the previous double color and why he never returned?" Leilani asked, confused and frustrated.

"It was about a thousand year ago. His name was Edward Crimson or, as he liked to be called, Eddie. He was chosen to have a double color so that Lucifer would lure him in," Gabriel explained.

"What do you mean Lucifer lured him in? For what and why?" Leilani didn't care how bold she sounded and certainly did not like where the conversation was leading.

"Why would God use a Guardian to lure Lucifer in?" Matai asked, knowing deep down there was more to the situation than what meets the eye.

"We were never fully given an exact answer. Eddie had a uniqueness to him that God knew and Lucifer wanted. Lucifer would lure Eddie in with money, power, women, and eternal life. Lucifer wanted to know the secret of the Guardians and how the kingdom has been running ever since the flood," Gabriel answered.

"So does this mean she is about to be a target?" Lau asked, hoping there would be an important reason they were doing this.

"She will be a target, but not in the way you are thinking. As you all know, the boy has been born, and Lucifer is on a desperate hunt to find him. He has been sending Abaddon and Mott to sniff out any new Guardians. He is trying to find another Eddie because if one of us, even just one acts without the right to interfere in a human life, Lucifer has free rein over the world, and that will expose the boy, just like God did with Jesus. Lucifer couldn't find him until the time was right," Michael explained.

"Great, so how do we tell her this? She has been wanting to go on a mission, and I know she is ready now. I don't understand this. It doesn't make sense," Reese asked the archangels, then looked at Leilani.

The two angels didn't answer right away. They looked at one another, and then the archangels said, "You can't tell her. This has to remain kept from her knowledge."

"*What?*" they all said in unison with their voices slightly raised.

"How do you even expect us to do that and why?" Annie asked.

"Michael, come on! You can't expect us…to know she is going to be targeted by not only the Watchers but Lucifer himself and not warn her? Didn't Lucifer only present himself to Jesus and Judas? So why now? And why Kinsey? How can this be done to a new Guardian?" Big Ben asked.

Matai, Grunt, Cronk, Mongo, Thud, and Thunk all had the exact same intense stare as they sat and listened to the conversation and began digesting the situation. Suddenly, Matai was struck with the answer to solve the problem. "So when it's her time to go on her first mission, we can keep an extra close eye on her. We're a larger group, so it will be easier for us than any others. Tank can stay close by her side, or every time we go for a mission, maybe rotate between all of us?"

The whole group stopped to look at Matai. Their growing concern was evident on their faces. They didn't understand how he could be so nonchalant about their current situation, but before anyone could confront Matai, Lau spoke up.

"From what I am hearing you not say, we are to let nature take its course because this is meant to happen?" Lau asked, studying Michael and Gabriel.

"Correct. We know it's going to be difficult, and honestly, it could have been anyone. It just so happened that she was chosen.

We just don't know the details. We just know this is meant to take its course," Gabriel said.

"I don't like this. I don't agree with this. I don't know how to just keep it quiet," said Annie. Then suddenly, her face and body language changed and she was calm. "Okay, I am going to assume she was chosen because of experiences in her life. That much is clear to me. Obviously, this is meant to happen because it's linked to the boy, isn't it?" She spoke with such determination she realized she actually had the answer she was seeking.

The Holy Spirit suddenly took over her and then each one of them slowly. Each of the Utuas, Big Ben, Leilani, and Reese all had the answer. The Holy Spirit whispered to each of them what they needed to know and what part they would individually play when it came down to the boy. Ironically, they knew they couldn't tell the archangels, they couldn't tell Kinsey, and they certainly couldn't tell any of the other Guardians.

Leilani suddenly spoke, breaking any train of thought the group had. One by one, they all began to leave the colosseum. "We understand and we know what to do now."

Lau looked at them and knew they had the answers they were seeking but also knew that he had to just let nature run as it should. Everything was under God's control, and there was no way to deviate from what he wanted, so why complain and why fight it? He just knew he was going to train Kinsey to be the warrior God intended all of them to be together with a few more kicks for strength.

The group walked out and was completely silent as they ventured toward the beach. They knew that's where Tank was taking Kinsey, and they figured they all may as well go find the two members.

Annie and Leilani were thinking the exact same thing, that it was time to teach Kinsey the same strategy and techniques that they all knew inside and out. It was more than just quick thinking. It was quick thinking and a plan to get out of a situation with a gnarly kill shot.

"Hey, Matai," Leilani called for her brother

"*Ua li,*" he responded.

"Time to take her through the strength simulators. Lucifer will come straight for her when he sees her. Annie, you and Ben start by giving her the accelerated and high-impact simulator where quick decisions are needed to make it through," Leilani said to Annie and Ben.

Reese approached Leilani and gently asked, "Maybe this is a good thing. Kind of like a chosen one, you know? We just don't know chosen for what," Reese said with a giggle.

Leilani looked at him and knew he was trying to lighten the tension or the load on Leilani's shoulders.

"I don't think this is necessarily a bad thing. So it's a double color. Big deal. It's not like anyone on a mission notices you unless you strictly interact with a Watcher," Reese said as they continued walking.

"What about Abaddon and Mott?" Leilani turned to Reese to ask.

Annie had been listening in, and then it dawned on her. "We just do what the Watchers do. Distract them! We have a ton of new Guardians that have earned their colors, and we just go in slow and low. In fact, I think the missions that are being handed to us lately have been light."

Good old Annie, Leilani thought to herself. She was always thinking ahead of the maze. It was true they could go with other groups or they could be assigned to the most mundane missions so that Kinsey didn't stand out.

Leilani stopped to face her group and her brothers. "Look, we have a plan in motion. We will go harder through the simulators, and then we will go on the most mundane missions. We don't want her to stand out in any way because she could possibly become a target. Let's all agree and promise for now to keep this secret from Kinsey and anyone else. We don't need anyone else accidentally speaking on this sensitive subject." Leilani put her right hand down in front of the whole group.

One by one, her brothers and the group members placed their hands on top of one another. Thud and Thunk were last. Everyone smiled because they knew it was coming. Each one of them yelled,

"*Ua li gums.*" Then they laughed and continued heading toward Kinsey and Tank.

Out of nowhere, Saige and Jaxon came from around the corner and began begging Thud and Thunk to keep Roxy and Hendrix for the night.

"You may as well take them," Cronk said. "They ignore the twins anyway. I think they love the fresh job of entertaining small children."

"We can't help it if we are so beautiful and the dogs love us," Saige said while flipping her hair back.

Tank and Kinsey had begun swimming back toward the shoreline of the homes, and surprisingly, she felt rested. Tank had some heavy stories, and Kinsey learned to appreciate the life she had in comparison to the brokenness he experienced.

As they swam back to their homes, Kinsey saw the entire group standing there, just waiting for the two to come back. As per usual, the twins yelled at the top of their lungs, "*Ua li gumz!*"

"Hey, look! A welcoming committee," Tank said sarcastically.

"Well, that was a quick mission," Kinsey stated back.

Thud and Thunk decided to throw everyone they could out into the water. As the brothers tried to gain advantage over one another, they looked like two giant walruses with long black hair. In one quick swoop, JoAnne and Leilani were scooped up and tossed into the gentle waves. Big Ben went against Mongo and Cronk. The whole group together danced around one another, each one trying to land on top and be king of the mountain.

Tank positioned himself behind Matai and, without being detected, pulled Matai's feet out from under him. As his body flipped over the wave, water found its way straight up his nose, and Matai couldn't stand the feeling. "Oh, man! It burns! It burns!" he screamed.

When he stood up, everyone began laughing as hard as they could because Matai had a giant line of snot falling from his nose. Kinsey realized she was standing the closest and dove away by the sight of the green snot. "No, no, no!" she screamed as she dove.

The water play continued as the sun went down on the horizon. Each of the members and Utuas had worked up a hearty appetite from attempting to drown one another.

Leilani, Annie, and Kinsey slowly crept out of the water and crashed on the sand.

"All right, ladies, we can't let these men beat us," Leilani said.

"What are you talking about, Leli, you are already beat," Mongo said, laughing with his brothers.

"Yeah, yeah, yeah!" the girls replied.

"Let's go eat. We need our strength for later," JoAnne said.

"What do you mean later? I'm crashing early tonight," Kinsey said to the group.

She loved playing in the water but was ready to lay in her comfortable bed and crash out. "Today was a good day. I wish I had days like this while I was alive." Kinsey waved goodbye to everyone and noticed the two kids were inside the house with the two dogs, Roxy and Hendrix. "Mommy is going to take a shower and go to bed. If you guys want anything to eat, there is a lot of leftovers from the celebration that somehow has stayed incredibly preserved," Kinsey said as she went up the stairs and straight into the shower. After she was done, she was so happy to finally say, "Time for bed!"

The two kids snuck in the room and climbed into her massive bed. "Night, Mommy," they said in unison.

SUPERNATURAL OR SUPER DECEPTION?

The morning sun was beautiful and warm as the Utuas were all standing outside their home overlooking the water, each one of them lost in their thoughts about the previous day. Tank tried to ask about what happened, and each one of them kept tight-lipped about the day before. Thud, Thunk, Cronk, Grunt, Mongo, and Matai all responded the same way, stating that it was just supposed to happen, nothing more and nothing less.

Tank found the answers odd but knew eventually the secret would reveal itself. He spent eight years in solitary confinement in prison. He learned how to do time. He knew he had a lot of patience.

Reese approached the band of brothers with Leilani and looked them in the eyes. They all had the same silent understanding and decided to just tell Tank that today was a viewing mission. She told Reese to go get Kinsey and get her ready for the day while the rest of them met up with the group.

Reese ran into Kinsey's home and headed straight for her bedroom. He knew he had to be excited for her because a first mission was a big deal. He decided to act as though he didn't know the secret and chose to follow her lead. If she was happy, he was happy. He jumped on the bed and started yelling, "*Wake up!*" as he pulled the blanket back that uncovered her and the two children. Usually, in the night, Jaxon and Saige crawled in and snuggled with their mom. Kinsey loved having her two little ones bundled up beside her.

Kinsey looked up, hair disheveled, eyes half open, and mumbled something slightly audible. "Whaduwant?"

"You get to come on a mission today. It's an observation mission, but you get to go, so get your butt up and get ready. It's a big deal and it's going to be eye-opening for you," Reese stated as he began pulling Saige and Jaxon up out of the bed. The two children were excited for Kinsey since they knew she had been waiting and ready to see what the human world really did look like with Guardians and Watchers all around.

"Mommy gets to go on a mission today!" Reese said to the children. He then jumped off the bed while grabbing them and telling them to get ready for a long day of playing with their friends.

"Always remember, if you get bored or you want to see your Great-Aunt Judy or Grandma and Grandpa, you can, okay?" Kinsey yelled down the hall.

"*Okay!*" the two children yelled back in unison.

"I will be out in five minutes…tops!" Kinsey yelled out to Reese, unsure if he was still even in the house. She was so excited she began shaking while trying to get her gear on. She wasn't sure how she was gonna bring her swords, but then again, she never saw Leilani nor any of her group members bring their weapons on missions. She came down the stairs and looked herself over in the mirror on the front door one last time before she walked out and smiled. She felt deep down she was definitely ready for today and decided to pull her hair back, just in case she did get involved in some kind of action. Just the thought excited her. She kissed her children and ran outside to meet Reese.

"I can't believe it. I finally get to go today," Kinsey said, the sound of the excitement in her voice notable to Reese.

"Well, you look fierce in your gear, my dear. We are meeting everyone just outside the colosseum below the four horsemen," Reese stated as they began up the hill toward the marketplace. He saw her excitement and knew to just roll with it, even if it did hurt him inside to think about what could possibly be coming her way.

"You know, whoever designed the horsemen, I mean, wow, the beauty and mystery just give me chills every time we pass by,"

Kinsey said as they passed through the marketplace, heading toward the majestic sight. She saw her favorite trader, the beautiful Indian woman, and asked for a juicy strawberry. Kinsey wanted to make sure she had just a little something in her stomach, and Reese, just behind her, asked for the same. They thanked her for the treat and stated they would be back to trade at the end of the day.

"Take your time," the sweet woman said as she waved them off.

The two children were not seen in the massive playground, and Kinsey assumed they were either deep in fantasy and make-believe or they were with family. Either way, she loved that her children were always safe.

All the Utuas, including Tank, were waiting underneath the giant archway under the four horsemen for Reese and Kinsey. Big Ben, Annie, and Leilani had just arrived shortly before the last two did.

Leilani could see the excitement on Kinsey's face, and with a smil,e she asked, "Are you ready for your first mission? You don't need your weapon today because it's observation. But what we are about to see is a group of men in the past and then visit them in today's world. I will warn you, it will be slightly scary because the Watchers are nothing but pure evil, and their physical appearances definitely doesn't help either."

"Well, I don't know how I will respond, but I will do whatever you tell me to do. Why are we going to see these people in the past?" Kinsey asked.

"Once you see, it will all make sense," Leilani replied. "Okay, are we all ready?" she asked everyone in the group.

The twins, in unison, tried to sound upbeat as they replied, "*Ua li*, let's go."

The whole group passed through the archway, and the usual simulators and obstacle courses were in full swing for those who were practicing. Annie and Big Ben waved at several of the Guardians that they had made friends with over the many years and even recent days of practicing.

Kinsey felt so excited she could barely contain herself. She jumped on Reese's back, and they giggled as they ran ahead of everyone. They stopped under the other archway, directly across from the first one. The arena went silent like it did the day she first went to the Hall of Infinium. Kinsey still didn't have any desire to see her past and wasn't sure as she began to wonder, would she ever be able to see any of those memories? A few of them stumbled around in the darkness before another archway opened up and they entered into the water garden that led everyone to the Hall of Infinium. Every single one of them seemed sunken, deep in thought as none of them spoke when they reached the entrance to the hall.

Matai and Tank pulled open the giant doors, and Leilani led the group past all the podiums with the giant gold spheres of light. Instead of heading up to the House of Memories and Hall of Mirrors, they went straight through into a spacious observation room. Multiple groups were gathering around the different podiums, and Kinsey wondered if the other people were all there for the same reason she was. She was mentally trying to guess which person in each group was the new member. Suddenly, Leilani broke her train of thought and caught her attention. They had stopped at one particular podium that didn't have a sphere on it.

"Okay, Kinsey, when I put my Makirus on the podium, a sphere will appear. All of us will touch the sphere at the same time, and then we will end up where we need to be. Since these are not any of our own memories, only leaders can access certain moments from a person's past when it's not historical or rather a very significant time for the average person."

Leilani placed the Makirus on the spoke, and from inside the podium came a red sphere. Every single one of them placed their right pointer and middle finger together on the sphere. Kinsey just happened to take note and smiled that each one of their hands bore the mark of the sea turtle. They all seemed to notice it the same as they all smiled before they traveled to the past of an unknown time and location.

The whole group found themselves standing outside a building that was oddly shaped. The setting was just off a dirt road, and the area was completely surrounded by trees. They each stood for a minute, trying to take the scenery in. Kinsey tried to take note of any cars or people so that she could discern what time frame they were currently visiting. A couple of trucks were parked off to the side, and they appeared to be fairly recent models, give or take a dozen years. She looked up at the name of the building, and instantly, her stomach dropped. She was hoping they were not here on purpose and it was some kind of overcalculation of time and definitely a place—Billy McGee's. This was a small country western bar in Wilder, Kentucky, but gained its popularity due to the paranormal activity. She knew this building because it was known as one of the most haunted and demonic locations within the United States. She realized they were all looking at her, and Kinsey had to ask Leilani, "Why are we here?"

"Well, you were a huge fan of *Ghost Avengers*, weren't you?" Annie asked.

Suddenly, a car door behind her shut, and there they were—Neil, Adam, and Zane from *Ghost Avengers*, the three guys she loved to watch every Friday and Saturday night. The first location they ever investigated on TV was a country bar named Billy McGee's. The three guys were new to the paranormal world, but their personalities made the show not only spooky but completely entertaining. This was their first time investigating this particular location due to the reputation that preceded it. Many different TV shows over the years had done multiple investigations because Billy McGee's never failed to present the evidence they were looking for and seeking after.

"Yes, these guys were really entertaining. You know, I remember the first episode they came here. Billy McGee's is definitely no joke in the paranormal world, and I know for a fact it's demonic," Kinsey replied while she turned away from the group. She took a few steps away before she continued.

"It used to be a slaughterhouse, and two guys cut a woman's head off who just happened to be pregnant, and they made her a sacrifice as an offering to Satan." Kinsey didn't realize her entire group was frozen still, staring at her as she continued, "That is definitely one thing I do know for sure. Lucifer likes to copycat anything he can from the Trinity. Jesus died for our sins, his blood was shed for us, so Lucifer wants the blood through sacrifice to be served to him. I have always believed when someone does something like that, they give a large piece of their souls over to the darkness." Kinsey took a breath, not realizing that the whole group was staring at her in slight shock. She answered so matter-of-factly along with more knowledge and background of the location than they had all anticipated.

"Well," Annie paused, slightly puzzled, "now you are about to see if you are still…entertained after you watch their first interaction with the Watchers," Annie replied.

"It's important to keep in mind that we are looking into the past, so none of the three guys nor the Watchers they encounter can see nor hear us. You may be startled at first, but we're all here with you, and this will help you understand how the Watchers not only deceive but how they operate," said Leilani as she followed the three men into the doorway.

Kinsey stopped to look around as the three men setting up the investigation walked straight through her. She always wondered what it would really be like to investigate a paranormal hot spot, but the truth was she knew not to mess around with any of it because it could be deceptive.

"Leilani… Annie…what is it going on that you are really trying to show me? I mean, other than just how the Watchers operate? Something in the core of my spirit says there is more than meets the eye," Kinsey asked with a serious face.

Annie and Leilani froze along with everyone else, but before they could answer, Kinsey spoke again, "For example, there is no little girl on a rocking horse who is looking for her mom, is there? As Guardians, we can send subtle notices when we visit our family and friends, but God would not keep a child's spirit in this hell hole we once lived in. I mean, the God of all creation wants to give us our hearts desire, but he might trap a few children on earth in the process. That has never made sense to me. I mean, would he really do that? What are some of the most innocent of all creatures on earth other than an animal? A small child, right? I get it now. It makes so much sense now. That's how the Watchers operate, don't they? They work to trick and deceive a person in as many ways as possible."

Kinsey paused for a quick moment before she continued seeking for answers with a neediness radiating in her eyes. She turned back to look at each and every one in her group. "The Watchers make it a big chase, deeper and deeper down a rabbit hole. They want the person to become so consumed with questions about the supernatural they are unable to accept that...this." She paused again with her hands doing a giant circular motion over the situation. "This is all deception." Kinsey realized how much she actually just said, and she waited for several minutes for one of them to answer her.

Annie and Leilani looked at each other, relieved, and then looked to Kinsey and answered, "You just answered your own questions, and you are correct in everything you said."

Suddenly, Kinsey heard a weird noise coming from the trees close by. She looked back to the rest of the group and stood, frozen in place. Her heart dropped into her stomach as a shadow, darker than dark, came from the trees just outside the nightclub. The sun was shining brightly, so nothing moving nor living could cause such a shadow to exist. The head was small, arms and legs almost in human form with the body frame of a gorilla. The creature jumped from the trees and then down to the ground. The eyes, amber in color, reflected off its surroundings, and then the creature formed into a snake and slithered just behind the three men who walked into the club.

"Oh, I don't know if I can do this. I could have sworn that... that...thing just looked at me," Kinsey said, trembling.

Big Ben walked up to Kinsey and placed his hands gently on her shoulders. "They can't see you. You weren't here when this happened. Your Makirus only shows the moments of your life. A leader, like Leilani, can access random moments in time. We chose this moment and these men because it was the easiest way for us to explain everything about the Watchers to you."

Kinsey took a deep breath and shook her head and forced herself to go in. "Tank, you are holding my hand, and if I climb on your back...just go with it."

"Okay, just don't squeeze those tiny arms under my neck," Tank replied.

"No promises," she stated with a wink.

"Okay, let's go take our places inside and watch as everything unfolds," Annie said, walking straight through the door.

"This place is known as Hell's Gate, and we need to find out why," Zane from *Ghost Avengers* said into the camera that Neil was holding.

The whole group gathered by the stage, and each one sat down. Kinsey squeezed her way in between Tank and Matai. If something was going to pop off, she was going to make sure they would be eaten before she was.

Suddenly, it hit her that she didn't really grasp or believe yet that the Watchers couldn't see nor hear her them. She then realized, what use was all of her training if she just ran? That was a coward's way out, and in her heart, she couldn't handle the thought of losing a member, let alone be responsible for the death. "No!" she said to herself. "I will fight to my death? Wait. Can I fight to another's death?" It was another "a-ha" moment because she realized she never heard of anyone dying again when they were sent on assignments.

As she was listening to the guy's interview with the employees of the bar, something caught her eye. The others just happened to notice the commotion too because each of their heads were in the same direction as hers. The same shadow that had gripped onto Adam's leg then changed its shape into a creature similar to a baboon. The teeth were all razor-sharp, the claws looked prehistoric, and the eyes were completely hollow.

The Watcher then climbed up the wall and posted itself above the three charismatic men during all the interviews. After they were completed with their interviews, it was then time for the caretaker to bring them down to the basement. The group then got up and followed the men and caretaker down to the cellar, and Kinsey's stomach instantly began to feel sick.

Every single hair on Kinsey's body stood on end. She could sense there were dozens of Watchers in the cellar, and she hesitated before entering. The Utuas were unusually quiet, and that alone made her scared. The Utuas were never quiet. The brothers were a source of safety and comfort, and their silence only validated her fear. She began to slightly shake and felt there was no way she would be able to follow them in. She didn't like the way the basement felt, and although she knew nothing could harm her, that wasn't the real problem.

Annie turned to look at Kinsey still standing on the outside of the building. She slowly approached her and held her hands. Annie softly spoke, looking Kinsey directly in the eyes, "Nothing can touch you, remember that. We are a team, and we would *never* allow anything to hurt you without a fight with all of us. The Utuas alone are like the wall guarding the king in his castle."

"That's not what is bothering me. There are at least over a dozen, and the very sight of them is making me weak," Kinsey answered honestly with her legs trembling. "How am I supposed to be a Guardian and face them for real if I can't even handle just the thought of them? I'm watching a memory and I am absolutely terrified. I shouldn't be scared. I should be prepared and ready. In fact, maybe my label as a Guardian is completely wrong. I could make a great Momenti. Just drop in and drop out." Kinsey had tears welling up in her eyes, desperately pleading to not have to go into the basement.

"You know, what you said actually proves that you are meant to be a Guardian. If the archangel made a mistake and you were destined to be something else in our structure, you wouldn't know how many Watchers are in this basement. You are correct. There are thirteen Watchers total. They are following these three guys from the bar and they are now behind all the debris in the back of the basement," Annie said with a smile. "Come in and observe their dumbest mistake."

As Annie and Kinsey made their way over to the rest of the group, Leilani was standing by, waiting for them to enter. Leilani had pulled out the red sphere while Kinsey and Annie had spoken outside. She kept holding the red sphere in her hand as she spoke to the group, "Everyone touch the sphere. I am going to move time forward to their investigation in the dark."

All the brothers and the group members placed their right fingers on the sphere, once again displaying the sea turtles they all shared that made them as one unit. The visual display gave Kinsey the comfort she needed, and she felt herself begin to relax. Leilani slightly spun the sphere clockwise, and suddenly, they were all in the dark. The cellar was completely black, bearing no light. Kinsey didn't realize that in the dark, her eyes now had night vision.

Leilani placed the glowing red sphere down, and all of the group members began to watch the following events about to unfold. Each one of them sat dead silent, causing Kinsey's anxiety to rise again. She couldn't understand why she still felt so anxious. That was a human emotion, so why did she feel it? She was in no way connected to these men, so she couldn't feel what they were feeling. It was overwhelming and bothering her to a point she felt of almost no return. Every week without fail, she watched *The Ghost Avengers* and had even seen this exact episode several times. So why now was she so afraid?

The three ghost hunters had been taunting the Watchers, and the energy was about to raise to a level no one anticipated. All of the Utuas' body language were screaming with rage, itching to attack the enemy. They had a warrior stance, showing no fear to the enemy, and by the expression on their faces, they wanted to kill, but they all sat and listened as the guys continued.

"Why don't you come out of this hole and get us? If this is a portal to hell, come out of the ground and come get us," Zane, the aggressive one, repeated. "We are right here for you. We are all looking for you. Come show yourself. In fact, I don't even believe you can do anything to us. So show us what you can really do if you aren't cowards," Zane said.

"See, Zane isn't afraid of you. None of us are. You can do what you want, but we won't run from you. You're going to have to harm us to get us to leave," Neil said, looking through the LCD screen in his camera. Neither Zane, Adam, nor Neil could see anything down in the basement since all the lights were off. It wasn't just dark in the room. It was blacker than black. The darkness represented a level of evil that no one, except God himself, could make bright. A perfect recipe for a Watcher to grow in.

Tank was shaking his head and couldn't believe the stupidity the men had as they taunted the Watchers. "One thing you never do is get cocky with Watchers. These guys have no clue what harm this moment will cause them, even long after they leave. But...he's about to. See that Watcher up there?" Tank pointed to the corner. "It's taking shape and coming down for that guy, Zane. The more arrogant a person becomes, the more the Watcher can mess with him, even harm him and drain his energy."

Kinsey sat with Matai to her left and Tank to her right. She watched the scene unfold with a death grip on both of them as she slowly looked up to the ceiling. All thirteen of the nastiest creatures she had never laid eyes on took the shape of vultures ready for the kill. Their eyes were red. The wings appeared to be as steel so sharp, a single bladelike feather could slice through a human body in seconds. The Watcher made its way above them on the ceiling and then crawled down the post in front of them. The Watcher changed into the shape of a scorpion, over six feet long and two feet wide.

A ticking noise coming from the mouth that made Kinsey squeeze Tank's hand. The eyes were hollow with an abyss deeper than space. The pincers could cut the head off another Watcher or a Guardian if one was in the way. The beastly nightcrawler came down the post in a circular motion. All eyes focused on the Watcher as the arachnid used its claws to lift up the back of Zane's shirt and the stinger made three long distinctive scratches down the center of his back.

Kinsey was dead frozen on her seat. *There is no chance in hell I am moving,* Kinsey thought to herself. Her group told her that the Watchers changed form, but not once did they mention anything about a giant scorpion in any of her training.

Another Watcher morphed from the vulture into a wicked ten-legged spider that was much smaller than the scorpion. The hairs on the legs stood out like thorns as it slowly fell down from the ceiling, gripping onto the freshly made silk. The spider landed on the ground and methodically made its way around all three of the men. The Watcher appeared to be checking Zane, Neil, and Adam out while trying to decide which of the prey he wanted to devour.

Zane began screaming while panicking about the burning marks on his back. The spider then made its way up Zane's leg, up his body, and stopped on his shoulder. The nasty creature then went under Zane's clothes, down the center of his back, and bit him.

While Neil, Adam, and Zane kept trying to figure out why Zane's back was burning, another Watcher hovered above them with no shape or form, just a cloud of darkness. The Watcher then transformed into a Komodo dragon and opened its mouth extremely wide. The tongue of the lizard stretched out all the way to Zane's head and wrapped around him like a rope, and as it did, Zane spoke, "I feel disoriented. I don't know what it is, and my back is still burning really bad. Neil, check my back and tell me what you see. It's burning so bad." Zane lifted up his shirt.

Neil and Adam both turned their flashlights on his back and slowly inched away from him.

"Oh my God," said Adam with a tremble in his voice.

"What is it?" Zane screamed with clear fear and agitation in his voice.

"You have three long scratch marks down your spine, and it also looks like a huge bite. Some more are starting to appear on your skin," Neil said as he flipped his camera light back on. Some of the scratches were even drawing blood, and it slowly dripped down his body.

Tank leaned toward Kinsey and softly spoke, "That's what happens when you're arrogant and you taunt demons. Huge ones at that. The one thing that most people don't understand is, Watchers are very proud and they live off that pride. They feed and gain power by tormenting any soul that is lost or in pain. This whole basement is just a feeding ground for them. They all lured their prey and will now feed off of them. Those scratch and bite marks just left a trace of venom in his bloodstream. Once a person has been marked by a Watcher, their venom flows freely through the bloodstream." He paused while looking back and pointed toward Zane, Adam, and Neil. "All other Watchers will now know he has been marked because the venom leaves a very distinct smell, and in spiritual warfare, it's really hard for the person to have the venom removed. Only the Holy

Spirit can cleanse them. Remnants of tonight will follow these men home. There is a reason why we are told not to engage them. We are just meant to kill when it's time to kill."

Zane began to get angry from the marks on his back. "Did someone just scratch me?" he yelled. "I bet you're thinking wow, what a tough guy he is, but he is still coming for more. I'm calling out to the one who scratched my back. Come get me. Come scratch my face."

The Watchers above him all started to laugh. The bladelike feathers clanked with their chuckle. The scorpion and the spider began to climb back up to the top with the rest of the Watchers. The dragon that stayed by their feet kept slightly licking them throughout their bodies, and as it did, the tongue was draining all three of their energy. Once the three Watchers fed off Zane, it then became a feeding frenzy. Like sharks in the water, several of the Watchers came down and began to feed off of him. The more the Watchers ate, the more they desired. Feeding off a human for a Watcher was like a drug with an incredible high. The demons love to feed off of humans because for a small moment in time, they would feel humanity come back into them. The high only lasted so long, and coming down from their short-lived euphoria only made the Watchers more vicious and hungry. Unfortunately for this human, the remnants of this night would haunt him for years to come.

Kinsey was frozen and couldn't believe she was observing the Watchers literally feed off of the three guys she once loved to watch as her weekly show. All those ghost-hunting shows only made a demon-infested location worse. She knew in God's Word, he said no to communicating with the dead. The main point people didn't understand was why? Why would he say don't do it if it couldn't be done? The reason is it's never safe. The person could never truly tell if a spirit was human or a demon. Watchers could be instructed to lure people in and never want to leave.

Leilani pulled out the red sphere again and said, "Okay, everyone, we need to move forward and show the consequences of taunting the Watchers."

All of them placed their fingers on the sphere, and Leilani moved the time several years forward. The group and the Utuas remained in the same location, except the place had an overwhelming darkness that was suffocating their senses. After the episode hit the air on television, all the local ghost-hunting groups wanted to go to the famous Billy McGee's.

Without any warning, Zane kicked in the door to the basement and made his announcement he was back. All of the Watchers growled when he walked in. They were now in the form of vicious wolves with fangs that could penetrate and rip a human body apart. The tips of the fangs were already dripping with blood from the previous night's ghost hunters. The poor group definitely obtained more than what they bargained for. The little ghost-hunting group all went home with remnants provided from the darkness. From the Reeds of Death up to the Watchers, they attached themselves to the group, and those ghost hunters would soon be suffering from the oppression that consumes those who try to challenge any form of demon.

Leilani swiftly and methodically pushed time forward. Everything played in front of Kinsey like a movie in fast forward. The group of men walked in, and each of the men now had small Watchers sitting on their shoulders. They were tiny in comparison to the massive wolves that now surrounded the building. More and more Watchers came to feed off the living since the people opened themselves up so freely like a buffet to the beasts. By coming to a place that they knew was demonic, yet still trying to taunt them anyway, the people became a ready-made meal. The little demons now attached to the three men had their tails wrapped around their necks.

Neil, Adam, and Zane filmed themselves for a few minutes and then went back up to the main floor of the dance hall to interview an exorcist. The man was a bishop with years of experience as a demonologist. Kinsey and the group made their way up toward Zane and the bishop so they could listen more closely to the conversation.

The demonologist, named Bishop Short, had worked on the location once before, and as long as the owner of the building allowed the Watchers to stay, there was little he could do in getting rid of the beasts. The three men had decided they wanted to try to cast the

Watchers out of the location, but in reality, all they were doing was taunting a predator in their own territory.

The whole group sat and listened as Zane asked the bishop, "Is it typical for demonic entities to mimic voices?" He asked the bishop this question because once at a haunted location, the other investigators used a device called the spirit box. The spirit box scanned through radio airways and hit a station a second. The spirit voices could come through the white noise of the rapid changing of stations. A voice came through that sounded exactly like Zane. The voice was a warning, and they heard it scream through the box, "Guys, be careful!"

Annie took the opportunity to explain to Kinsey, "An inexperienced person dealing with spiritual warfare can so easily be deceived, thinking that a spirit is trying to help them. It can go as far as tricking the person to think that the spirit is asking for help. What they fail to see is the entities are just another family member in the darkness, tricking people to come back for more so they can feed off the humanity left within their victim. Some people end up with an uncontrollable rage or a change of personality because they get so invested for answers it becomes like an addiction. That's when the Watchers have full control and can now have the authority to stay with the ghost hunter, even when they tell the entity it can't follow them home. We as Guardians can only do so much when a person chooses to listen to the darkness and allow it fool them. That's why God says do not speak with the dead."

They turned their attention back to the bishop as he explained, "I have experienced, especially in demonic possessions, they mimic the voices of loved ones. They will absolutely go to the emotional core of the person they oppress. The deepest emotional scar that you have, they will play on that."

"Well, at least someone knows what they're talking about," Big Ben said as the group stood by, watching the conversations.

This made Kinsey giggle because she loved Big Ben's sarcastic sense of humor. He didn't show it often, but when he did, it was on point.

Zane looked over to Adam and asked, "And that night, they did that, didn't they, Adam?"

"That night, the spirit box came through and said family problems and then marriage issues. I ended up getting a divorce because of this place because what affected me affected her, and she couldn't take the oppression anymore," Adam answered.

The bishop put his focus back to Zane and tried to explain even more, "Demonic entities are patient. They don't come when you call them. Just because you say come get me now doesn't mean they are going to come. They work on their time."

"Bingo!" Big Ben replied again as he made his hand in the shape of a gun and shot it toward Zane.

The next interview that took place was the strangest part the whole encounter they were watching. Billy McGee, the owner of the nightclub, had never experienced any type of demonic activity. None of the Watchers had ever affected him in all the time he had owned the building. The Watchers completely left him alone, and he even told Zane, "It's really hard for me to get my brain around anything demonic or spiritual. I still don't believe how it could be scientifically possible."

Kinsey's curiosity took over, and she had to ask, "Why wouldn't the Watchers affect him?"

"Because they want to keep their home. If they scare him, then then he will want them to leave and would try everything in the world to have them leave. They keep him nice and comfortable because he allows all the ghost hunting groups to investigate, and then what happens? They feed off the living again. I mean, look, these three have come back. Why do you think that is?" Annie asked.

"Because the Watchers that are now attached to the men feel like they need to come back?" Kinsey asked.

"Exactly!" Leilani answered.

Reese noticed a man bringing in a video, and none of them were prepared for what they were about to see next. It was a recording of an exorcism from a former caretaker. "I believe it's about to get worse."

"Oh Lord! Why would anyone want to share a video of an exorcism?" Big Ben asked, highly annoyed at the stupidity of the situation.

The group sat in a stunned silence as they watched the video with Zane, Neil, and Adam. The caretaker began screaming at the priest while his eyes had changed to pitch black. Only the Guardians could see exactly what was going on. They observed a Watcher morph into the man's body and fully take control of him. Over and over again, as the priest tried to banish the Watcher, the man kept screaming a response in a voice much lower than his real tone, "This body is mine! This body is mine!"

The Watcher had no intention of leaving the caretaker anytime soon as he provided a buffet for their feeding frenzy. The man was not only possessed but under severe oppression since the Watcher was given full control over the man's spirit. Kinsey noticed a Guardian in the video and leaned toward Tank and asked, "So the Watcher has been given control over the man. Does this make the Guardian completely powerless?"

"The Guardian is very limited at this point. That man has to make a full and conscious decision he wants to get rid of whatever it is that is oppressing him," Tank replied.

The man in the video was on the ground at this point, and the priest made his final commandment, "Under the authority of Christ, I demand that every spirit affecting this man has to leave!"

The caretaker howled in pain as the Watcher left his body. The whole group watched in awe as the banished spirit lay on the ground as a dark and murky smudge. The Guardian in the video then stood over the banished spirit. He withdrew his weapon from his side, and it grew into a massive sledgehammer. The Guardian prayed a quick prayer and, with all the strength he could muster, slammed the sledgehammer on top of the weakened spirit's face.

"You will attack no more...in the name of Yahweh!" said the Guardian.

Kinsey found herself floored over the reality of the situation. She knew spiritual warfare was complex and complicated, but she never realized the intensity she would come up against.

All the interviews were finally done, and the sun had just set toward western horizon. The three men were once again preparing themselves for a battle they were incapable of winning.

"These fools have no clue what they are truly messing with. If they even caught a glimpse of what these beasts really look like, they would never sit alone again in the dark," said Matai as the darkness overcame the entire nightclub. "They have no idea how this place will haunt them for days to come."

Leilani looked at the men and the monsters before her. "It definitely will be different this time. Not only did they bring new Watchers with them from all the previous locations they investigated, but now"—she paused—"now the Watchers from before are much stronger than what the men experienced the first time around. These Watchers had recently fed from investigators the night before, and don't get it twisted, but they planned to enjoy a feast from these three tonight. All those locations they have been to, where Watchers dominate, they smell the venom in their blood and they make their own mark. It makes the blood sweeter and their meat tender because the venom also weakens the body and spirit."

"Why would they do an exorcism in a place infested with Watchers the size of bigfoot?" Cronk asked, looking toward Leilani.

"It wasn't smart. If he had the exorcism done and never came back, he could possibly have been freed from the oppression, but because he felt the need to keep coming back, the Watcher venom wasn't fully removed from his system. Plain and simple, the Watcher has the right to stay with him," Leilani answered.

"I will never understand why these people just don't get it?" Annie said, highly annoyed at the stupidity from the continuous investigations.

Kinsey dug her nails into Tank's hand as the darkness fully surrounded them once again.

"You have to remember, Kinsey, they can't see you, and you have us. We wouldn't let anything get to you. Most of all, you weren't here when it happened. This isn't current, it's past," Tank said.

Kinsey sat there, annoyed with herself that she was afraid. How could she be afraid when she was blessed with the most incredible team members imaginable? With the darkness engulfing her, she became determined to be brave like her team. She had the power of Christ in her, so there was no excuse for her to feel afraid.

Kinsey couldn't believe what she was looking at. The three men looked as though they jumped into a shark tank and cut themselves to gain a feeding frenzy. They were swarmed with Watchers of all sizes and shapes.

The group's reaction matched Kinsey's, and it gave her a sense of ease and confirmation that these Watchers were nastier and bigger than the last ones she saw. The group became surrounded by some of the nastiest creatures imaginable. She was looking at countless stingers, teeth, and claws filled with unimaginable crippling venom.

The three men acted on the surface as though they were Vikings, knights of the king's court on a mission from God to destroy the enemy. Clearly, these three men did not understand who or what they were up against.

"I never realized how arrogant people are when they don't realize the power of the enemy," Cronk said.

"That's because they are still thinking in a physical sense, not a spiritual one," Leilani replied.

"Didn't the bishop say that to them earlier in the interview?" asked Mongo.

"Selective understanding," replied Leilani.

They continued to watch three men poking and antagonizing a tiger that should have been left alone, but something caught Kinsey's attention. One of the Watchers had morphed into Adam's body. His eyes changed, and body movements became rigid. She was horrified because she realized he was under a state of possession. The bishop recognized the change in him and began to perform the rite of exorcism. Kinsey found it ironic that a bishop would perform the banishing of a demon in a place surrounded by demons.

"Well, I think we have seen enough of the Watchers today. I am allergic to stupidity, and we need to head back and cleanse," Leilani said as she pulled back out the red sphere. Each one of them all willingly placed their fingers on the sphere and returned to the Hall of Infinium.

The group remained silent as they left the Hall of Infinium. Not one of them had anything to say. Kinsey was relieved to be back and thankful she didn't have a real mission that day. She thought she was ready, but clearly with the fear she felt, she wasn't ready. She kept trying to ask herself, why would she feel fear? She wasn't supposed to. This just wasn't making sense. She would speak to Leilani about it later, but for now, she was too exhausted to even think.

Before they all parted ways, Big Ben approached Kinsey with Annie. "Hey, would you like to train with us tomorrow? We could use an extra hand."

Kinsey pondered for a moment and then answered, "Yeah, sure, what time?"

"Just meet us in the colosseum in the morning whenever you get up. You will know we will be here," Annie replied.

"Okay, sounds good," Kinsey answered. She definitely needed to get some sleep. She decided to find the kids and just go to bed. It had been an exhausting day, even if it was just observation. She wanted the comfort of Saige and Jaxon in her arms for the rest of the evening since the day left her utterly drained. Deep down, she wanted Grace and Zerek with her too. It was a beautiful thought, and a warm feeling began to consume her just imagining all her children together.

After a few minutes, the smile and warm feeling was replaced with a sickening concern. Kinsey's two children still on earth were susceptible to whatever the Watchers were given the ability to do. "Not if I have anything to do with it!" she said out loud to herself. She realized in that moment why family members couldn't be Guardians to their own family. A close relative, most of all a mother, would tear a monster limb from limb if her baby was in any kind of danger. She felt sorry for the first creature who tried to influence her children. She laughed to herself, thinking, *How do you spell killer? K-i-n-s-e-y!*"

Kinsey visited her grandparents, knowing they were playing card games with the two kids.

"Hey, Jaxon. Hello, my pretty girl," she said to her son and kissed her little girl. "All right, kiddos, tonight is an early night, and tomorrow starts early, so I could use a good cuddle from my little cuddle bugs," she said with a smile.

"Sounds good, Mom. I dominated against the family," Jaxon said.

"That's because Judy let you cheat," Saige said with a huge smile to Jaxon.

"I can take her down," Jaxon said without knowing that Aunt Judy was standing directly behind him.

"Oh, you think so?" Judy asked.

Jaxon's face turned white, and he refused to turn around. The whole family began laughing, and after the goodnights and kisses and goodbyes, they all left together.

Judy caught Kinsey's attention and had the kids walk ahead so she could talk with her in private. "So you got a double color. How does it make you feel?"

"Confused. Everyone seems to be freaked out or incredibly distant since they have seen it. I had an observation day, and Judy, the Watchers are some of the nastiest creatures I have ever seen. I was afraid. Judy, I'm a Guardian, and I am not supposed to have fear. So what do I do?" Kinsey asked with pleading eyes.

"Kinsey, sometimes there is no rhyme or reason to certain situations we are placed in, and you just have to wait this one out. God will never leave you with no answers, but just keep going, and whatever you do...don't stop!" Judy said, looking deeply in Kinsey's eyes.

In some way, and somehow, Kinsey knew exactly what Judy was telling her. "I love you, Judy. I just need some sleep after today. I am drained and exhausted."

"Don't forget to cleanse yourself after a day like today. The music is a good way to share how you feel and praise God for what he has done for you. The most important thing you can do is acknowledge and be honest with yourself about what is going on," Judy replied.

MORAJES THE MANIPULATOR

Morajes enjoyed the recent chaos caused by the Prince of Rome upon his recent release from captivity. His destruction kept spreading throughout all of the United Kingdom. All of the innocent people were ill-prepared for such gruesome attacks, and the rest of the world watched in shock as city after city was bombed to oblivion. She was in love with the melee. The recent bombings in Paris and attacks elsewhere entertained her. They fed her desire for chaos.

She was lying in bed with Gatticus, watching the attacks on the news after they had spent what felt like an endless weekend together. They enjoyed shopping, enticing and seducing the men and women around them. Since Gatticus had been alive during the height of the Roman Empire and quickly banished underground, he had a lot of catching up to do. A man with money can entice almost any young woman with no morals to do with her as he pleased, and he had a lot of pleasure that he wanted.

Gatticus had not been around Morajes in centuries, and now, here she was for the taking, just as luscious and full of desirable curves. He recognized that she was still incredibly beautiful but infinitely more deadly. It was her thirst for destruction and power that shocked him. When he first met her, she was softer, kinder. She was still a new demon with some ignorance left in her because she was not a part of the originals of the fallen. She was created from the perversion of Sodom and Gomorrah, but when he met her, the Romans were full of sexual desire and no modesty. She didn't need to seduce anyone for corruptive purposes.

He found himself in love with her back before he was sent underground with the Prince of Rome. He had the fantasy etched in his mind they had eternal life and they could be together forever.

Unfortunately, now she was overwhelmingly wicked, uncaring, and definitely cruel. He learned of Lucifer's plan to begin seducing children and animals into mainstream human desire and sexual lust. Gatticus found the news sickening. He was blown away because even though he may be a part of the darkness, he would take no part in that form of perversion. He knew deep down, though, it was a bad idea to tell Lucifer he would absolutely take no part, but he would find his way to dance around the requests. Suddenly, he realized why the man he met underneath the colosseum looked so defeated. That man had been watching life change for over a thousand years, and he was exhausted. Gatticus was just barely getting a taste of life, though, and wasn't ready to defy Lucifer just yet. He would just keep close to Morajes and follow her lead.

She crawled out of the bed and headed toward the shower. Gatticus was ready to travel the world and get his hands on as many women as possible. He was ready to bring back the perversion and sexuality he knew in Rome during the time he was alive. He wanted them to believe that sex was good and nothing to be ashamed of. He would entice to the mind that "the more, the merrier" was completely normal. Who cared if a marriage was destroyed, a girl shamed at school, or anyone received a disease? It wouldn't affect him. He was amazed when he heard of the different fetishes the current humans had. The information only made his job more entertaining.

"So where do you want to go next?" Morajes called from the bathroom.

"I don't really know. I know the world has changed a bit since I was banished. I know the Prince of Rome is having fun with all the chaos that he and the Prince of Persia have started. Persia has actually had to slow him down because of his thirst for chaos," answered Gatticus.

"Well, then, I must bring you home. It's beautiful, sunny, and full of all the beautiful people that you and I feed off and we desire," Morajes stated as she stepped out of the shower and placed herself in a shiny silky dress. "You will be proud of the darkness that is taking over this world. No man is immune to the Watchers."

"These Watchers didn't exist before I was banished. I mean, I know for a short time I saw things here and there, but now, I see them everywhere. They are hideous. How do you stomach them?" Gatticus asked.

"They were around back then, but you couldn't see them. They are beneath me. They are all beneath me. I am in human form and I am untouchable. There is nothing they can do to me. Lucifer needs me, and the best part is I can manipulate him to do whatever I want or need," Morajes answered.

Stunned and intrigued by her arrogance, he asked, "Does that mean I am beneath you as well?"

Morajes turned to smile at him. "Of course you are. I am the only one in the darkness who takes no orders. I always get what I want. Always," she said, looking straight into his eyes.

It made Gatticus uncomfortable, and the hairs on his arm stood on end. He found himself suddenly debating mentally on if he should seek out that other immortal. Then again, maybe he should stay close by her side so she didn't turn the darkness on him. He could sense how quickly she could turn on him, and deep down, he knew that was the last thing he wanted. He had no desire to get banished again. He just had a small taste of the current life for the past week, and it left him thirsty for more. "Well, then, we can make anything happen now," he stated, trying to play upon her natural instinct.

"Maybe later. There are more important things we need to accomplish back at home," Morajes stated while she was frantically packing her bag with all the new items she and Gatticus purchased while in Rome. She knew he needed a new look from the toga-style clothes he had on from when he was sent underground.

"All right, I will…try this shower thing and we can go. Ugh, how I missed my baths," he stated.

They took a flight to California by a private jet that Lucifer, of course, owned. Gatticus kept throwing up the whole time in the tiny bathroom provided on the plane. He couldn't quit shaking and was amazed by the fact that man was now in the sky like birds. He knew one thing for sure: he would never go into the sky again. Just the thought made him sick once more.

Morajes watched him, and true to her nature, she was incredibly annoyed. This was no man who deserved her time nor attention, but she needed him if she was to gain control over the darkness. She was tired of pretending to take orders. She was tired of the abuse and his destruction. She wanted revenge on him for letting her live. He should have killed her in the sand that day when her parents were murdered by God. All she had to do was convince Belial, Legion, and Gatticus to follow her. She had been seducing Belial and Legion for thousands of years, and now, with Gatticus, they could try to take the world for themselves. They weren't afraid of God like Lucifer was. She hated God more than Lucifer because Lucifer's anger toward God was taken out on her. She had to make sure all three were behind her, and then the four of them would overthrow Lucifer.

The only major problem she really had were the two Princes. Persia was always trying to appease her father, and it annoyed her. The Prince of Rome would have to come last because of his lust and thirst for destruction. He wouldn't want to be destroyed or banished again. She was ready to take over and had been planning strategically since she knew for certain that the boy had been born. The boy was a crucial element to gain control. Whoever controlled the boy would control the world.

Eddie, on the other hand, didn't have the strength nor the stomach. She would have to be careful with him or simply destroy him, whatever was necessary. Lucifer gave Eddie the tendrils so he couldn't lie, and if Lucifer got wind of anything, the whole plan would crumble before it began.

The jet landed, and Gatticus finally came out of the bathroom. He left a disgusting mess and still didn't quite understand how to use the toilet. Morajes snapped her fingers for Gatticus to follow. She led him to a red Ferrari parked close to the location where the jet landed. Morajes climbed into the driver's seat and signaled for Gatticus to get into the car. He was still getting used to regular doors and had not mastered how to use a car door. The bags were placed in the back, and he got in.

"Ready for some real speed?" she asked with an evil smile on her face.

"I don't think I can handle—"

Before he had the chance to finish his sentence, she was off, dashing through the streets of Los Angeles toward northern Hollywood. She made her way up and around Fairfax with ease as she drove on the opposite side of the street. No one could actually see the car, and Gatticus was getting ready to throw up once again.

Morajes looked his way and instantly spoke when she noticed the look on his face. "Don't even think of it. Ugh, you are so pathetic." She slowed down the fast beautiful sports car, and Gatticus finally adjusted. He kept his eyes closed, and when his stomach stopped turning on him, he opened his eyes back up. It was just in time as she stopped the car in front of a beautiful golden gate that protected a long driveway up toward a majestic mansion far out in the distance.

"It's beautiful," he stated. All the while, he was so overwhelmed with all the sounds, lights, and people. He was itching in the Armani suit Morajes made him wear, and he could tell she was annoyed that his sickness left several remnants on the designer outfit she hand-picked for him. He didn't like the tie and wanted to put his toga back on. Gatticus thought pants locked ridiculous on men, including the women he saw. He didn't understand the point of underwear because it was a deterrent for the ability to use the restroom quickly and efficiently. The toilet made him jump the moment he hit the silver handle and noted mentally that he never wanted to know where all the waste would all end up.

"It does what it's supposed to. It keeps the humans out and allows the darkness all the protection needed," Morajes stated. She drove in and parked the Ferrari in the driveway. She made Gatticus grab the bags from the back and bring them into the home.

Gatticus dropped the bags and luggage the minute he walked past through the threshold. The design, the furniture, and the colors overwhelmed him. He had been underground with the Prince of Rome so long that he forgot how beautiful the world really was. Now, though, he was in a foreign future world that he would now have to adjust to. The day was warm outside, and to feel air-conditioning against his skin felt beautiful. He could smell the perfume of Morajes, and it overwhelmed his senses. Two staircases greeted him in the entryway, and his curiosity took over him as he began to explore the mansion. He set the bags down and headed toward the top of one of the sets of stairs. He slowly walked down a long hallway with several doors and eventually found himself in a large bedroom where Morajes was changing. Her naked body danced before him as she was searching through a massive closet of clothes.

"Are we heading somewhere?" Gatticus asked with a smile.

"Well, no, *we* aren't. I am. I have some people today that I am about to destroy their future. Father made it clear that I needed to engage young girls, and today, that begins. I have them set up to begin in pornography, and I am running late," Morajes said as she dashed around the room, removing the previous clothes, and added on a tight high-slit red dress. Her curves seemed to stand out more than usual, and Gatticus wondered if that was supernatural. She dashed past him, and when he turned around, he found himself face-to-face with Belial. It almost scared the life out of him. Belial's hot breath came down on Gatticus's face, and if he had glasses on, they would have been fogged.

"Uh, umm... Mo-Moraj...es." Gatticus trembled at the sight of Belial. He had never seen a creature so dominating and terrifying at the same time.

"Good, Belial! You are here! We must have a quick meeting between the four of us before I go. I'm just waiting on Legion. Zip up the back of my dress, will you?" Morajes said toward the giant creature.

Belial didn't have a normal set of hands or feet. Three large stumps on each hand replaced what could at one time be considered fingers. Hooves replaced feet, and Gatticus was still scared. Through the animalist face, Belial snorted out toward Gatticus as his way of saying, "Get out of my way, boy."

Gatticus was, of course, all too happy and willing to accommodate. "Sure, no problem. What do you want me to do while you are gone?" Gatticus asked.

"Well, TV is there. Remote here. Umm, unless you want to come with us?" Morajes asked.

Gatticus could see Belial behind Morajes and quickly got the hint that he really wasn't invited. "No, I'll be fine."

"Good. I wasn't going to take you anyway," she replied as a loud snortlike grunt came from behind her. "Ah, Legion, you are here. Good. I need to ask you both, what do you know of the boy? Have you heard anything? And what have you been doing this week? Maybe we can make sense of it before my father does."

Belial grunted again and said, "Persia has been more attentive to Lucifer since our last meeting. He has had me help him cause anger to surge through the Middle East. We have been putting nothing but hatred in their hearts, so what usually is a rational man is now not. We believe the boy would come from that location due to the history and track record of the corruption. It just made the most sense to us."

"That's an excellent start, and you are so right. That is exactly where you should have started. Thank you, darling," Morajes said as she kissed Belial on the face.

Gatticus felt grossed out that she would even let the beast touch her. Just the thought made his skin crawl.

"Okay, Legion, what do you have for me?" Morajes asked.

The gray mist of Legion was in full form, and faces kept appearing that looked tortured and slaughtered. "From all the Guardians and Momenti, I keep hearing them talk about a new Guardian that has a double color. None of them know what it means, but that made me think of Eddie. There must have been a reason he was given two colors. It makes me think there is a reason, and they may want us to find this Guardian. I think it's a setup, to be honest."

"Are we ever truly honest, Legion?" Morajes asked as her words came out thick like honey. "Excellent start. Oh, I can't wait until I see Eddie again. Gatticus, you and I will find Eddie after I get back and ask him why he has the double color. Feassure is with him, so he should be easy to find. He's a moron, but he is a cute moron."

Belial bared his teeth at her words. Gatticus didn't want to go find Eddie because he didn't want to know anything but at the same time wanted to ask him about how these past thousand years had been. Was it worth it?

"I report to Lucifer today. He may show up before you and will get suspicious if you show up shortly after. Didn't you want to bring Gatticus?" Legion asked.

"Yeah, why don't you take me with you because then I can ask Eddie about his immortality and what tips he may have. Couldn't hurt," Gatticus said.

"All right. After I am done ruining these girls' lives, I will come and get you. Let's go, Belial. I need some one-on-one time," Morajes said.

Gatticus felt his stomach turn with the thought of the two of them together. He was beginning to seriously doubt the decision he made and was definitely thankful he at least had Eddie to help him understand this new world. For now, he would keep the facade of wanting to stay where he was.

Nothing Is a Coincidence

Big Ben and Annie stood together on the sands of the colosseum, waiting for Kinsey to arrive. They both had the same idea, and their discussions kept their minds running deeper and deeper down a rabbit hole. Annie's mind was unlike any other. She was quick and stealthy, not only with actions but with complicated situations mentally. Leilani called her the "Maze Runner" for a reason.

"Are you waiting for Kinsey?" Leilani asked as she broke them from their thoughts.

"Yeah," Big Ben answered.

"Are you going to train with her today?" Leilani asked.

"Well, we have an idea. I noticed her fear, and since we know that isn't normal, we may know a way to work through it. We both think it has something to do with the color," Annie answered.

"Yeah, those were my thoughts as well. I should have just asked you from the beginning. What is your plan with her today?" Leilani asked.

"I think we need to take her to the Hall of Infinium. She needs to see some of our personal experiences, and maybe it will help," Big Ben answered.

"Okay. I trust whatever you guys have planned. I know she is probably still recovering, so give her some time before you feel the need to—"

Just then, Kinsey approached behind them and repeated Leilani's words. "Before they feel the need to what?" Kinsey asked with a halfhearted smile. "I'm fine. I am exhausted from yesterday, but I am fine."

"Well, today, Ben and I want to show you something unique, something you wouldn't expect, and it has nothing to do with the Watchers," Annie said with a serious yet kind face.

"Sounds like a good day to me," Kinsey replied.

"Well, I will leave you guys to go play. I'm out with my brothers today. Reese and Tank, I believe, are going to be bringing all the final touches to your house today, Kinsey. We will all meet up at dinner," said Leilani.

"Sounds good," the three replied in unison.

"Well, what's on the menu today? I'll be honest, it took all the strength I could gather to get out of bed this morning. I don't think I am up for any major training today," Kinsey said, sounding really tired.

"That's okay because we want to take you to the Hall of Infinium. There is a memory we want you to see. We just want to give you a new adventure…with no Watchers. I know yesterday was exhausting, but maybe this will help understand how everything works," Annie replied.

"Sounds perfect. Thank you for taking it easy on me," Kinsey said as she yawned and took one last stretch before following behind Big Ben and Annie.

"Well, today you will observe, but you are going to observe a situation. What we want you to see is that nothing—and I mean nothing—under God is a coincidence," Annie said.

"Today will be a nice change of pace. We hope it will give you a new perspective on why things turn out the way they do," Big Ben said as he winked at Kinsey. "I believe there is a reason you had fear, and eventually, the answer will play out. Just give it time, but for now, let's take a trip down memory lane," he said with a smile.

They continued to walk in silence as they passed through the water garden. Kinsey loved watching the aquatic performance, and as odd as it sounded, the water made her comfortable, similar to the feeling when she would swim in the ocean, the gentle ride of the waves slowly rolling up and down again and again.

Big Ben opened the door for Kinsey and Annie. The bright lights from the spheres glistened in all of their eyes. Kinsey realized she still had more historical moments in time that she desperately wanted to visit but couldn't quite get herself to come alone. The three proceeded to the House of Memories and passed along the many, many hallways with numerous doors. Suddenly, they stopped at a door, and Big Ben and Annie pulled out their own Makirus and placed both of them on the spokes together. They turned the knobs and opened the door. Inside the room, it was empty, except for a medium-sized single blue sphere.

"What does this color represent?" Kinsey asked.

Annie and Big Ben looked to one another, then after a short pause, Annie answered, "How we met. Our story began at his death. We wanted you to see that nothing is a coincidence. When we both place our Makirus on the spokes, you will be able to watch his and my story together."

"Woah, no way! Yeah, I definitely wanna see this story," Kinsey replied.

They each placed their right index and middle finger onto the blue sphere, and suddenly, Kinsey was standing by herself in front of several people inside a doctor's office. She looked around and realized she was without Big Ben or Annie.

Kinsey took a minute to observe each one of the people in the waiting room, and none of them seemed to look familiar. She made a closer observation at a man directly in front of her, and he looked familiar, but she couldn't quite place him. After a few minutes of analyzing his features, it finally dawned on her; it was Big Ben! The man in front of her, though, was aged, frail, and not the tall, strong, quick warrior whom she admired as she watched him train with Annie every day.

As Kinsey stood in the room, she couldn't help but to study Big Ben's features. She could trace the deep end lines in his fragile face. The bright blue eyes she became captivated with by day after day were now heavy and almost a milky gray. In the midst of her thoughts, she heard Annie's voice break the silence as she said, "Just sit back and watch the story in front of you."

Kinsey started turning in circles looking for Annie, thinking maybe she was another patient in the room. After realizing no one she saw even came close to Annie's description, she sat down next to Big Ben and replied, "Okay."

Big Ben was sitting patiently in the waiting room of his doctor's office to find out some test results of some blood work that had been taken just two weeks prior. As Kinsey decided to sit down next to Ben, she observed him shaking his right leg and staring off into the distance. He was finally called from the waiting room into a smaller examining room, and Kinsey didn't have to wait long before the doctor came in. Big Ben had sat on the examining table, and Kinsey and Big Ben could both tell by the look in the physician's eyes that the news couldn't be good.

Kinsey observed that the physician was in his early seventies, and the years of working as a family practitioner were showing through on the lines in his face. His once golden-brown hair was now a silver gray, and his eyes barely seemed to open on normal occasions and usual visits as he spoke. His eyes this time, though, were steady and fixed upon Big Ben's. The next words spoken registered into his mind the three words no one ever wants to hear, the three words that every person shivers and dreads when spoken to themselves or a loved one: "You have cancer," the doctor said.

Kinsey held in her breath.

It was as if the room went silent for Big Ben, even though the doctor was speaking. There was a slight ringing in his ear blocking everything the physician was trying to say. He continued explaining what Ben could anticipate in the upcoming months of what little life he had remaining. The only other sentence Ben was able to hear and comprehend in the whole speech was aggressive and that he needed to prepare. Kinsey sat in awe, thinking he was there alone to face the fact that he had cancer. Somehow, Kinsey could see his thoughts as he began to reflect on his life and his past.

Kinsey could then see a small light come from the top of his forehead. A small screen began to play like a mini movie within the life-sized movie she was already watching. She finally understood what it meant when a person made the statement "their life flashed before their eyes."

Big Ben, in this particular moment, was sixty-five years old and had lived most of his life working as a mechanical expert on early model Corvettes. He was born in 1913. He grew up in an incredibly abusive and poor home and was the only boy out of four children. Lorena and Patricia were his older sisters, except Marie was four years younger than him. His older siblings were from the same mother but different fathers. It was quite a scandal for that day and age for a woman to be caught in any type of an affair. One night, on a usual drinking binge, Big Ben's father took his mother's first husband out further into the deepest part of the desert where no one would be heard or seen and after that night just never returned home. Shortly after, he married Big Ben's mother, and to avoid suspicion and scandal, the family moved from the desert out to the south so that no one would come asking unwanted questions.

Big Ben's father worked for the railroad and was as mean as a cobra when he drank. Needless to say, but more than obvious, he carried two nasty Watchers on his shoulders: one for his addiction and one for the dirty desire of young girls. He beat Ben senseless and did unspeakable things to his sisters. At the age of sixteen, Ben's oldest sister, Lorena, got married and left the home, never to be heard from again. His other sister, Patricia, followed soon as the abuse and drinking got worse. The girls were so empty inside, desperately missing the father that disappeared in the desert one night. The Watchers attached to his sisters' emptiness convinced his oldest sisters that drugs and men could be the only true way to numb from the situation.

The hardest part for both Patricia and Lorena is they were never allowed to ask about their father or what happened to him. He became replaced with a stepfather that was designed from the depths of their worst nightmares.

Kinsey's heart broke, and she felt herself become so angry at Ben's mother for only caring about herself and not her own children. Kinsey could understand why the children were all so angry, hurting and consistently existing in a living hell. How could a mother choose to walk away when her husband sexually abused her daughters and never tried to stop him from beating her only son? How could it not affect the rest of their lives? So when his sisters left, unfortunately, this left Big Ben and Marie to get the worse of the abuse.

One cold winter day, when Ben was fourteen, his father had been effortlessly drinking a full bottle of whiskey and was narrowing his abuse down on his little sister, Marie. Ben finally felt himself being filled with a sense of fury he had never experienced before, and it was taking him to his boiling point. He could feel himself getting ready to blow like a volcano, inactive for years that one day explodes, destroying everything in its path. Kinsey held her breath because it was as if she knew what he was thinking and could feel what he felt. Internally, he was screaming inside, begging his mother to stop the drunken attacks, but he knew, just as she had always done, she would turn and walk away.

As he went to pass the disgusting man known as his dad, his father tried to gain control of his neck as he usually did right before the swings to the face came. Ben had just slipped past the cold bony grasp and snatched the whiskey bottle that had been set on the table. He thrust and smashed it as hard as he possibly could on his father's head. The old man fell to the ground with such force, and his mother screamed for the first time ever, showing some genuine emotion. She stood frozen, eyes wide with horror. Her exact reasons for the emotional outburst Ben wasn't exactly sure of as he stopped to glare at her. He finally didn't care anymore. His rage finally took control of every cell in his body.

Kinsey grew chills all over her body. She died inside watching her friend explode from pain and observed that Marie had crept up and stood at her brother's side as he began to pound downward into their father's face. Ben struck his father over and over again, and as he did, he couldn't help but scream with each blow as blood began to spit out everywhere from his father's face. Ben's knuckles were cut, sliced, and crimson from the punches as he broke several of his father's teeth and jaw. Tears kept streaming down his face, and his eyes began to burn from the blood. All he could see was red. The anguish he felt inside as he watched this man enter into his sisters' rooms and how many times he caught him glaring at them with a sexual desire, all the physical pain Ben experienced came down to him finally setting himself free of this bastard. He wanted to set them all free.

Kinsey stood as still as a statue. She feared if she moved the scene would end. Her heart shattered into a thousand pieces for her teammate and the pain he had to endure. She felt no sympathy for the man who lay bleeding and disfigured on the floor. Kinsey didn't even feel like Ben would ever need to ask for forgiveness for his actions or his anger to God because the pain this man caused the four innocent children was justly served.

During the attack, Marie, the most innocent of them all, just stood motionless, clutching her favorite stuffed bear. Since the encounters began when her father came into her room, they were captured in her memory. The bear was her only source of comfort since her mother cared more about appearance than pain. Even as the blood of her father reached up to her face, she didn't flinch. Her big blue eyes never blinked as the drips from the blood upon her forehead started to fall down her cheeks. Even though she was a little girl, she had just as much hatred for her father as her brother did, and she refused to weep for this man. Every touch would be held captive within her memories, and it would haunt her for years to come, and he didn't deserve one single tear. She was so still and motionless it was barely visible that she was even breathing. It wasn't until she finally blinked and looked at her mother that she realized that her brother had stopped the attack upon their father and was sitting on his chest, sobbing.

Kinsey had tears streaming down her face. She was so wrapped in the moment and the broken children that endured so much pain. It made her feel like she was dying inside. She couldn't and didn't want to believe that people like Ben's parents existed. She vowed on several occasions that if anyone ever laid a hand on her children, she would go to prison for their death.

After several moments, as a wave of euphoria rushed through Ben's veins, he surprised both Marie and Kinsey as he quickly stood up and spat on his father's chest after kicking him a few times into his side. His father lay motionless and just happened to breathe his last breath as the bubbles of blood arose from what appeared to be his mouth.

Ben's mother stood frozen, crying massive sobs as if it had finally become apparent that she had allowed such abuse to happen. This was her fault, and now it was time for her to face the music. She was starting to realize in this moment of terror she cared more about appearance than the pain she caused her children. They were innocent, and she chose not to protect her babies. She fell to her knees, unable to move as though she had the weight of the world was forcing her downward. She looked at her only son and was barely able to say the words, "I'm sorry."

Ben stood up and ran straight over to his mother, and she trembled to his presence. He looked like a titan and not a fourteen-year-old boy.

"*Don't you ever—*" Ben paused as he gazed down at his mother with a fire burning inside him. He wanted to make sure she understood the seriousness of his words. "Don't you ever allow anyone to hurt my sister again!" he continued to his mother, startling her as his voice grew deeper.

Ben got his second wind and ran back toward his father. He spat on his father's chest one more time before screaming as loud as he possibly could, "*I hate you!*" His breathing sped up, and his hands shook as he kept looking at the mess he made of his father's face. It was only a few moments before he had assessed all the damage he had done. Blood was splattered around the whole room with large trails on the ceiling. After he had enough of the image that would forever stain his memory, he turned to see Marie.

He approached his sister, kissed her on the head, and she wrapped her arms around him so tightly. He slowly let go and placed his bloody hand on her chin. He looked deeply into her saddened but aware eyes and whispered softly, "He's not going to hurt you anymore, Marie. No one will. I promise!" He held onto her for a few more moments and then loosened his grasp and began to walk back toward his mother.

He stopped purposely to meet his mother's gaze as she slowly looked up at him. He glared into her eyes with the same fire burning in them from taking down his father. After a moment of silence, he spoke slowly but clearly, making sure he had his mother's full attention. "If I hear from Marie"—he paused as he kneeled down to get eye level with her—"that anyone ever touches her again, I will kill not only them...but I will kill you too!" His rage began to boil up again as he screamed at his mother, *"Now take care of this, do you hear me? You take care of this, not Marie! Get one of those men you flirt with when Dad isn't around to help you!"*

Kinsey felt like her breath had just been sucked out of her body. Big Ben was just a boy, yet in that moment, he became a man.

Ben knew that his mother often flirted with other men, and he knew that one of the men she had been speaking to behind his father's back would gladly help her take care of his father's body. He heard her on several occasions speaking to some strange man when his father was at work about how she wanted to leave him due to the abuse.

After he took his gaze from her, he went into his bedroom to gather all of his clothes. He knew that his mother wouldn't involve the police and he also knew that he couldn't stand to look at her anymore because all he felt was disgust. He spared his mother's life only for his sister's sake because Marie needed their mother. Ben knew deep down he would never depend on his mother again. He knew what he was capable of now when his rage took over, and he realized that he needed to cage the wild animal that would devour anything in its path when released through anger.

He was so incredibly exhausted from the emotional outlet he couldn't stop his hands and knees from trembling. How could any mother allow anyone to hurt her own flesh and blood? How does a parent purposely and knowingly hurt their own children? He didn't understand how and why a woman who is supposed to nurture and protect *chose* to turn cold and walk away. Big Ben decided deep down he would never give his heart to anyone since the ones who were supposed to protect him the most failed him. He felt a woman would just drag him back into the darkness that he despised and vowed he would never go back into that darkness.

Kinsey barely had a chance to absorb the fact that her friend murdered his father. Just the thought gave her chills. She questioned and was anxious to know where Big Ben would go next. He was still just a kid, but Kinsey knew deep down that she had to follow where this story was about to go.

When Ben left home, he ended up living with a friend he met at school. He was lucky. Since his family had moved so much, Ben hardly stayed in the same school long enough to maintain a genuine friendship. The abuse was obvious to anyone around, and every time someone was about to step in and help, the family was conveniently relocated to another state along the railroad. This caused Big Ben not only to be cut off but shy.

Somehow, a boy named Tommy was able to break through Ben's tough exterior walls. Tommy was an outgoing, kind, and care-free kid. Ben found Tommy and his family to be a breath of fresh air. For the first time in his life, Big Ben grew the first healthy bond. He had spent as much time as he possibly could at Tommy's house, and his parents welcomed him with open arms as they could tell by the occasional bruises what was going on at home.

Tommy's father, Raymond, had become the father Big Ben so desperately needed. He took the boys hunting, fishing, and occasionally to a special place out in the middle of the country. He wanted to give the boys a place where a man can be left with his thoughts, drink as much as he wanted, and not be hounded with day-to-day life.

Soon after Big Ben went to live with Tommy, several other friends ended up living at Raymond's house as well. There was a magical connection within the home for all the local boys from the wrong side of the tracks. At one point or another, they all had a place they felt loved and welcomed. Raymond's wife, Virginia, always made sure the boys had a fresh hot meal since some of the boys didn't get full meals on a daily basis. She would thrift shop for clothes they could all share since they were all the same size.

The best part about living with Raymond and Virginia was that they provided a trusted safe place. They now had a loving male role model to teach them to be men and the tender touch of a nurturing mother. The boys didn't even mind having to share a room with each other, just as long as they got to bathe, eat, and know they had a place to call home.

The next two of their friends from school came and joined the family, one being known as a mouthy and quick-witted redhead they nicknamed Fox and a nervous and uptight kid named Billy Sommers. Raymond gave Billy the nickname Cole because he genuinely believed if they placed a lump of coal up his backside, they would get a diamond by the end of the week. Billy was nervous, always looking over his shoulder and incredibly tense due to the same upbringing Big Ben left behind. The exception to Billy was he experienced massive sexual abuse. Ben never asked Billy about his family but felt that if Billy ever wanted to talk about it, he would. The biggest thing Big Ben always felt that he kept as a motto was to leave the past in the past.

The best way for the boys to tell that Raymond genuinely cared for someone was he would give each of the boys a nickname. It was his term of endearment. Big Ben's real name was Benjamin Dean, and one night after a fight with a kid from the right side of the tracks, Ben puffed his chest out to show dominance. He kept making himself look more menacing and dipped into the Ben that killed his father. If he could tap into that rage, he knew he could rip this kid apart. That's when Raymond decided on Big Ben. The name just stuck, and it became his identity. He just tried to care for the boys and make sure they became good men.

Raymond also made sure each one of the boys did their homework every night after dinner, and each boy felt they had a place in the home. He gave them a share of chores, and as the boys grew older, they worked for Raymond's locally owned gas station. The gas station serviced the town that they all lived in, and Raymond taught each of them how to work on the cars that came in. Eventually, as the boys entered high school, they added two more friends into their family, Robert and Arnold, and in usual fashion, Raymond renamed them Hoss and Ernie.

As everything played in front of Kinsey, she was lost in a trance. She always loved the way guys could be fun with one another and not dramatic like women all tend to get. No lies behind the backs, just funny jokes to enjoy the company. Where were guys like these when she was alive?

The boys were rarely ever separated, and minimal moments of any bickering took place amongst the group. If they teased each other, it was out of love and never out of jealousy, spite, or hatred. They played sports together from football to baseball either for a team or just with each other and more guys from school. Since Raymond taught them all to work on cars at the gas station, they each grew a preference in which make and model that became their favorite.

Big Ben wasn't completely sure, but intuition told him that he and Raymond shared a very similar past. It was only on a couple of occasions when one or two of the boys got in trouble at school, and Raymond went out of his way to open up and not just yell and scream. He would talk to the boys through their choices. Tommy, Big Ben, Billy, Fox, Hoss, and Ernie all loved and respected the man that took them in. Their real parents never fought to make them come home, and it was confirmation in all the boys' hearts that this home is where they were meant to be. Individually, they all knew they were lucky to have a man like Raymond in their life.

Big Ben always checked in on his sister to make sure she was okay, and he was thankful no one ever laid a hand on Marie again. The guys at school who wanted to date the pretty blue-eyed brunette knew she had six older brothers they had to get approval from before they ever stood a chance. It gave Marie a sense of true love and protection that she had always needed. She was ever grateful that her brother took his place with pride.

His mother stayed single for several years before she ever allowed another man in the home. It took even longer before Ben was able to actually speak to his mother again. On a few occasions, she would arrive unexpectedly at Raymond's house, wanting to plead with her son to come home. Raymond never stood in the way, but he gave Ben the choice on what he wanted to do. Each time, it was the same. This is where he was happy, and this is where he knew he was safe.

Every time Ben considered the thought of going back into that house, he would get instant flashbacks of every horrible thing that had gone on. Since his father didn't have any friends other than the few he worked with, no one ever reported him missing. His mother went to work, and his father was never even a whisper; just a faded and wasted memory.

Kinsey had tears in her eyes, realizing that every single person in the world that she lived and died with had some form of pain they experienced. She never understood why she was never able to let the past go as easily as others. The many suicide attempts over the loss and depression she experienced so frequently were like stains in her memory. Her mind being her biggest enemy was minor compared to a father beating his son senseless over and over again.

Suddenly, everything went dark, and the little movielike projection from Ben's thoughts brought her back to him sitting in the doctor's office. Kinsey found it odd that she saw him grow up, and then was whisked back to where she started.

Suddenly, Big Ben was overcome with a horrible feeling that he would become just a faded memory. He never married and he never had children. Now his life was coming to this moment, and the doctor looked down at Ben sitting on the examining table and waited for a response. He just sat there and became lost, deep in thought for several moments. "I guess this doesn't surprise me," he stated out loud, looking back over his life, and how he still had so much unforgiveness toward his father and mother.

"Mr. Dean, do you have any family members that you can stay with or any close by that can assist you?" the doctor asked him, looking more and more concerned.

"I haven't seen my sisters in over forty years, and my youngest sister lives on the East Coast. She is an attorney with kids. I can't interrupt her life," he stated, looking down at the floor.

"Well, what about any close friends?" The doctor pressed on.

Big Ben suddenly had a moment of anger as if it had finally kicked in this man was telling him he was dying. "What are you getting at, Doc? How much time are we looking at here that you have to tell me to call my family or friends? Level with me, and don't BS. Cut the crap. I don't have time or the energy for it." He stared straight into the doctor's eyes with determination, and his brow furrowed.

"When cancer spreads to your lymph nodes, it ends up throughout your whole body and all the systems that make up the human structure. At most, you may have a couple months left. You have not been feeling so great for a few years, and because you had waited so long to get yourself checked out, there is little medically that can be done in such a short amount of time. With the lack of energy and the sudden pain within your body, I wanted to rule everything else out before it came to checking your body for this," the doctor replied.

"Great. Just absolutely great," Ben said with pure sarcasm. He was so angry he wanted to cry and he had not shed a tear in his life since he had beaten his father at fourteen. He cussed to himself, mumbled a few words that would make a sailor faint, and closed his eyes to gather his composure before he looked back up at the doctor and asked, "So what's next?"

"Well, the next thing is to contact hospice and have them come in, assist, and care for you as needed." The doctor hesitated for a moment as he had only seen this man several times before he got really sick. The more Ben came in to find out what was wrong, the more the physician saw the anger in him and decided to be firm but also gentle with his words.

"Find peace with whatever or whoever you need to. I just know when cancer comes so quickly and aggressively, there is some kind of traumatic event that may have taken place. I say this because I saw it in my father. My father had a rage inside him that was indescribable. He was an alcoholic and abusive and he was definitely broken. His cancer did the same thing to him. So...just something to think about?"

Ben sat there, shocked and in awe. Kinsey just stood by and read his body language. She could see he looked so defeated and just plain tired. Just as Ben was about to ask for information, the nurse walked in and provided him a list of the local home health care agencies in the local area.

Kinsey followed Big Ben, and she could tell that the drive home was one of the hardest drives he ever had to do. She rode alongside him, observing that he had tuned out all sound around him. He felt as though he was standing still, and all the world was racing around him. A few times, he was honked at for waiting too long while stopping at the traffic lights. The drive was about a half hour with all the traffic, and it seemed like less than a minute since he blanked out for most of the journey.

As soon as he got home, he sat in the driveway for several minutes, not really thinking and was just motionless. He stared straight ahead for about a half hour before he realized he had not even tried to get out of the car.

Kinsey wanted to hold him. She wanted to say, "Trust me, the afterlife is so beautiful.," but Kinsey knew she wasn't with him when he experienced this moment. There was nothing she could do or say. He wouldn't see her anyway.

When he finally had the strength to get himself onto the driveway and into his house, he realized for the first time that his house actually looked empty. It felt void. Nothing special on the lawn, just very low-cut perfectly trimmed grass. His house showed absolutely no signs that a woman had ever given her personal touch in it. He never had a desire to get married since his mother cared more for herself. He never got over his distrust for women. He was never cruel to women, just never cared for a wife. Big Ben was an attractive looking man for a Guardian and a human. He was often told by his friends they had the perfect woman for him. Fox and Hoss had tried for years to set him up with all kinds of dates, yet in the end, it was always the same result.

Big Ben would never allow himself to move relationships forward. He thought from time to time about wanting kids, but he enjoyed his solitude and freedom for the occasional poker game with the guys he grew up with. As the years passed by, one by one, all the guys he lived and grew up with all got married and had kids. Big Ben, of course, was happy for them but just didn't see it in his future. Except right now, he wished he had even just a dog to come home to.

He approached his fireplace, and Kinsey took her place at his side. He just stood in front of his fireplace, looking gently at the pictures he had placed on the mantle, each one neatly framed and each one with the same men. The only thing that changed in the pictures of the five men was the groom was always different. Inside, he didn't feel anything as he looked at them, just pure apathy because he knew if he allowed himself to feel any kind of regret, the floodgates would open, and he just couldn't bear that amount of emotion at this point.

Kinsey looked at the pictures one by one. It broke her heart. She never found true love either, but her fault was trying to find a man when she was so broken inside. She tried to fill the hole in her chest with any man who would take her in. Here she was, looking into five different wedding pictures, each with the same men celebrating a union with another person, and Big Ben never experienced it. She realized fully that she and her teammate could connect more now that she knew his past.

Big Ben backed away and his first action he decided to do was to have a good stiff drink. He despised whiskey since that was the choice of his father. Big Ben's anger took over, and he said out loud, "My father! *Ha!* He's the one responsible for this." He then changed his direction as if he was speaking directly at his father. "*It's all your damn fault! It's because of you I never knew love. It's your fault that I couldn't get close. You selfish bastard hurting innocent kids. You deserved what I did to do you. I would do it again if I had to.*"

Kinsey stood shocked. She had never seen Big Ben angry nor had she ever heard him be angry. She realized why Raymond, the man that raised him, called him Big Ben. There was fire that came out of Ben when he got angry. It wasn't just anger; it was pure rage, and he looked like a beast when he screamed out. He definitely deserved and earned the name Big Ben.

Ben only had a bottle of scotch and felt kinda shocked he had it and couldn't for the life of him remember why he had it. "What the hell?" he said to himself.

He then pulled out one of the five beer glasses with his name on it that was given as a gift from each of the weddings he was in. It had become an inside joke for his friends, and they each told Big Ben at one point they were waiting for the sixth glass. He paused for a moment before he added a few ice cubes since he couldn't stand warm alcohol and started to pour. He took his drink, walked over, and sat down in his favorite chair and decided to call his sister. He wanted to tell her that he loved her, even if it sounded strange coming out of nowhere.

Over the years, Marie had sent Christmas and birthday cards from the kids and herself, wishing he could come visit. Unfortunately, he always made himself out to be as busy as she was, so it helped him feel less lonely inside. Slowly, he dialed her number and waited as it rang and rang and rang. He finally hung up and just rested the cold drink upon his forehead. "I may as well pound the whole bottle. Maybe it will help the process go faster," he said as the alcohol began warming his veins and he had become more lucid and slightly carefree. He knew he didn't mean the words, but he couldn't help but honestly feel so lost and alone. He took a giant swig of his drink, and then he couldn't fight back the tears anymore.

Kinsey didn't blame him for wanting to escape the reality he was now in. She felt horrible that he stayed alone and literally had no one. Out of nowhere, the scene Kinsey was watching sped up as if someone hit fast forward on a movie. Big Ben had spent the next several weeks at home, and it took him just as long before he finally called for someone to come in and help him. By this time, he had made all the appropriate calls as each of his childhood friends nagged him constantly that it was time for the help. Each one had offered to come over and help or tried to insist he stay with them, but in his true stubborn fashion, he didn't want to depend on anyone. He didn't want the pathetic looks his friends gave him, knowing he was dying. Within the depths of his soul, he hated that more than anything else.

One day, when the pain was out of control and he was completely alone, he finally made the call, and they said a nurse would be out in the morning. That night, he drank what felt to be his own body weight in liquor and passed out on the couch.

Big Ben was awoken by a banging on the door, and with his pain coursing through his veins and the pounding headache that was starting to consume his every movement, he tripped over bottles and finally stumbled to the door and managed to open it.

"Good morning, Mr. Dean! My name is Annie from Home Health Care Services," Annie said as Ben peered from the opened door. He looked like he hadn't slept in about a week, and the pain in his body was starting to show through his face. He had not shaved in about three weeks, and the unpleasant aroma of booze coming from his body, swiftly passed through the house and into Annie's nose. She winced slightly as she caught a whiff of the booze from his pores. He was wearing black sweatpants, a gray t-shirt, and had a robe over him that was opened and just hanging from his body.

"Oh, this is where Annie entered his life," Kinsey said out loud as if speaking to them in the moment. She was beginning to wonder if Annie was even a part of his life.

"Hi," was about all he could mumble as his eyes were squinting in the sunlight, and he could barely see the woman at the door. She was wearing nurse scrubs and had a bag with her, but he didn't notice a car anywhere. She was what Raymond would have described as a younger Black gal with a pretty smile and a familiar Southern twang that sounded of home. Her voice was far too perky for his liking, especially at this time in the morning. At least he thought it was morning. He had given up on checking the clock after he left his job and decided to just stay at home.

"May I come in?" she asked patiently as she stood at his doorway for several minutes, still trying to hold a smile on her face.

Realizing he had not invited her in, he stepped aside and watched her as she entered. He knew she was going to make some kind of comment about all the alcohol bottles all over the living room and the empty beer cans and pizza boxes in the kitchen. He braced himself and waited for a moment as he saw her taking in the room.

"Well, as I said before, I am Annie, and I am here to make life a little more comfortable. The first thing I would suggest, Mr. Dean, is to, uh, shower and brush your teeth. I think I am getting dizzy just smelling you," she said with a smile, and more of her Southern twang came out. "While you do, I will clean up and change the sheets, start any laundry, and anything else you may need to help keep you comfortable. I can even go to the store and get some groceries for you, but it would have to be tomorrow because I don't have a car and I would have to plan ahead."

Benjamin didn't know how to take this moment. He never let strangers in his home before, and he certainly wasn't used to a woman, especially a Black woman, telling him what to do. *But whatever*, he thought, *it's 1978. Times, they are changing.* And without saying a word, he walked to his bedroom to shower up and shave.

Annie decided to just clean up the bottles and put them all together. She cleaned up the kitchen, throwing away all trash, and washed any dirty plates. She looked around for some blankets and pillows to make it more comfortable in his living room as it seemed to be the place he was sleeping. She grabbed what blankets have been left scattered around the room, including clothes, and placed them in the washer. As she was done with everything, he came strolling down the hallway, clean-shaven, fresh-smelling, and in new clothes. She opened the blinds to let sunlight in and even opened a couple windows to allow fresh air to cleanse the home.

"Now doesn't that feel better already, Mr. Dean?" Annie asked, smiling as he walked into the room. She could tell by his body language he wasn't comfortable with someone in his home. She was sure this wasn't easy, a stranger cleaning his home, let alone a woman he didn't know trying to take care of him.

Benjamin looked around the room, and he mumbled, "You cleaned." His eyes kept squinting from the sun shining through the window.

"Yes, sir, I did, and if I am gonna be here taking care of you, I need to be where it's clean and comfortable. So how are you feeling today?" Annie spoke with a soft but firm voice. She wanted to make it clear that she was gentle, but she did have her standards. As she asked the question, she sat on the couch and began to take her paperwork out that needed to be signed.

Kinsey couldn't believe how cold Ben was being toward Annie. They were so close, and she was so used to seeing them working together. She wondered if maybe they died together, and that's why they had stayed together. Then she decided to finish listening to the conversation.

"Peachy," he grunted to her. He slowly pushed his way passed around her and sat down on the couch. All he could focus on was getting rid of the pounding hangover and the excruciating throbbing pain soaring through his body. It was spreading more as the days went on. He didn't want to accept the fact that he was dying, let alone dying with a stranger in his home. He had tried calling his sister several times, and each time, there was either no answer or she was so busy the phone call lasted less than five minutes. Not the perfect time to say, "Hey, Marie, I'm dying." No. Instead, he called an attorney and asked him to send her everything she needed with a letter explaining that he tried to get in touch with her but there was limited time. He knew it was not the most subtle way, but he wasn't much for sugarcoating in life as it was anyway. That was one of the traits he had obtained from Raymond. Just come out and say it; you're not always going to make everyone happy anyway.

Annie grabbed her bag and decided to take his vital signs and just spend time getting to know her new patient. She had a special place in her heart for people who were alone and who were sick. It broke her heart to watch someone with no family to take care of them, so she went out of her way to do the best she could, and from each patient she was with, she took a little keepsake. It would be a small and unnoticeable keepsake like a keychain or a magnet, and she wrote their name on it and brought it home when they passed away. She could tell he would be a little harder to get to know since he didn't talk much, and he didn't engage her very often for conversation.

Two months passed, and Big Ben's condition had grown considerably worse than what he had anticipated, but he had begun to open more and more to Annie as he realized he truly enjoyed her company. He would make sure he had always showered, shaved, and had clean clothes on when she came over. He wasn't quite sure why, but he wanted to impress her. Her smile captivated him and even made him smile. This was definitely not familiar to him, and it left him slightly confused, wondering if maybe it was the steady flow of morphine flowing through his system.

As he grew to learn about Annie, he found out she lived in the same town as she did in Mississippi for a small point in time. He would tell her funny stories about Raymond, and she even knew about the gas station he worked at as a young man. Annie would engage in his stories and make Big Ben definitely feel so much more comfortable with each passing day. He began to feel that he could ask more about her personal life and past. He wanted to know if she was ever married, and she stated she was divorced. Did she have children and because of life's choices? She did not. Why was she a nurse? And most of all, why she didn't drive a car?

"Truth be told, Mr. Dean, I haven't always had an easy life. My father died when I was a little girl, and my mother just couldn't cope. She made horrible decisions for myself and my siblings by all the different men she would bring in. My brother is the oldest, and he tried to take care and look out for me and my younger sister as best as he could. He was just fourteen at the time my father died. My father was incredibly kind and hardworking. He was a man of God and raised us kids to believe, and every Sunday, we were very involved in church. Unfortunately, when he died, it left a gaping hole within my mother. I came to learn that her faith was dependent on him, and when he was gone, so was her belief. I loved my mother, but she chose men over us from that moment on, and I had to just fend for myself. It wasn't easy for a young Black girl in the heart of Mississippi to find people who are willing to help you out."

Big Ben took it in for a minute and realized that he wished he had a friend like her his whole life. His buddies growing up came from similar backgrounds, it's true, but to have a woman friend and not only that but one who was funny, intelligent, and easy on the eyes. He realized they shared the same childhood experiences, and it made him grow a love for her. Not so much a romantic love but a pure love like she would be a best girlfriend. He never thought they would have so much in common.

One day, when he was feeling better than usual, he got her to sit and have a beer with him on the porch and talk about their own wishes and dreams. He decided to ask her about her favorite food, favorite singer, and even song. She laughed and said, "I loved my mother's breakfast meals when my father was alive. Oh, she loved him, and she showed it in every aspect of her life trying to be a good wife. My favorite singer is Smokey Robinson, and I love 'You Really Got a Hold on Me.' Something about that song just reminds me of my father and how he would embrace my mom and express his love for her."

Ben thought for a minute and said, "This might surprise you, but I actually love some Smokey too!"

Annie smiled as she took another drink of her beer and asked, "Is that right? What do you know about Smokey? You don't know nothing about no Smokey!" she stated, laughing at him.

Then suddenly, Ben got very serious and told Annie something he never thought he would say to her. "Annie, you're the first woman I have ever allowed to get close to me. I have grown to really enjoy your company, and to be honest, I appreciate everything you have done for me."

Taken back by the statement, she put her beer down and looked at him with eyes that dug deep into his soul and saw so much pain. He started to tear up slightly and looked away. "Mr. Dean, I find that hard to believe. It may feel like that right now, and it's a normal feeling, but people struggle with illness and death all differently."

"No, Annie, I never really lived. When I look back, in my eyes, I just existed each day. I did what I wanted to do, and deep down, I am sad that I didn't live more freely. I took things so seriously, and that really hurt. I never got married nor had children because of my distrust of women due to my mother. I have watched my best friends over the years all move on with life, and truth be told, I don't know what it was inside me that wouldn't allow me to do the same." Ben stopped for just a moment and then asked Annie, "Did I ever tell you about Raymond? The man who raised me and my friends?"

"No, you didn't, but I am all ears." Annie was genuinely curious about Big Ben's past and what caused him to cut people off so easily or caused him not to trust anyone.

Annie sat quietly, listening to him as he talked about all the things he had always wanted to do but never had the courage to. He even expressed about the one woman he had fallen in love with, but because of his fears of true intimacy, he let her slip away, and that was his biggest regret. Last he heard of her, she was happy with a new baby, and even though he was angry with himself, he was happy for her.

Kinsey sat by patiently and just got lost in the story taking place in front of her. Her heart melted over the friendship that had been displayed in front of her. Suddenly, the thought came up that she didn't see how the two of them meeting was a coincidence. She called out to Annie and Big Ben. "Am I missing something here?"

She heard Ben's voice in a soft reply back to her, "Just wait."

Ben suddenly fell forward in front of Annie. She panicked but was able to get him into his bed and stayed at his side as his body began to give up at a rapid pace. A frail Ben called out and told Annie, "I am in so much pain and I know I am getting to my time. Annie, can God forgive everything?"

"Of course. Some people want to disagree, but everyone deserves a do-over here and there, she said as she held his hand.

"I killed my father at fourteen. I realize now that's why I kept others at a distance. He was a horrible man, and I know I did wrong, but he was disgusting," he confessed.

Annie sat for a moment and thought. "You know, I realize we could be wrong, but in all honesty, something in me says otherwise."

Ben closed his eyes as two tears dropped down. "There is a letter for you. Go ahead and open it."

Annie stood up and found a small envelope with a letter inside. There was a set of keys that dropped out, and as Annie read the letter, Ben stopped breathing. When she finished the letter, she turned to ask Ben why there were keys, but he was gone. She then noticed there was a pink slip he signed to give her a vehicle. She dropped to her knees and felt her heart shatter. She knew the car in the driveway was to be given to his sister if she wanted it, but she had never seen a different car. She decided to go into the garage and she saw a cover over the car before her. She pulled it back and noticed it was a beautiful 1941 Woody. She opened the door, slid onto the seat, and tears came falling from her eyes. She wasn't sure why but she pulled down the visor, but a picture fell down. There were three young guys posing next to the Woody.

Suddenly, Annie's stomach dropped. When her father died, there was a little girl who was an eyewitness. She had explained to the policemen that she didn't fully run home because she wanted to get a good look at the three men who attacked the nice man who saved her. Annie began screaming. She gripped the steering wheel and yelled at the top of her lungs, "*Why?*"

Kinsey couldn't believe it. This man murdered her father, and Annie befriended him and took care of him. "Oh my God! What are the chances?" Just as Annie had said, there is nothing that is a coincidence when it comes to God. This is what she meant. Kinsey then saw someone sitting in the seat next to Annie in the red pickup along with another much younger Ben standing outside the car. The man Kinsey saw was that archangel that reacted weird toward her when she first arrived in heaven. Itherial was sitting next to his Annie.

Her heart sped up as she saw Big Ben approach Itherial and tell him how so sorry he was. He had tears fall from his eyes and just kept saying he was so sorry for the pain he caused not only in Annie's life but the rest of his family and friends. Itherial then put his hand on his daughter's shoulder, and Annie instantly stopped crying. She wasn't filled with rage but compassion and instant peace. Things didn't always make sense, and she learned that from an early age.

Kinsey kept still as she watched Itherial kiss his daughter on the cheek and then turn toward Ben and say, "Time to go home."

Instantly, Kinsey was whisked back to the Hall of Infinium. She was standing before her two team members. "How in the world did you just let that go? I can imagine that was so painful," she asked.

"It wasn't easy, but the fact that my dad placed his peace in me... I was able to let go. I never told my brother about who owned the car. In all honesty, mine had crashed, and I had lost two jobs taking the bus. I was down on my last leg, and just in time, it was a gift. I could have destroyed it, but what would that do? Satisfy a need for blood I genuinely didn't need?" Annie replied. "No. That wouldn't help."

"When I got here, I saw Jesus and had to ask if she had forgiven me. He told me she had, and when she got here, Jesus and I met her with Ray and Mittens. Our souls were connected in a way we didn't fully understand. It makes sense now but would never be okay on earth," Big Ben told her.

"This is heavy. I am starting to feel left out. I haven't met with Christ yet, and I am getting a little discouraged. I understand that my two colors are getting concerned looks. No one seems to want to tell me what's going on. I was born at night, but it wasn't last night. So how does this relate?" Kinsey said with a discouraging tone.

"Well, we believe your color has some significance with what's coming," Annie said.

"What do you mean what's coming?" Kinsey asked with her eyes burning through both of her teammates.

Big Ben and Annie were both silent. They just realized no one had told her that a boy had been born, a unique boy, and that Lucifer was stopping at nothing to find him. They didn't know how to approach the subject, but then they realized they still couldn't tell her. Itherial had said that they couldn't tell her.

"Well," Annie said slowly, saying the words she knew would cause some pain and that secrets had been kept from Kinsey.

"Hey, guys, what's happening?" Reese said from behind the group. "I have to take Kinsey to the Worship Hall."

Both Annie and Big Ben were relieved they didn't have to divulge information that was meant to be kept unknown.

"All right," Kinsey said. The fact that they were hesitant kept bothering her in the back of her mind. She realized that she messed her life up more often than not. She finally knew why she had the double color. Deep down, she wanted to cry, but she couldn't. She realized that she desperately needed to go to the Worship Hall.

"Okay, dear, let's go." Reese said.

Kinsey didn't turn around nor say goodbye to her teammates. She wasn't angry with them. She was confused. A million thoughts flashed in her head, and then she had the answer. She would mess up. She would mess up big time. She realized, though, she couldn't focus on that in the chance she would be wrong. She knew what self-prophecy was all about. If you speak something into existence, then the Watchers would hear and know the weakest thing in her. She was so exhausted emotionally.

Kinsey didn't say anything to Reese as they walked quietly together. Reese didn't know what Ben and Annie had revealed to her, but he was sure it wasn't anything fun. She didn't have her usual carefree demeanor.

"I think your buddy, Johnny, will be there, playing. Maybe he can sign something that will perk you up?" he finally said.

"That would be helpful because I could really use some answers or something that will help me shake whatever it is that is bothering me. I wish I could just know what this whole double color is all about. I am getting so frustrated with the awkward stares or looks I keep getting. I know that no one means any harm, but it feels like I am still alive, about to deal some incredible chaos. I know this feeling, and it's way too familiar," Kinsey said.

Reese felt bad for Kinsey. He knew that it must be painful to be alone in this current state. He had to keep his faith that she would be fine, and he knew deep down God knew what he was doing.

They arrived at the Worship Hall, and Kinsey went straight in. Reese was right, and Johnny was there. She cried as he sang several songs, and when his turn was over, he went down to go talk to her. "What's wrong?"

"Look at me!" Kinsey said as she pointed to herself. "I lived so many years of chaos and pain, and all I want is peace. I don't feel peace being different. I don't wanna be different. I just want to enjoy my afterlife, and I can't do that when everyone keeps looking at me."

Reese couldn't say anything, and he felt horrible that his friend didn't know what she was coming up against. He couldn't tell her, and he was starting to break down inside because he couldn't imagine what it must feel like.

"Well, from what I can see, you were chosen for a reason. You may have a special talent that no one else here has. Doesn't mean it's bad or that no one else has talents because we all do," Johnny said.

Kinsey just shrugged her shoulders, not feeling any kind of comfort from his words.

Johnny sensed her thoughts and continued, "Let me put it this way. When your car breaks down, do you go to a carpenter to fix it or a plumber? No! You go to a mechanic. I think the same applies to you. There is something in you that other people wouldn't be able to understand. Take that to heart." He looked Reese in the eyes. He was giving her the look that showed this was what he was told to help her see the colors from a different point of view.

Kinsey thought for a minute and decided that was the one thing that had made the most sense to her since the day she got the color. That gave her comfort. The only problem is she wasn't sure what she was good at. She had maybe three talents—sarcasm, being soft-hearted, and being great with organized chaos. That was pretty much it. So if her job was to make people feel loved or needed a laugh, she was the girl to go to. If they wanted total destruction on planet Earth, she knew what to do. The longer she got to avoid a mission, the better.

"I guess that makes sense. Thank you, Johnny," she finally said. She turned to Reese and realized she hadn't eaten all day. "Reese, I forgot to tell you I am supposed to go meet everyone for dinner. I need to eat anyway, plus I need to love on my kiddos. Sorry to walk out on you, Johnny. Your input helped more than you know! Thank you," she said again with tear-filled eyes. "I truly am grateful." She slowly stood up, and Reese followed her.

THE HUNT
CONTINUES

M orajes and Gatticus made their way on the jet toward Manhattan where Lucifer would be impatiently waiting with Feassure, Eddie, and the rest of the Greater Demons. True to her personality, Morajes was annoyed as Gatticus kept throwing up. The height was scaring what life he had in him, and he realized that man was never meant to be in the sky. He knew Morajes was absolutely annoyed by him, and that fact only made him want to find Eddie that much more. He hated the cold woman he knew now. He saw some of the young girls she lured in, and even he could see their innocence and didn't get why she would ever want them to know this kind of pain she endured for thousands of years. It wasn't sitting well with him, and he needed Eddie badly.

Eddie had come to enjoy Feassure's company since they truly only had one another to relate to. He enjoyed messing with people who would see the lizard in the shape of a dog and then blend into the background. Some people would stop him when he went to enter into a restaurant and tell him the dog couldn't come in, and as they said it, the dog would disappear. Eddie had not laughed and enjoyed being out among people since the jump from being a Guardian to… well, he didn't know what to call himself. He wasn't a demon, but his best guess was a fallen angel. It still broke his heart because he was truly happy before Lucifer enticed him to switch. He felt this was about as good as it was going to get, and he would enjoy it while he could.

He still took one bite of an apple every single day and kept doing it to make sure that if he ever was given a chance to go back home, he had to take it immediately. And if Lucifer tried to entice him again, he would remember to throw him off anything he cared about. His heart still broke over the fact that he told Lucifer his favorite city. Seeing the reports of the suicide bombers that day destroyed him inside. He made sure through the prayers he could finally say again he would catch anything Lucifer was trying to set him up for.

Feassure also discovered what it was like to have someone other than Lucifer take an interest in him. He started to understand why humans enjoyed each other so much, including having dogs as pets. For the first time in his existence, he was able to eat actual food. During the time they had been together, Eddie was able to throw up two more of those black slimy sludges and was even beginning to pray again. He didn't know how many of them were in him, but he knew that the more he got out of him, the better it would be. Feassure did him the honor of peeing on them for Eddie to give him a good laugh. He even prayed with Feassure watching. They were concerned, though, because the lizard was able to shed his skin, and soft white fur had begun to grow. They both knew that Lucifer would have questions, so they both made a plan and decided to stick to it as best as they possibly could and avoid as much as they could.

When Gatticus and Morajes made it to Lucifer's other home that was completely covered like the mansion in Los Angeles, it was interesting that they could see the wear of fear showing through his body. Belial was more agitated than normal, working to the point of exhaustion with the Prince of Persia throughout the Middle East. Where there was usually peace among certain villages or towns, there was now anger and chaos. The surrounding countries of God's chosen people, the Israelites, were beginning to report throughout the world that it was looking like another war was going to start. The Prince of Persia was sucking up to Lucifer in his usual way, thinking that the promise of war would appease him, but it was only making him more annoyed.

The Prince of Rome thought they were all acting like children complaining because they were doing what Lucifer designed them to do. He was the one left underground for thousands of years. If anything, it should have been him complaining. He used his enormous stature to create the most devastating "natural" disasters, anything from hurricanes in Florida to earthquakes and a tsunami in Japan. With his massive foot he was able to kick off the top of a volcano in Hawaii for it to begin to make the world show its true fear. The Prince of Rome set out to destroy as much as he possibly could, hoping to appease Lucifer, only to discover it was making him demand more. He was half tempted to step on him, but he knew his power since he morphed and changed into this massive creature when he banished him underground.

Even though he was a Greater Demon, he still had fear. He saw what Lucifer as a monster could literally do. He would destroy anything and everything in his path once he had the boy, and the only reason Lucifer had not already destroyed half the world was because he had to find the boy first. The boy was the only reason he couldn't do as he pleased. He had to find him first because he was the key to the destruction of all the humans God loved so much.

Legion's mist was extremely dark gray, and all the bodies and souls that morphed in his features were almost skeletal. Their eyes were sunken completely in, and their mouths were wide open. No tongues were visible, and what could be seen in the mouth area was a dark hole. The bodies had no clothes, and only a small piece of cloth covered the groin. The ribs appeared as though there were bugs crawling in and out. Legion was just as exhausted as the others, but he also knew better than to deny Lucifer even the smallest request.

"Sorry we are late, but sissy boy over here can't take a single ride in a car or jet with his weak stomach issues," Morajes said as she approached her father.

He instantly slapped her in the face, and she fell to the ground. She just looked up at him and glared. Lately, it was as if she was challenging him now and wouldn't let a single tear fall.

Gatticus made his way over toward Eddie and whispered, "We need to talk."

Eddie looked at him and gave him the thumbs up.

As Morajes slowly got herself up, she looked at Belial, and he growled toward Lucifer.

"*Don't you* ever *make me wait again!*" he screamed at her. Lucifer looked toward the rest of the group, and he wasted no time in confronting them. "Do you think you are doing enough? Gatticus, I know you haven't done anything, and I don't even know why I let you live since all you have ever done is disobey me. Belial, don't you ever growl toward me again or I will break both of your horns on your head. Prince of Rome, your disasters have been the most helpful in this world so far. We need to hit every country and choose whatever resource you can to make it devastating for the people. Prince of Persia, we need to dig deeper in the people because I am beginning to think the boy is in those areas, so you and Legion are going to stay there for now. Eddie!" Lucifer noticed that Feassure wasn't a lizard but a dog, and Eddie was scratching behind his ears. "What is this?"

"It's a dog," Eddie replied slightly sarcastically.

"Don't try my patience because I can kill you right along with Gatticus! The two of you are absolutely useless to me as humans!" Lucifer replied.

Since Eddie was able to throw up the slimy sludges, he was actually able to throw Lucifer off his trail. Eddie was happier, and he wasn't about to give it up. "Sorry. It's a human thing, I guess." He wasn't about to reveal the fact that Feassure had shed his skin and was now growing fur. He knew it would be a dead giveaway. "Why don't you disappear while we talk shop?" Feassure then barked and morphed into the background. Eddie knew he was still there and could feel him resting his head against his leg.

"I'm going to put you and Gatticus together because I need him to learn as much as possible from you. Otherwise, he no longer gets to live," Lucifer said.

"Well, we don't want that now, do we?" Eddie said sarcastically. His thoughts began running, wondering what he would he be able to share with him regarding Feassure and his secrets. "I'll give him the rundown. Feassure and I have been able to blend behind the scenes and get into places and snoop around, just to see what we may discover. We have been cautiously following the Guardians, and it all keeps coming down to the same thing. If there are two of them, we notice they are cautious with their words, but the only information I have heard about is another double color. So that Guardian, I believe, is going to be your mark. Just like I was."

"Do you know what colors?" Morajes asked. Her face had swelled up from the hit she took, and lines began to appear in the shape of Lucifer's hand print. "That could help us narrow it down on who to follow."

Lucifer directed his gaze from Eddie to Morajes. "Your interest in this is interesting because the last couple centuries, everything was beneath you, and all you cared about was fashion and money. So explain to me why you would even begin to care now," he inquired.

Morajes wouldn't look at him as she replied, "Haven't you been requesting to know this information? I thought maybe it could be helpful. It was just a natural question."

"All right, continue to keep going into what we have discussed. If even one of you messes this up, everyone will pay the price. All of you, hunt for the double color that Eddie spoke of. He was red and silver. I assume this new one will have silver too. What has been going on with the young girls in the pornography world?" he asked Morajes.

Still refusing to look him in the eyes, she replied, "I have put ads out on Craigslist, and every day, I have girls calling me with the lure of money and fame. I have put them up in the house in Los Angeles. I have already begun to see the effects along with addiction begin to build in them."

He seemed appeased by her response and then looked each one of them over. After a moment, he stood up and said, "I have to go now to cause as much destruction as I can to crash the stock market. The US is far too comfortable, and this needs to be done anyway."

The whole group stood up as Lucifer walked out and cautiously waited until they knew he was gone, unaware that he was watching them through a hidden camera.

"Well, we can see the wear and tear now as he grows more anxious to find the boy," Morajes said.

"All right, Gatticus, come with me to walk the dog, and I can catch you up more on life," Eddie said. The two men, along with Feassure, walked out of the room.

The Prince of Rome and Persia knew better than to discuss anything with Morajes. She was reckless and selfish, and they knew the game she was playing with Belial and Legion. So both of them walked out quickly.

"Why do you antagonize him? You only make it worse on yourself and us," Legion asked.

Belial had a weird feeling and didn't say a word. He felt like he was being watched, and knowing Lucifer, it wasn't unlike him to play any kind of games or destroy any of them if he wanted to.

"Because," Morajes said, "I don't need him anymore." She cut the conversation short and walked out.

The two Greater Demons looked at each other and both realized they were being recorded. They knew all too well Lucifer never walked out after these meetings and left all too quickly.

Gatticus and Eddie quickly walked down the street into Times Square. Eddie wanted to make sure there was as much noise as possible. "Quick test," he said to Feassure. This meant a quick test to find out if there were any Guardians around, and they blended into the background. Gatticus became confused because suddenly, there were all these Guardians in different bright colors with weapons, walking along with their humans or assignments. When they would do this test, they blended into the background, and not only were they hidden from the Guardians, but they were hidden from the Watchers and Lucifer too.

"All clear," Gatticus said.

"So let me guess. You realized the mistake you made and want absolutely nothing to do with him now?" Eddie asked.

"*Yes!* How have you been able to deal with this life for so long? I have wanted to get you sooner, but Morajes just wouldn't do it. I don't know if it was because she wanted control over me or to make a point, but she is out to get Lucifer. She has some kind of death wish while thinking she will be in control," Gatticus said.

"Well, me and Feassure have been doing our requested assignment while not doing our requested assignment," Eddie said.

"What does that mean?" Gatticus asked.

"It means we avoid it as much as possible while enjoying each other's company. We still do our searching for the double color Guardian and the boy," Eddie replied.

"That's another thing I want to ask. Who is this boy he keeps talking about?" Gatticus asked.

"I'll explain his importance, but basically, he is a young boy, possibly about ten, and Lucifer will stop at nothing to find him," Eddie said.

"So how do we...yes, I mean we...get through this without being killed?" Gatticus asked.

"We keep doing exactly what we have been doing. Just understand, if you ruin what happiness that me and Feassure have, we will both kill you, and you won't necessarily die, but you will be disformed for as long as you live. I will teach you everything you need to know to keep him off our trail. Trust me, you don't want to be alone in this world with him out there. We both discovered that, and we want to stay this way."

"I know you don't know me, but let me show you that you can trust me. This everlasting life is not worth it to me, and I wish more than anything I had followed the guy who came back to life after the three days. Is that such a crazy thing to say?" Gatticus asked.

"Did he put any weird little black sludges in your throat?" Eddie asked.

"No, and I don't plan on letting that happen either," he replied.

"Come. Take a walk with me and Feassure, and I will tell you why that isn't a crazy thing to say." Turning back into the dog, Feassure, Eddie, and Gatticus began to make their way through Time Square. "I'll buy us all a hotdog," Eddie said.

Feassure barked in approval, and Gatticus asked, "What's a hotdog?"

Eddie slightly laughed and explained to Gatticus everything he could in the upcoming week.

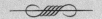

A Time to
Remember

Kinsey awoke the next morning with a weird feeling inside her. She felt like something was off or missing. The sun was warm with a cool breeze shining in the room. The two children were snuggling in her arms, fast asleep. She kept listening to the rise and fall of the waves, and all seemed to be as it should. She kissed Saige and Jaxon on their heads and rolled out of bed.

Her gear was neatly placed on the dresser made out of bamboo that the Utua's made for her. She debated on just facing the day with a pair of sweats and going to the marketplace but felt with her "spidey senses" she had to go to the Hall of Infinium. Just as the thought hit her, she heard Tank yelling through the window.

"Yo, Kinsey, put your gear on. We have something we have to do." Tank said.

"All right, I just woke up. I'll be right down," Kinsey replied. She kissed Saige and Jaxon once more on their heads and told them she loved them. Out loud, she summoned the Holy Spirit and asked him to tell Grace and Zerek how much she loved and missed them. His crystal-clear form gave her the thumbs up and took off. She looked at herself in the mirror and still didn't fully recognize her face. It was her, but it didn't look like her.

"All right, so what are we doing today? Is it your day to watch me?" she asked with a smile.

"No, I don't have an assignment today, but I felt in my heart you need to face the pain in your past. If you don't do that, you will continue to be frustrated. You have to let it fully go and forgive yourself or whoever you need to, and trust me, you will be much more efficient and effective. I had to forgive myself for the three guys I murdered, and that was so hard. When Jesus said I was forgiven, I cried like a baby, but I did it alone. If I had at least had Matai with me, it would have been easier. Soooo...with that said, I'm going with you," Tank replied.

"Ugh. Ugh and double ugh. All right. I totally don't want to, but you are right. I need to. The biggest person I couldn't forgive was myself, so I am glad at least you can relate to that," said Kinsey.

"It sucks the life out of you, but I will be here every step of the way. I promise once it's out of you, you will feel like an angel," Tank said with a smile.

They made their way to the colosseum, and Kinsey always seemed to look and admire the four horsemen embedded on the entrance. They saw all the other Guardians running through the obstacle courses, and Kinsey kept trying to look for Big Ben, Annie, or anyone else from her group. None of them seemed to be there, so they quickly made their way through her favorite water garden and took her time through it until they hit the door. "Do you have your Makirus?" Tank asked.

"Yup. Locked and loaded," she said with a smile.

"Let's roll," Tank said while taking the lead.

They watched all the people standing around the podiums with the giant gold spheres. They were all chatting and excited. Kinsey could tell who was new due to the fact that they were so in awe of the Hall of Infinium. They were taking their time to read all the gold plates under the spheres that read what point in history they wanted to see. Kinsey still couldn't believe she got to watch Noah build the ark, and he had to make the hard decision to not let anyone in. That would be difficult for any person with a heart to walk away and let everyone die.

They made their way past all the podiums and headed to the Hall of Memories. All the way down at the corridor, Kinsey began to slightly panic and could feel her heart starting to pound throughout her body. She stopped at her door and put the Makirus on the spoke. The door instantly opened, and Kinsey hesitated to walk in. She didn't want to feel any bad emotions overtaking her.

"I promise it will be okay. I am right here with you, and nothing can hurt you," Tank said.

"I trust you. I just don't trust myself," she replied. She took a deep breath and then walked in. The gold spheres were beautiful. She could see herself laughing in a bunch of them and got to see the memories with her kids. Every Disneyland trip for her daughter was always so much fun. Kinsey wanted to take Zerek, but due to the pandemic of COVID-19, the trip they wanted so badly wasn't quite in the cards.

She turned toward the first black one and looked at the gold plate below to find out what happened that day. She had no intention of visiting the gray ones. She was well aware of what those moments were. When she bent down to read the plate, she knew she had to go in. She braced herself and put her fingers on the sphere, and Tank went along with her. They both had that roller-coaster feeling that always tickled the senses. Kinsey put her head down because she knew instantly where she was, the issue that started it all the pain in her life.

It was June of 1991, and she was spending the night at a friend's grandfather's house. There were a lot of young girls who played together in the neighborhood, and they all had spent the night at his house. Little Kinsey wanted to go so bad because she had heard how fun it was. They would go swimming, rent movies, and order pizza.

When she got there, she instantly felt weird. They were inside his apartment with only one bedroom. Her friend was wide awake, watching TV, and Kinsey was falling asleep. Well, trying to fall asleep. Kinsey stood completely still as she watched the younger version of herself. Suddenly, she could see Leilani was at her side, trying to relax her. That gave Kinsey a sense of comfort to know she wasn't alone that night.

"Can I sleep anywhere else? I am so tired, and the TV is so loud," Little Kinsey asked. She was unaware that he only had one bedroom and didn't get a good feeling when he placed Little Kinsey in his bed and said just go to sleep.

Kinsey and Tank stood by little Kinsey and watched Leilani try to protect her from what she could. Tank opened up to Kinsey and told her, "Even in prison, if you have a rap sheet that shows the person was a pedophile, rapist, or had molested a little kid, especially a little girl, they get targeted and beat up. Sometimes even killed."

"After I spent the night at this dirty old man's house, I truly have no sympathy for them when it comes to that. He had a stroke shortly after what he did to me. The cop that investigated her case told my mom, and she truly believed that was God punishing him."

The next thing they saw was the grandfather came back in the bedroom, and this time, they noticed several small Watchers on his shoulders. Kinsey and Tank were stiff as a board and didn't want to move. Leilani had tears in her eyes because she knew how much this moment would destroy little Kinsey. As he came back in again, little Kinsey got herself out of the bed to head toward the bathroom. Just as she got off the bed, the grandfather grabbed her arm and made her sit on his lap. Leilani was ready to swing her shark staff and cause a massive bloodbath with all the little Watchers that crawled over the grandfather.

As he sat her on his lap. He began to rub on the inside of her leg and kept rubbing. He kept telling little Kinsey to kiss him. "You can do better than that. No, you can do better than that. Give me a better one. Give me another one." As he said it the last time, his hands began rubbing up on the inside of her leg again, and Leilani had enough and decided to kill the little Watchers that were influencing him. Little Kinsey finally went to the bathroom, locked it, and sat on the floor and cried.

The grandfather had told her she wasn't allowed to use the phone, and little Kinsey felt her gut instinct to call her mom, regardless if he said she couldn't. The rule now made sense, and it was Leilani who gave her the strength. Little Kinsey called her mom and told her she wanted to come home.

"Why, baby? What's wrong?" Janelle asked.

"He is touching me weird," she replied. Then after she finished the sentence, he walked right in. With a trembling voice, she said, "Mom, he's here." She felt completely paralyzed. "My mom wants to talk to you," little Kinsey said with her hand trembling as she handed him the phone.

She kept listening as her mom tried to play it off by saying that Kinsey usually gets emotional when she spends the night in new places. The grandfather insisted on bringing Kinsey home, and her mom finally just agreed and asked how long it took to get back. Kinsey cried the whole way home, and when she reached her house, she ran in as fast as she could. She never wanted to see him or his granddaughter ever again.

Tank looked like he wanted to kill him, like he did on the three men he had killed in prison. Kinsey noticed him and decided to ask, "Can we please go? I honestly didn't need to see an old man molest me again."

He nodded, and they placed their fingers on the black sphere, taking them back to all her memories inside her room. "That was many years ago, and watching myself as a kid was not remotely what I needed," Kinsey said as she looked around the room. Her aura was dulling due to the fact she went back on one of her worst memories. She wondered if that's what made all her anger come out so easily as she got older. "Which one do you want to see next?" asked Tank with pleading eyes.

"None," Kinsey said flatly.

"Well, you gotta keep going," he replied honestly.

She looked at the next black sphere, and she absolutely did not want to visit it. She felt it was better to just go as fast as she could so she could just get it over with. "You will see that the next two align with this one. So do I go into each additional memory? Tank nodded his head at her but reminded her that Leilani was there with her when she felt so lost and alone. It then gave her total and complete peace.

She hesitated for just a minute, but Tank was right. She needed to see them, to see how many Watchers or Guardians were in her most painful moments. Once again, Tank got her down the next couple black spheres, and they both placed their two fingers in the next black sphere. At first, she wasn't sure where she was. Then she realized and recognized where she was.

It suddenly dawned on her she had just gotten married, and she was in her townhouse. It was perfect for her, her husband, and her daughter. The next thing she knew, she ended up having to take Grace back to her grandparents' house because she was accused of kidnapping her own daughter. It didn't make sense because her daughter's father knew she was going to move that whole time. For two weeks, she sat and prayed and fasted. She wanted to do it right instead of fighting in courts all the time.

For two weeks, she prayed the verses, morning and night, not knowing what the outcome would be. She hurt inside so badly because all she wanted was to make the best decision she could. At the end of those two weeks, she heard him say loud and clear, "Give her to her dad."

Kinsey died inside that day. She never wanted to experience that kind of pain but also didn't want to put her daughter in hell. Deep down, she didn't understand and also felt like she wasn't good enough to have her. Kinsey just wanted what was best and believed God knew her heart enough to give her peace, that it would be okay. Little did she know the next the events that transpired the following year would tear Kinsey to pieces.

Tank turned the black sphere slightly forward, and Kinsey saw her and her husband sitting in her favorite Chinese restaurant, talking. She had a funny feeling this was the moment her husband was about to tell her he didn't love her and that he never did. Kinsey was slightly embarrassed standing next to Tank and having him watch her most painful moments. As if he read her thoughts, he leaned in and said, "Kinsey, we all have moments like this."

"Doesn't make it any easier," she replied.

They continued to watch, and Kinsey dreaded what was coming next. "Look, I know you care about me, but you have been sleeping with 'man shoulders' Ashley, haven't you?" she asked.

Kinsey felt her heart beating in her ears and didn't feel like watching this moment over and over again. Tank could see her discomfort and said, "We don't have to watch the same thing over, but we do have to get the worst moments out of you."

"I care about you, but I don't think I ever loved you," her ex-husband said.

Once again, as if this was a current event, Kinsey felt her blood go cold. Tank took out the sphere and turned it slightly forward. They were back inside her house, and anything that had any pictures or memoirs of her husband were taken down. Kinsey saw herself on the floor, alone in the house, having a huge reaction to the pain with a massive panic attack. She had never experienced one before, but felt it like she was dying. She couldn't catch her breath. She was shaking while curled up in the fetal position. The only thing that started calming her down was she had to pray. Slowly, she prayed, and little by little, her breathing began to slow down, and after twenty minutes, she started to feel normal. She slowly stood up, wiped her tears, and gently heard God say, "I heard you. I am here." Then she got to see Leilani had been with her the whole time.

When Kinsey woke up, she felt a new sense of purpose. She felt refreshed and went directly into her Bible, just as she did when the pain became too much inside when she had to fight for custody of her daughter. She was directed by Leilani on which verses she needed to pray to help her walk through the pain. Leilani then whispered in Kinsey's ears, "Wait three years."

Kinsey remembered that moment vividly. Tank held her hand as it was his way to say, "I'm with you. You aren't alone."

That wasn't the reason Kinsey was so sensitive about this moment. She couldn't wait the three years Leilani told her to focus on. Kinsey felt so abandoned and so empty inside that true to her insecurity, she instantly started dating someone else.

Tank turned the black sphere slightly forward, and now this time, she was looking at the guy who walked out on her a year later. Since he was in the military, he told her he was going out to the field. She knew that generally, when they did that, it meant about a week or two. But he never came back, not even a phone call or text. She knew absolutely nothing, but this was the second massive blow to her heart.

Kinsey began to cry, even with Tank by her side. He couldn't believe it because here by his side was the sweetest, funniest, most beautiful girl by his side. These men just abandoned her without even being man enough to face her. That thought alone didn't make sense to him.

They both touched the black sphere again and were sent back to the room of her memories. Tank replaced the black sphere and handed her a new one. Kinsey knew instantly which memory it was and handed it back to Tank. "I know this memory very clearly, and that is a time of pain I can't watch or see," Kinsey said. In the sphere, it was showing the night she was raped by her friend's husband. She had taken her Ambien, which usually made her sleepwalk and pass out. The following morning, she woke up. and she had no bottoms on herself, not even underwear. She had no clue what had happened, but she felt incredibly sore in an area that shouldn't be sore at all. The reason she knew it was assault was because he had kept trying to get close to her all night while she was backing away. After the pain of her husband sleeping with someone else, she never wanted anyone woman to experience that type of pain.

Tank respected her wishes and grabbed another one. "What about this one?" he asked.

"Oh, wow. That is one of the most painful moments for me. I don't know," Kinsey replied.

"Kinsey, if you want to be efficient in battle, you can't have any fear nor have anything holding you back," Tank replied. "Besides, after this one, you only have one left."

"Let's just get this over as fast as we can," Kinsey requested.

She and Tank placed their two hands into the sphere, and there she was in one of the most painful points in her life. Her breathing began to speed up, and Tank touched her shoulder and reminded her it was just a memory and it would never happen again.

Her ex-boyfriend was standing on the balcony doing drugs under the preface he was just smoking a cigarette. The following night, she had been spending time with her daughter as they both lay in bed, watching movies. Not too long after, it was time for bed, and her daughter went to sleep. All seemed well and calm as everyone went to sleep. Little did Kinsey know she was headed for her worst nightmare and rude awakening. Kinsey had purchased a journal for her daughter to be able to say and express whatever she needed.

One day, Kinsey had a funny feeling that she should read it, and somehow, she turned directly to the page she needed to see. What she read next made her absolutely sick. Her daughter had written the night before that the man Kinsey was living with had come into her room in the middle of the night and sat on her bed. He rubbed her leg, and when Grace asked what he was doing, his response was making sure she was okay.

Kinsey lost her mind when she read that. She vowed her daughter would never know the pain she knew when it came down to a situation like that. She had to get ready for work and had to have her wits about her on how to approach the situation.

On her way home from work, Kinsey felt a tiger ready for the kill. The journal was in the passenger seat, and Kinsey was ready for whatever came next. She kept thinking of herself as that little girl scared of an old man. She blew through the front door with her boyfriend standing in the middle of the living room. Kinsey headed toward him and tried to make it look like she wanted a hug or kiss. What happened next was the total opposite. She gave him the best uppercut she could, knocking out two of his teeth. Of course, this only enraged him, and even though he had hit and strangled her in the past, she didn't care. He wasn't going to win this time. Every slap he ever did to her face, it didn't matter because she wasn't going to cry. Every punch he made when he was stoned right in that moment, she didn't care. Every text message he sent to other girls…they could have him. Then the last blow came to the face, but this time, he slammed her head in the wall while strangling her as hard as he could.

Tank looked at Kinsey and proudly told her, "Kinsey, I am proud of you watching this. That had to be extremely hard and scary, reading what your daughter wrote. I would gladly stand by your side in battle…or a prison riot. Take your pick," he said with a smile.

"I was miserable day in and day out with him because I didn't listen to what God said. I was supposed to wait three years before dating again. I was just so broken I seriously couldn't wait. I hated myself for that torture for the longest time," Kinsey said.

Tank took notice of all the stuff she and the ex-boyfriend had destroyed during their fight and the shock of watching this guy slamming her head into the wall over and over again. One of the biggest rules in prison was you don't mess with kids and you don't mess with women. If this guy had gone to prison and Tank knew what he was in for, he would become his next target.

The next thing they knew, there were five policemen at her door, and even if she had not called them, she welcomed them. The men at her door could see her eye swelling, her mouth swelling, and the handprint on her neck. They instantly went to arrest him, and he became combative. It was the drugs in his system, and they ended up having to hogtie him.

Kinsey, in that moment—and the Kinsey with Tank—were both appreciative of watching him being taken out. While he was in jail, she packed up all of her stuff and finally left.

As they were looking around, they both saw everything scattered all over the ground from picture frames to movies. They both stood still for a second as they realized Itherial just arrived. They could see the two Watchers that were attached to the boyfriend morph and change into small creatures with claws as they were trying to swing at Itherial. They saw Itherial kill the two Watchers as they turned into two giant black sludges. Kinsey's body stiffened.

"Why was Itherial here and not Leilani?" She barely had any strength because her tears were a fight to hold back. Kinsey noticed the small lemur-looking creature that had its tail around her neck. She watched herself go into the kitchen and pull out the bottle of alcohol. She began feeling sick because she knew instantly what was coming.

She and Tank followed the younger version of Kinsey up the stairs and into the master bedroom. They watched as she looked at the marks on her neck, Itherial standing close by, and the Watcher with its tail now circulating inside her head. She watched as the younger version of herself picked up the black marker and wrote the lyrics to the song that Kinsey knew all too well. It was a song about suicide, and she didn't care if she lived or died anymore. The boyfriend was so controlling, and she even found out shortly after he was on some serious drugs.

They both watched Itherial stand by very still and praying. Over and over, they watched as Kinsey took out several opiates at a time and swallowed them with whiskey to wash them down. Tank began to think of memories of his own mother. "Kinsey, you remind me of my mom. How could you do that much?" Tank asked.

"I had given up. I didn't care anymore. I wanted something that was going to take me out of this world. You won't like what comes next," Kinsey replied.

Just as she said it, younger Kinsey went into the tub with her clothes on. They both saw the knife in her hand that they didn't notice before. "You may not want to look, Tank," she told him.

They were sitting on the side, watching Itherial pray, and continued watching her younger self begin to cut. Over and over, the slices from the knife were deep. She kept singing the lyrics from the broken song, and then they noticed she had dropped the knife into the water. The water was then dark and brown and had begun to stain her clothes. She had begun to pray, and it was all Itherial needed to take the kind of action necessary with the Watcher. He took out his sword with the black flame and stabbed the creature right in the head. When it turned into the black sludge like the others had, Itherial swiped over the sludge, and it was gone.

Itherial then turned his attention back to Kinsey. He placed his hand onto the wrist that had been sliced and cut. Tank and Kinsey watched in amazement after he prayed, and then Kinsey lifted her arm up. It was healed. There was nothing there, not even scratches. The only thing visible were a few red lines.

Kinsey and Tank expected that to be it, but instead, they saw Itherial place his hands inside Kinsey's stomach. As he did so, she began to throw up everything in her system up. They watched as Itherial cried by her side after whispering in her ear something inaudible. As the two of them watched her begin to let the water out, they both agreed it was time to go.

"This last one isn't going to be easy either," Tank told her.

"Wouldn't have it any other way," Kinsey said sarcastically.

"Okay, last one. Here we go," Tank said gently.

Kinsey saw where she was and instantly wanted to leave. "No! I don't need to see this!" she said with anger.

"Your actions are telling me otherwise, Kinsey. It's time to let it *all* go," Tank said kindly.

She stood and watched yet again another younger version of herself was in front of her. She was sitting with her legs crossed, doing her makeup in the mirror. She was stoned out of her mind. She didn't have an addiction to street drugs but a massive addiction to pain medication. Kinsey's addiction began when she lived with the abusive boyfriend. She would give everything to escape him, and the pain medication was her outlet. This moment, though, was many years later after she had her son, Zerek. The night before, someone had given her some pain medication, and she didn't know that they had laced it with something else. She began having her usual grand mal seizure but this time wasn't coming out of it. Her parents laid her flat on her back and watched her struggling to breathe.

Kinsey saw the Watcher that was in her ear and how the tail once again wrapped around her hand and kept pushing her to take more medicine. This time, though, Leilani was at her side, knocking the creature off Kinsey's body, and placed her hand in her stomach, just like Itherial did from the last image they saw. The next thing she knew, she was puking all over herself and everywhere else and was struggling to breath. Her parents were terrified, so they called the paramedics. Five hours later, she woke up in the ER and had no clue what happened. She had scared her family to death. She made a vow she would never touch anything like that again. Since they watched her screaming, she couldn't breathe and just happened to notice the medication that wasn't hers. The paramedic who brought her in had stayed with her until she woke up, and when he told her what had happened, she was so ashamed for what had happened.

She did have legit pain after breaking her foot and the multiple surgeries that went along with it. For the next four days, after returning home, her cognitive reactions or thinking were highly delayed and hard to understand. She had caused her parents and her daughter so much pain they didn't deserve. She hated herself every single time she hurt anyone. It made her sick of herself and disgusted that she couldn't make the better decisions. The lovely curse of being bipolar was usually not far behind.

"Okay, okay, I have had enough. I know all of these memories and I know exactly the pain I caused. It hurts like hell, but I forgave myself and was given forgiveness for the pain I caused to others. I don't understand why my life finally came together, and then I died. I lost good friends, respect, I was gossiped about, and due to the seizures, I was so limited to life at one point," Kinsey told him.

Tank wasn't sure, but he felt in his spirit this was the point to stop. Those were the memories she needed to see and to deal with to be able to move forward. "Okay, Kinsey. We can go. It was draining for me too. I just thought that it might help you to face these moments so you could let go," Tank said.

They touched the sphere and were back into the room of all her memories. "I really didn't want to go back for a reason, but I am thankful I had you with me. All of the gray spheres, I have no desire to see any of them. I saw one of them labeled when I was ten, and kids at school found out about the nasty old man who touched me and whom I had to kiss. There is no need to see stuff like that anymore," Kinsey said.

"Let's go to the Worship Hall. I'm sure it will help, and then we can find the group," Tank replied.

"Sounds *great*," Kinsey replied. "I just want to hold my babies."

They made their way into the Grand Worship Hall, and Kinsey was so grateful to see her new friend singing on stage with a choir behind him. The song was catchy, and the beat sounded great. It was exactly what Kinsey and Tank needed to be able to get rid of the lingering pain from watching the events that happened to her in previous years. Just about the time the music stopped, after her friend played, he came down to talk to Kinsey. "So are you feeling better?" he asked.

"Yeah, worship music always does. Especially yours. I enjoyed your set," Kinsey replied with a halfhearted expression.

"Well, at least someone can appreciate it," Johnny said with a small laugh.

"I need to talk and meet up with my group, see my family and my kiddos. I will be back again soon. Please know I always enjoy your songs," Kinsey said as she and Tank got up and headed toward the door.

"Thank you, friend! I always appreciate a fan."

FIRST ASSIGNMENT

Kinsey woke up feeling extremely exhausted from the previous day's adventure. An emotional journey by itself was enough to keep in bed for a week. The kiddos by her side were snuggled extra close, and she pulled them both in and kissed them on the tops of their heads. Her heart slightly panged as she thought of her other two children alive without her. She missed her daughter's jokes, personality, sarcasm, and sass. She was so beautiful by looks and heart. She once helped a man who was having a seizure since she had to witness several of Kinsey's seizures. She always felt bad because she couldn't control when they happened along with how she looked. Kinsey would just drop and then would have to stay there for forty-five minutes until it was all over. She always awoke with a pain in her chest, blood in her mouth, and her right shoulder dislocated. She would have to roll it back in, and that was the most painful part.

Then there was Zerek. Kinsey knew he would love having a brother like Jaxon. Friendly and playful was all her son needed to be able to work on his social struggles that came along with having autism. It broke her heart to think of her son alone because Kinsey knew deep down, her parents couldn't live forever. Zerek's dad had not shown much of an interest in his son. After Kinsey had kept her distance, she wanted nothing to do with him, and it turned out to be the right decision.

As she lay in her bed, sharing little snuggles, she began to hear voices chattering outside her window, and just like before, her group was throwing rocks at her window. She rolled out of bed and looked outside the window. Just like last time, Matai happened to hit her forehead, dead center. Her group, along with the Utua brothers, all laughed as he said, "Never fails."

"Ha-ha," Kinsey replied sarcastically. "So what's with the welcoming committee? What kind of torture are you going to put me through today?" Kinsey asked.

"Well, you finally have your first assignment, and not only that, but it's not just an observation. We all get to go with you to help get you used to everything, but even better. Think of it this way: you get to show your skills on earth. It's finally time, friend," Reese replied.

Kinsey's heart began to pound in her ears. She still wasn't sure if she was completely ready, but who was to say she truly wasn't?

"There is a little boy that needs our protection because of some abuse that has been happening," Leilani told her.

Those words alone were enough to tell her that Tank was absolutely right about facing her past. She needed to let go and do her best to protect this little boy. There was one thing in actual life she hated more than anything, and she wanted to kill any person who would hurt a child. This Watcher wouldn't stand a chance when it came down to protecting a child. "All right, I'll get ready, even though my colors freak everyone out." Kinsey couldn't help herself. She had to say it, and by the looks on everyone's faces, she had to smile and shut the window.

"Wait, wait!" she heard the twins say. "You gotta bring your Makirus since this is your mission, not ours."

"Roger that!" Kinsey replied.

She got ready quickly, kissed her kiddos goodbye, and headed out to meet her group.

"All right, let's do this," Matai said.

"When we go on assignment, why do we bring the Makirus?" Kinsey asked.

"It becomes embedded in your memories. Kinda like being recorded, and you put the videotape in and watch it," Reese answered.

"Can I see my other two kiddos really fast when we go? I just need to see them," Kinsey pleaded.

"I don't see why not. I know you miss them, and it must be hard," Leilani answered.

"We will all go with you, just because you want to visit. We don't want you caught off guard," Tank replied.

They all began walking, laughing, and joking like normal. This always gave Kinsey a sense of comfort as if she was in the house she grew up in. She always felt safe and taken care of. The group made their way through the colosseum into the water garden. They reached the doors of the Hall of Infinium, and everyone turned their attention toward their group. Kinsey wasn't positive, but she thought the sight of the Utuas and Tank was pretty intimidating walking together into the same space. She was wrong, though. All of the Guardians, Momenti, and even some Fruits of the Spirit had their eyes on Kinsey. It made her want to hide. She was tired of the double color, but it wasn't much different than what she experienced alive. People loved to gossip, and with all of her bad decisions, she didn't blame them. This was different, though. She hadn't done anything to stand out or anything worth discussing. It grew quiet. Eerily quiet. "Let's just get there as fast as we possibly can," Kinsey said hurriedly.

They walked into another large room, just like the last one with the blue observation sphere. This room had one single white sphere. They all pulled out their Makirus', but this time, Kinsey noticed they were all able to put them on the spoke.

"This time, yours goes last because this is your assignment," Annie said. "We are here to protect you due to the colors and this being your first time. These Watchers, Tortones, and Reeds of Death will hunt you out like flies to a dead animal. So we all want to be with you and be able to watch your back," Annie said.

"Yeah, you could have left that out," Kinsey said honestly. "Well, let's all put together our sea turtle power."

"Are we ready?" Leilani asked.

"About as much as I could possibly be," Kinsey answered.

They all put their hands on the sphere with the sea turtle symbol on each of them. They all placed each Makirus on the spoke, and they were whisked back to Kinsey's home to see her family. She missed them so much. She wanted to just hold them and tell them she was there. Zerek was playing with his cars and dinosaurs. Her parents were up to their usual activities, and more than anything, she just wanted to wrap her arms around Zerek, her little prince. She prayed over him with the group. Zerek looked up once again like he had during her visit in the car and stared at each one of them. They all felt like he was watching them. "Hi, Mommy!" he said.

"Who are you talking to?" his grandmother asked.

"I can see Mommy and her friends," Zerek said honestly.

His grandmother teared up, and his grandfather stood up to walk out of the room. After a few minutes, he came back in.

Then they all prayed over her parents to help them with as much health protection as they could possibly need. The next place they ended up was in her daughter's room. She was lying on her bed, doing her homework, and Kinsey was able to say to her lightly in her ears, "I love you, pretty girl, and I will always love you. I miss you." She began to have tears in her eyes, but this time, she noticed a sense of peace and calm.

"Okay, we need to head out because we have a little boy who needs us," Big Ben said as his thoughts brought him down to his own beatings as a kid.

Kinsey happened to notice that everyone she was with had now stiffened up and looked incredibly serious. That always gave her cause for concern, but she had to remind herself that she was with her group, not alone, and she was protected.

Leilani had a small red sphere and moved it slowly to the right. They arrived at a location Kinsey was not familiar with, and it appeared no one else was either. They noticed the home they were supposed to go in but, all at the same time, saw multiple Watchers around the location. All of them noticed Kinsey's double color. They howled out loud as if they were summoning or announcing her presence. All the Utuas had their staffs of shark teeth, and they were standing directly behind Kinsey for her own protection. "Your job is the boy. Our job is to watch your back," Matai said.

Kinsey felt actually strength and not fear as she had before. No matter what, she was going to help this little boy from whatever was coming his way. All of her group entered into the home while the Utuas said they were going to keep an eye on the others by surrounding the outside of the home.

317

When she saw the little boy, she saw his bruises and saw that the mom didn't look different than her son. Then she saw the little boy. She saw his bruises and saw the mom didn't look different than her son. The next thing she knew, the father blew in through the door, and three giant Watchers followed behind. Then out of the blue, Eddie, Gatticus, and Feassure was there with them.

"Who are you?" Annie asked.

"I was once like you. Lucifer enticed me to cross sides, and it was the biggest mistake of my entire existence. Lucifer is after this little boy, and me and these two with me have been trying to throw him off your path. I was the other double color, but I was red and silver. We need a way to keep her hidden," Eddie said.

"Why are you so willing to help us?" Big Ben asked with full suspicion.

"I have been tortured by Lucifer for the past thousand years, and I would have given anything to go back over. This is Gatticus, and he has lived through hell, just like I have," Eddie replied.

"What's that?" the twins asked in unison.

"This is Feassure. He can help us hide not only from Guardians and Watchers alike, but he can hide us from Lucifer," Eddie answered. "They all know you are here. They have been on standby once they heard there was another double color and you instantly stood out. We just want to keep you hidden and away from him. The minute he is able to affect you, everything will change."

All of the group members instantly believed him. They weren't sure why, but since he was a Guardian over a thousand years ago, he truly had no reason to lie. "So why would you want to hide from Lucifer?" Tank asked.

"We have seen what he can do and who he can do it to. He will entrap you with any sort of weakness you have, just like he did me. It was the biggest decision I ever made in my life. Thankfully, Feassure and Gatticus are with me because doing this alone, all I wanted to do is die, but he made me immortal. If he shows up here tonight, I will hide you from him just so you can get back as quick as you can. Some of the Watchers already told him you're here," Eddie explained.

"He's right," Mongo and Cronk said. "There are tons of them all around this place."

Grunt grunted in agreement.

Then suddenly, they all took notice of the father drinking heavily, extremely heavy with hardcore alcohol. Big Ben was the stiffest Kinsey had ever seen him. Knowing his father used to beat him, Kinsey could understand the anger he could possibly be feeling. Then at the same time, they all noticed a Watcher close by, and it kept looking at Kinsey in the eye. Its eyes turned amber red, and its claws grew. It stretched outward and upward. It was unlike anything any of the other Guardians have ever laid eyes on.

"So, guys, what do I do?" Kinsey asked. Just after the question, the man began yelling and hitting his wife. All Kinsey could see was herself from the vision the day before: the man who slapped and hit her on multiple occasions and even slammed her head into the wall while choking her. After he started drinking more, he then started hitting the son. He was just a little boy. Kinsey couldn't figure out why he would hit either one of them, but flash images kept running through her mind, and she was beginning to get seriously angry. She hadn't felt that emotion since she had arrived in heaven.

Then the husband hit her so hard she instantly had a black eye that started swelling. He choked her to the point of passing out and then faced the son. Kinsey could feel herself building up her anger as he smacked him more and more. The next thing she knew, the Watcher looked only at her and jumped into the man's body as he began to hit harder and drink more.

"I am warning you again, I was a double color and became the bull's-eye on the target. He sent every Watcher in the world to be on the lookout for you," Eddie said.

Suddenly, Feassure began acting weird, running in circles as a warning to him and Gatticus that they needed to hide, but just as they were about to blend into the background, Belial blew through the door. He threw the Watcher back after he howled and yelled a sound none of the Guardians had ever heard. The sound was so terrifying none of them knew what to do with him since he was a Greater Demon. Not a single Utua or the rest of the group could understand. If this was Kinsey's first assignment, why make her face the worst of all?

Finally, after Kinsey couldn't stand the flash images in her head of the man who used to hit her, she finally ran and bum-rushed the Watcher that was in his body. They both flew out of the building, and instantly, the Watcher made the form of a python and began wrapping its body around her neck. He even bit into her shoulder, and Kinsey could feel the poison sinking into her, and her arm struggled to fight against it. She had run so hard at the Watcher that they flew through several buildings, destroying everything they could in the spiritual world. The physical world was confused and thought it was some form of earthquake.

Belial stayed behind as a way to keep Kinsey from getting the help she needed. All the other Watchers that the Utuas saw on the outside of the home were now inside the home. The man had stopped the attack upon his family and held onto them, crying. Tank took the position to keep protecting the family, especially in front of the little boy. He happened to notice, though, that the boy wasn't crying and sad. He was angry and wanted nothing to do with the man who hurt him and his mother. When Tank took a second look, one of the smaller Tortones was on his shoulder and whispering in his ear, telling him that his father deserved to die and needed to stay as far away as possible.

The Utuas had to start fighting as many Watchers as they possibly could, and then as a group, they had to go against Belial whom none of them had not only never fought before but they had never even seen him before.

Kinsey and the Watcher were still flying through the air as they attracted every Watcher in the area. Legion caught wind of the Guardian with the double color and immediately notified Lucifer. "Who found her?" he asked.

"It looks like Eddie and Gatticus found them first," Legion replied.

"Take me there now!" Lucifer demanded.

The Watcher that had shaped like the python was now similar to a baboon with razor-sharp teeth, and the claws kept scratching through her skin. She was able to get her sword when she got the advantage and cut its head off. She immediately took off back to the house they had started in and was stunned when she walked in. Belial was one of the scariest creatures she had ever seen before. The other Watchers that everyone else had been fighting against were now dead. She was barely able to catch her breath when suddenly, she heard the coldest, slimiest voice come from behind her. A cold chill went down her spine, and she knew it wasn't anyone in her group. She could see them all trying to catch their breaths.

"Thank you for making my job easier. I heard you would be a double color, so of course, I had to have everyone on the lookout for you. I heard Eddie and Gatticus found you first, so I guess I have them to thank," Lucifer said.

Reese was the only one who could see Eddie, Gatticus, and the weird furry-looking lizard. The three of them kept shaking their heads no, and since they were the only ones who could see each other, Reese asked them, "Why would you do that to us?"

"We knew you would be coming anytime soon and we wanted to find you guys long before Lucifer so we could warn you. We just want to help without getting caught," Eddie replied. Almost as soon as he finished his words, he made a mad dash for the outside of the house with Gatticus, Feassure, and Reese behind him. He felt incredibly sick, and while he was still hidden, he began to throw up the last three of the slimy sludges that Lucifer had put in him. "Thank you, God. Thank you."

The next thing they saw was Itherial before them. "Are you ready to come back home?" he asked. "You served your time well, and because you didn't live as Lucifer asked of you and kept in your heart a love for God, he wants you home now."

"Wait. What about them? Gatticus has been underground and just recently was released, and Feassure here and I have grown a bond since pretty much it's only been us."

Itherial stood still for a moment while he thought. "Gatticus, weren't you the one who was to guard Christ's tomb?"

"Yes," Gatticus shamefully.

"Correct me if I am wrong, but you fell asleep, right?" Itherial asked.

"Yes," he answered.

"Well, then, I don't see why not. As far as Feassure goes, he shed his skin, and the fur coming through is representation of new life. Do you want to come, Feassure?"

Feassure hesitated. He had never been given this chance before. Then after thinking, he nodded his head vigorously.

"Then come with me," Itherial said as he held out his hands. Just as he did so, Lucifer walked out and saw the three of them leave with the archangel.

He was fuming, and the only thing that consoled him was the fact that this new Guardian broke one major rule of attacking a Watcher without the prayer of the victim and also discovered the boy she was protecting...was the boy he had been searching for. The boy's heart was no longer innocent and pure. It was dark and extremely angry. He wanted nothing to do with his father anymore, and he was about to make sure he let him know that.

The whole group, including the Utuas, were exhausted due to fighting as many Watchers as physically possible. Finally, they all realized it was definitely time to go because none of them had a clue what was going to happen when they got back. They all touched the sphere and ended up back in the Hall of Infinium. No one said a word because they all knew she broke the pact. She was to never intervene without the authority to do so.

Kinsey didn't want to say a word to anyone. All she wanted to do was go see Lau and hide in his garden. She made her way over without telling any of them where she was going. "I just need to be alone," she said as she ran from them.

When she got to Lau's, she had tears in her eyes and just begged him if she could be out in the garden alone. "I need to clear my head, and I just don't want to be where anyone can see me right now," Kinsey told him.

"I understand. Take your time. We will be practicing if you care to join us," he replied.

"Maybe I will. Maybe the exercise is just what I need," Kinsey said.

She stretched, trained with her swords, and sparred a few Guardians she had never seen before. Since she was so tired from the fight with that Watcher, she finally decided it was time to relax.

UPON THE WATER

Kinsey was exhausted, and every inch of her body ached with pain. The bite from the shapeshifting Watcher was still lingering and stinging in her right shoulder. The fangs had felt like two daggers stabbing her at one time, and even though the poison was removed, she couldn't help but wonder if there were any traces left within her system. Her hair was a complete mess from all the rubble and debris that she and the Watcher flew through. To add insult to injury, she knew she screwed up royally. She didn't know the whole book of Revelation by heart, but she was pretty sure it never mentioned that a single Guardian from heaven would interfere in a pact between heaven and hell and be the cause for Armageddon to start.

She fell to her knees and let out a huge sigh. Images kept flashing in her head of the fight with the shape-shifter. The Watcher changed so many times, and it was incredible how fast he should shift. She knew that she shouldn't have acted so impulsively, but seeing how brutal the husband was with his wife, she couldn't just sit by and watch him beat her senseless. She knew that the innocent little boy would be affected by this moment the rest of their lives. She couldn't just stand there and watch, and what she felt in the pit of her stomach was more than anger. She had rage. Rage because of the memories of her own abuse.

She touched her neck and remembered the time when her ex had left a handprint from when he tried to strangle her. Kinsey closed her eyes again and began to cry. Deep sobs consumed her, and it was like a floodgate had just opened. She couldn't stop the tears, and what would the point be to try? She needed to release everything, and she didn't have the energy to exercise.

"Why do I screw everything up? Even in heaven, I can't seem to control my impulsive behavior. How could I ever think that I would get this right when I couldn't do it alive?" The tears started to almost drown her. Trembling, she placed her head in her hands and lowered herself all the way to the ground.

There had only been one other time in her life she had curled up in the fetal position on the floor, crying, unable to stop. It was while she had been alone in her house shortly after her ex-husband had said he never loved her. The pain of that moment was carried with her for years, and this moment now made her feel just as exhausted and lost. She had to pray to calm down, and little by little, the tears stopped as well as the trembling.

Suddenly, she could hear the ocean, and the salty smell followed. She wasn't sure if she was just incredibly exhausted, but she could feel herself rocking. Slowly, Kinsey opened her eyes, and she could hear water splashing and noticed she was in a small wooden fishing boat. The view startled her, and she instantly sat up and started looking around. She was floating in the ocean. There was nothing around her but water, and an eerie feeling came over her.

Why was she here? Was this her punishment for causing the destruction with the Watcher? Then she noticed a light off in the distance, and it was moving slowly toward her. The light started to form a shape, and Kinsey could see that it was a man. The man had shoulder-length brown wavy hair and was clothed in a white robe, and he was standing on top of the water. He was signaling to her to come toward him.

She instantly realized that Jesus was calling her out onto the water. Kinsey stood up in the small boat, and just as she was about to jump in the water, she saw dark shadows swimming and circling the boat. Some of the forms she could identify, and others she couldn't. There were creatures she had never seen before, and they appeared to be incredibly sinister. Some of the creatures had glowing red eyes while others were changing forms as they swam around the boat. This told her that there were Watchers in the water, and with the recent struggle with the Watcher she killed, she didn't have the energy to fight these ones off. Even if she used her swords, she wouldn't be able to fight all of them off. It dawned on her that this could possibly be her punishment and that she was to be consumed by the creatures in the water. Kinsey froze with the thought of being torn apart, and knowing the pain that the Watchers were capable of, she sat back down in the boat.

Looking out into the horizon with the sun straight above, she heard his voice call her name. It wasn't out loud as if it was in her ears, it was quiet and still as she could hear it from her heart. She looked toward Jesus and saw him signaling for her to come to him. Unsure, she stood and just waited. "I don't want to disobey and make everything worse, yet at the same time, I don't want to get eaten."

Just as the thought entered her mind, she heard in her heart, "Kinsey, you're not being punished. Do you trust me?"

Kinsey looked directly at Jesus again and then down at the water. All her life, she wanted to do right in the eyes of the Lord and didn't always manage to do so. She didn't want this to be another bad decision she made. With the shape-shifters still circling the small boat, she decided she would step out and into the water as she was being called. Her heart started to pound, and her breathing became more intense as her left leg reached down the side. She had expected to drop slowly into the water, but her foot didn't sink. She stepped onto a solid surface, and for a moment, Kinsey was in awe that she was actually standing on water. The moment really sank in as the creatures under the water were trying to attack her. There were claws, teeth, and tentacles all trying to grab onto her, but none of them could touch her.

She looked back at Jesus and started to run. Even though she was still exhausted, she didn't care. She ran as fast as her legs would possibly allow. Tears started to well back up in her eyes again because she was going to be in the presence of her Savior. As she reached him, she instantly fell to her knees and just rested her head and cried at his feet.

It took several minutes before Kinsey could gain some kind of composure so she would be able to look up and gaze into a face so well-known but never really seen. She didn't understand why she didn't see him during her time of judgment, but she was so excited to be at his feet at this very moment. Throughout her life, she often wondered how she would respond in this situation with the exception of running on water because never in a million years would she imagine walking upon water; it was the coolest moment ever. She was still crying at his feet, and she felt his hand upon her head. A wave of peace came over her as his touch was gentle and healing at the same time.

Calmly and slowly, she focused her eyes on him and stood up. His face was incredibly kind and even handsome. He had shoulder-length brown wavy hair that was a little untamed but with beautiful golden tones that glistened when the sun hit it just right. He looked at Kinsey and smiled while moving his hand to the side of her face. The embrace was so calming and so gentle.

Kinsey wasn't sure what came over her at that moment, but she wrapped her arms around him as tight as she could and felt the need to unload everything that she was feeling. "Jesus, I feel so lost right now. I know I screwed up and I know I acted impulsively, but I couldn't just sit there and watch this man hurt his wife, let alone that little boy! I know it was part of my own emotions from my past that caused me to kick the crap out of that Watcher and just want to kill him." Tears came down like a waterfall as she held onto him so tightly. All her life while she was alive, she wondered what it would be like when she faced him. This moment right here, as tightly as she held onto the Savior, she would hold onto the memory.

"Kinsey"—even his voice was calming—"my precious daughter, today was meant to happen."

Kinsey loosened her embrace and took a step back. She wanted this moment to be etched in her mind and know that he came for her at the time her soul needed him the most. "What do you mean? What was meant to happen? The fact that I would mess everything up as usual?" she asked, frustrated. "Just once, I would like to do what I am supposed to do. It brought me back to my own abuse, and I just couldn't sit there and watch it happen."

"Do you go to a plumber when you need your car worked on?" he asked her.

Johnny had used the same analogy, and she realized how much it made sense but didn't get why it applied to her. "No, you go to a mechanic," she answered.

"Right. You go to those who have the knowledge," Jesus said.

"I don't see how that applies to me because I don't have any knowledge that is of any use other than chaos. Oh, and sarcasm," she said.

"Well, that's just it. We chose you because you feel things on a deeper level than most. My father wanted you for this because he knew your pain and anger from what you lived through was going to cause the best reaction. It was real, it was needed, and it had to happen. Nothing done under heaven is ever a mistake. You just happen to walk through more in life than most people," he told her.

"Yeah, that was something I didn't want. I just wanted normal, and instead, I just screwed everything up. Do you forgive me for today?" Kinsey asked.

"There is nothing to forgive. You did what was meant to happen. The time of man is now upon them, and the clock started ticking a long time ago. Let me hold you and just remind you this was meant to happen and it will all be okay." Just as he said the words and held her, she found herself back in the bamboo and cherry blossom garden outside of Lau's school. When she opened her eyes again, every single one of her group members were looking at her.

"It's okay, Kinsey. We all knew this had to happen, and we were told to let it happen. Our job was to look after you. None of us are mad. We were just told to watch your back as best as we could," Leilani said.

"So why didn't anyone tell me?" Kinsey asked.

"Because it had to be natural or it could have been a serious disaster," Matai replied.

"Oh, and that wasn't a disaster?" Kinsey asked.

"No, it went down like it was meant to," Annie answered.

Kinsey let out a huge sigh and asked, "So what happens now?"

"Now…now we train for war. Lucifer has what he needs," Tank answered.

"And what's that?" Kinsey asked.

"The Antichrist," Big Ben answered.

CPSIA information can be obtained
at www.ICGtesting.com
Printed in the USA
BVHW051157180722
642395BV00001B/32